THE LIBRARY
BOOK

Centennial History of the Minneapolis Public Library

THE LIBRARY BOOK

Bruce Weir Benidt

THE
LIBRARY
1885 **100** 1985

Minneapolis Public Library and Information Center

The color illustration of the old Minneapolis Public Library on the dust jacket and opposite the title page of THE LIBRARY BOOK is a reproduction from the original oil painting by Anthony D. Hughes. This painting is part of a collection of renderings of former downtown landmarks painted by Mr. Hughes, depicting Minneapolis during the late nineteenth and early twentieth centuries.

The black and white photographs in THE LIBRARY BOOK, many of which have not been previously displayed or published, are from the Minneapolis History Collection of the Minneapolis Public Library. The collection provides over two hundred thousand photographs for use by researchers, publishers, broadcasters and exhibitors. *Minneapolis Star and Tribune* photographs donated to the collection have been used with permission of the *Minneapolis Star and Tribune.*

Project Coordinator: Kristi Gibson
Editor: Abigail Baxter
Production Editor: Lenore Franzen
Designer: Evans-Smith & Skubic Incorporated
  Graphic Design and Production
Jacket Photographer: Robert Paulson
Indexer: Dorothy M. Burke
Typesetter: Interface, Inc.
Printer: Colwell/North Central Inc.

THE LIBRARY BOOK: Centennial History of the Minneapolis Public Library
Library of Congress Cataloging in Publication Data

Benidt, Bruce Weir, 1950-
  The library book.

Bibliography: p. 239-240
  Includes index.
  1. Minneapolis Public Library and Information Center—History. 2. Public libraries—Minnesota—Minneapolis—History. 3. Minneapolis (Minn.)—Libraries—History. I. Title.
Z733.M667B46 1984   027.4776'579   84-19038

ISBN 0-9613716-0-9

Minneapolis Public Library and Information Center
300 Nicollet Mall, Minneapolis, Minnesota 55401

TABLE OF CONTENTS

This book is dedicated to my families—Benidt, Weir, Kiker, Jenne, Stiles—with love and thanks for their faith and support, and especially to my parents and my brother David, for getting me interested in libraries and books.

The author of this book would like to thank the library's editorial committee and administrators for giving me the opportunity to work on this project; I've enjoyed our association tremendously. Special thanks to Kristi Gibson, Dorothy Burke, Sally Jungers, and J. Marie Pihlblad for many hours of help, and to Abbie Baxter and Lenore Franzen for support and professional advice. My appreciation also goes to Louise Walker McCannel for giving me access to family material on T.B. Walker. Great credit is due the Minneapolis Historical Society, the Minneapolis History Collection of the Minneapolis Public Library, and the Minneapolis Athenaeum, whose collections have preserved the flavor as well as the facts of history. I am also grateful to Robert O. Shipman and Jane Earley of Mankato State University for allowing me the flexibility to work on this book around teaching duties. And thanks to Sharon Benidt for her patience and her careful reading of this manuscript.

Stephen H. Baxter, Jr., quoted in the conclusion of this book, died of cancer between the time the book was written and the time it was published. His efforts remain an example of the dedication of Minnesotans to improving the world around them. Without people like Steve Baxter, the library's past, present, and future would be far less rich.

As librarians, the first thought that occurred to us on the eve of the hundredth anniversary of the Minneapolis Public Library was— what else?—a book. None of us had ever written a book before, much less published one, but it was unthinkable to allow the occasion to pass without producing one. A book is surely the best embodiment for a tribute to our past and a look into our future.

The Minneapolis Public Library has a proud history and a rich tradition, as you will see. Bruce Benidt, the author hired by the library, has captured that spirit admirably, retelling the story of Minneapolis from a perspective unlike any we have been afforded before. We think it is an excellent addition to the city's archive.

Although there are many persons deserving of thanks in the production of this work, I would like especially to thank our Editorial Committee, which was chaired by Kristi Gibson. Members of this committee were: J. Harold Kittleson, Violet Lied, Dorothy Thews, Dorothy Burke, Robert Thompson, and David Benidt. In addition to her work on the committee, Dorothy Burke, in her capacity as librarian of the Minneapolis History Collection, provided invaluable assistance.

Finally, a word about money. Any undertaking of this quality is expensive, and most public library budgets in the waning years of the twentieth century cannot justify such an expenditure. We were fortunate in having two sources of funding: Mr. Walter A. Smith, in a bequest to the library, and the Friends of the Minneapolis Public Library, in the form of a grant. We are extremely grateful for this generosity and we cannot help reflecting that it is that same spirit that helped to make Minneapolis the community that it became and that it continues to be.

The excellence of the Minneapolis Public Library is but a reflection of the city and its people.

Joseph Kimbrough
Director, Minneapolis Public Library

THE LIBRARY 100

1885 / 1985

The history of the Minneapolis Public Library is intertwined with the history of the city and state. This timeline places the library's milestones in perspective with the milestones of local history. Highlights in the library's development are noted in the top part of the timeline, and significant Minneapolis and Minnesota events are recorded below. A color graph charting the patterns of circulation of both adult and juvenile library materials since 1891 is also included.

1859 / Bayard Taylor speaks in Minneapolis to newly formed Young Men's Library Association.

1860 / Young Men's Library Association drafts charter and takes new name, "Minneapolis Athenaeum." Thomas Hale Williams chosen as librarian.

1870 / Dr. Kirby Spencer leaves his estate to the Minneapolis Athenaeum.

1866 / Athenaeum building opens at 215 Hennepin.

1845	1850	1855	1860	1865	1870

1848 / First settlers at St. Anthony.

1849 / Minnesota becomes a territory; first sawmill operates at Falls of St. Anthony. Minnesota Historical Society founded.

1850 / John Stevens builds first house on Minneapolis side of the river.

1851 / University of Minnesota created by territorial legislature. Sioux sign away most of Minnesota at Traverse des Sioux (St. Peter).

1852 / Hennepin County established.

1854 / First commercial flour mill at St. Anthony Falls.

1855 / City of St. Anthony organized. First suspension bridge in history to span main channel of Mississippi River joins Minneapolis and St. Anthony.

1856 / Minneapolis incorporated; charter of incorporation repealed in 1862; incorporated again in 1867.

1857 / State constitution adopted.

1858 / Minnesota becomes 32nd state; Henry Hastings Sibley becomes first governor.

1859 / Alexander Ramsey elected governor.

1862 / Sioux uprising. Train service begins between St. Paul and St. Anthony.

1863 / First Minnesota Regiment saves Union lines at Gettysburg.

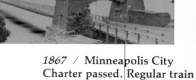

1867 / Minneapolis City Charter passed. Regular train connections to Chicago begin

1869 / First classes held at University of Minnesota.

1870 / Gas lights drawing from wooden gas mains come to Minneapolis.

1891 / Herbert Putnam resigns.

1892 / James K. Hosmer appointed librarian, Gratia Countryman appointed assistant librarian.

1885 / Minneapolis Public Library founded. First Library Board meets. Minneapolis Society of Fine Arts, Minnesota Academy of Natural Sciences and Public Library agree to share a new building. Library and Athenaeum sign a 99-year contract to share resources.

1893 / Children's Room opened downtown, first books loaned to public school collections.

1886 / Ground broken for library building.

1894 / North Branch moves into its own building, first branch building.

1888 / Herbert Putnam named librarian of Minneapolis Public Library, goes on book-buying trip to Europe.

1889 / Library building at 10th and Hennepin opens.

1896 / First woman on Library Board, Jennie C. Crays.

1884 / Herbert Putnam named Athenaeum librarian.

1890 / North and Franklin branches established.

1899 / State Library Commission formed.

1877 / T. B. Walker leads fight to make Athenaeum more accessible to the public.

circulation in millions

adult
juvenile

3
2
1
0

| 1875 | 1880 | 1885 | 1890 | 1895 | 1900 |

372 / Minneapolis and St. Anthony merge.

1873 / Minnesota Academy of Natural Sciences founded.

1876 / John Sargent Pillsbury becomes governor.

1881 / Powers and Donaldsons department stores founded.

1889 / Mayo Clinic opens in Rochester. First electric streetcar in Minneapolis.

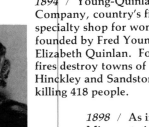

1882 / First hydro-electric station in U.S. begins operation at St. Anthony Falls.

1892 / Republican National Convention in Minneapolis renominates Benjamin Harrison.

1883 / Minneapolis Society of Fine Arts founded. Stone Arch bridge completed across Mississippi. Minneapolis Park Board established. St. Paul Public Library opens.

1894 / Young-Quinlan Company, country's first specialty shop for women, founded by Fred Young and Elizabeth Quinlan. Forest fires destroy towns of Hinckley and Sandstone, killing 418 people.

1878 / Washburn "A" Mill explodes in flour-milling section by the river.

1885 / Lumber Exchange building opens, part of 1880s building boom in Minneapolis.

1898 / As in Civil War, Minnesota is first state to raise troops for Spanish-American War. First moving pictures shown in Minneapolis at Bijou Theater.

1904 / Gratia Countryman becomes librarian, succeeding Hosmer. First addition to downtown library begun.

1905 / First factory stations open, beginning of outreach into the workplace.

1910 / Reading room opens in Bridge Square flophouse district.

1911 / Walker Branch opens on land given by T. B. Walker. Total library circulation passes one-million mark.

1912 / Carnegie grant gives $125,000 for four new branch buildings.

1915 / Society of Fine Arts moves from library to new Art Institute building.

1918 / T. B. Walker offers land and art collection to city if housed in new library building.

1921 / Library wins a two-mill tax increase.

1922 / Hennepin County Library organized, working out of Minneapolis Public Library.

1923 / Hospital service begins.

1925 / Fourth wing of library completed, center court roofed for stacks.

1928 / T. B. Walker dies. Edward C. Gale succeeds Walker as board president.

1930 / Circulation starts rising quickly, budget starts falling as Depression sets in.

1905   1910   1915   1920   1925   1930

1902 / The Dayton Company founded.

1903 / Minneapolis Symphony Orchestra debuts under conductor Emil Oberhoffer.

1904 / New state Capitol completed in St. Paul.

1905 / Minneapolis Municipal Building, with its city hall and courts, opens.

1906 / Dan Patch paces a mile in one minute, 55 seconds at State Fair.

1907 / First Automobile Show at National Guard Armory in Minneapolis. Minnesota passes state-wide highway tax.

1911 / First air-mail flight out of Minneapolis. Lakes Calhoun and Isles linked by boat channel as park development continues.

1915 / Farmers Nonpartisan League formed.

1916 / National convention of Prohibition Party held in St. Paul.

1918 / Former Congressman Charles A. Lindbergh runs as Nonpartisan League candidate in primary for governor.

1919 / Clara Hampson Ueland becomes first president of Minnesota League of Women Voters.

1920 / *Main Street* by Sinclair Lewis and *This Side of Paradise* by F. Scott Fitzgerald published.

1922 / Farmer-Labor Party formed. Three women elected to state legislature. First radio station in Minneapolis begins broadcasting.

1923 / State legislator Myrtle Cain gains nationwide attention by introducing anti-Ku Klux Klan law prohibiting appearance in public masked.

1925 / First car finished at Ford assembly line in St. Paul. State gasoline tax passed.

1926 / Northwest Airlines makes first commercial flight from Minneapolis to Chicago.

1927 / Walker Art Gallery opens in new building.

1929 / Foshay Tower completed.

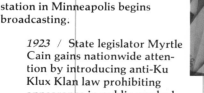

1927 / Charles A. Lindbergh of Little Falls makes first solo flight across the Atlantic. *Giants in the Earth* by O. E. Rolvaag published.

1944 / Carl Vitz becomes president of American Library Association.

1933 / Gratia Countryman elected president of American Library Association.

1945 / Nellie Stone wins Library Board seat, becomes first black elected to public office in Minneapolis. Civic Center Development Association recommends building new library at 4th and Nicollet. Library tax levy voted up to three mills. Carl Vitz resigns.

1951 / Preliminary architectural plans for new library downtown approved.

1936 / Gratia Countryman retires from Minneapolis Public Library.

1955 / City Council gives final approval to 4th and Nicollet site for new library.

1937 / Carl Vitz named librarian.

1957 / Glenn Lewis retires. Raymond Williams becomes librarian, begins reorganizing library service.

1939 / Fiftieth Anniversary celebration for Central Library building. Bookmobile service begins.

1946 / Glenn Lewis becomes librarian.

1958 / Groundbreaking ceremony held for new main library.

1947 / Library Board approves Civic Center site for new library. Library begins circulating 16mm films, is fourth public library in U.S. to do so.

1959 / Controversy over grade school libraries flares. Grade school libraries turned over to public school system. Cornerstone laid for new main library.

1941 / Junior High school libraries discontinued as library system starts cutting back from expansionist era.

1935   1940   1945   1950   1955   1960

'30 / Sinclair Lewis wins [N]obel Prize for Literature.

1940 / Armistice Day blizzard drops 16 inches of snow, takes 49 lives in Minnesota. Minneapolis holds its first Aquatennial Summer Festival.

1951 / Willie Mays called up from Minneapolis Millers to San Francisco Giants. Painter and sculptor George Morrison wins Fulbright scholarship to study in France.

'31 / U.S. Supreme Court [st]rikes down Minnesota prior [re]straint law, establishing [il]egality of censorship in most [ca]ses. Floyd B. Olson elected [st]ate's first Farmer-Labor [Go]vernor.

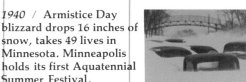

1944 / Democratic-Farmer-Labor Party created.

1954 / Open heart surgery pioneered at University of Minnesota.

1934 / Teamsters' strike in Minneapolis becomes violent. Aerospace scientist Jeanette Piccard is first woman to enter space in record-breaking balloon ascent.

1945 / Hubert Humphrey elected mayor of Minneapolis.

1956 / First plant processing Taconite opens at Silver Bay on shores of Lake Superior.

1946 / Fort Snelling closed as an army post.

1936 / Floyd B. Olson dies during campaign for U. S. Senate.

1958 / State Centennial celebrated; Eugene McCarthy elected to U. S. Senate.

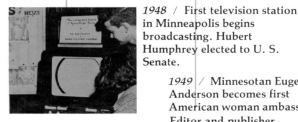

1948 / First television station in Minneapolis begins broadcasting. Hubert Humphrey elected to U. S. Senate.

1949 / Minnesotan Eugenie Anderson becomes first American woman ambassador. Editor and publisher Cecil E. Newman is first black from Minnesota to appear in *Who's Who in America*.

1939 / Harold Stassen becomes "boy wonder" governor.

1959 / St. Lawrence Seaway opens; U. S. Naval vessels visit Duluth.

THE
LIBRARY
1885 **100** 1985

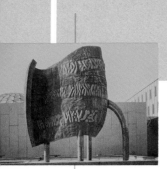

1961 / New main library
opens downtown.

1963 / Ray Williams
resigns.

1964 / Ervin Gaines becomes
librarian.

1966 / Voters approve
increase of library mill rate to
six mills.

1968 / Nokomis Community
Library opens, first new
library building in 37 years.

1969 / MELSA library
network founded.

1971 / Electronic
detection equipment installed
at checkouts in main library.

1974 / City-county library
struggle ends; cooperation
through MELSA the solution.
Ervin Gaines resigns.

1975 / Joseph Kimbrough
becomes librarian.

1979 / Minneapolis: Portrait
of a Life Style program
begins. Card catalog
discontinued; microfilm
catalog begun.

1981 / Walker Community
Library opens in underground
building.

1982 / Bookmobile
service discontinued.

1983 / Friends of the Library
assume planetarium
operation, open new and used
bookstore in central library.
Funding approved for
automated circulation control
system.

THE
LIBRARY
100

1985 / Minneapolis Public
Library centennial celebration.

| 1965 | 1970 | 1975 | 1980 | 1985 | 1990 |

1961 / Orville Freeman
becomes Secretary of
Agriculture in John Kennedy's
cabinet. Twins and Vikings
play first major-league seasons
in Minnesota.

1963 / Tyrone Guthrie
Theater opens with Hamlet,
starring George Grizzard.

1964 / Hubert Humphrey
elected Vice President of the
United States. Minneapolis journalist
and diplomat Carl Rowan
named director of U.S.
Information Agency.

1965 / Twins win American League pennant.
University of Minnesota graduate Roy
Wilkins named executive director of the NAACP.

1967 / North Stars play first
season in Minnesota. Nicollet
Mall dedicated.

1968 / Eugene McCarthy
challenges Lyndon Johnson for
presidency over Vietnam War
issue. Humphrey gets Democratic nomination, loses to Nixon.

1971 / New Walker Art
Center opens.

1972 / IDS Center opens.

1974 / New Minneapolis
Institute of Arts, Children's
Theater, and College of Art
and Design complex opens, as
do Orchestra Hall and Hennepin County Government Center.

1975 / Minneapolis Regional
Native American Center
opens, dedicated to meeting
cultural, social and recreational needs of American
Indian community and to
achieving better understanding
between cultures.

1976 / Walter Mondale
elected Vice President of the
United States.

1979 / Former Congressman
Donald Fraser elected mayor
of Minneapolis.

1980 / Dr. Richard Green
named first black
superintendent of Minneapolis
Public Schools.

1981 / U. S. hostages released
in Iran, including Minnesotan
L. Bruce Laingen.

1982 / First baseball game
played in Hubert H.
Humphrey Metrodome.
Thanksgiving Day fire
destroys old Donaldsons
department store and part of
Northwestern Bank Building
at 6th and Nicollet.

1983 / Marlene Johnson
becomes state's first woman
lieutenant governor.

1984 / Walter Mondale runs
for president. Norwest Center
model unveiled, at 66 stories
to be highest in city.

Centennial History
of the Minneapolis Public Library

George Miles Ryan Studios, Minneapolis 1960-61

"Libraries are the granaries of knowledge, and are as necessary for the growth and improvement of the mind, as granaries of corn and wheat for the sustenance of the body," Thomas Hale Williams wrote to John Eaton, U.S. Commissioner of Education, in 1876. Williams, one of the creators of what would become the Minneapolis Public Library, added that libraries are important as "storehouses for the experience of the past, to make it available for the present and the future." The sculpture by John Rood that stands in front of the Minneapolis Public Library demonstrates the library's role of capturing wisdom and transporting it across time. On the rippling form of a scroll Rood fashioned symbols representing the most ancient forms of writing from the beginnings of civilization. Behind the scroll lies the granary of knowledge, open to all.

Granaries of Knowledge

Outside the library in downtown Minneapolis is the John Rood sculpture of a scroll, rippling above a reflecting pool. The city was told at the new library's opening in 1961 that the Rood scroll, with its written symbols and its age, represents "the stream of human thought." The sculpture "points to the library where man's recorded thought is made available to those who seek it."

That's not a bad definition of a library. For, whether it's Einstein's speculation about the workings of the universe, Henry Adams's observation of the world changing around the machine, or Mary Stewart's evocation of a far country and time, human thought and the record of human action are captured and waiting for us inside the walls of the library.

A library is a storehouse, but that's only the inert aspect of it. A shelf of books is part of a library the way a granary full of wheat is part of a farm. Beyond and around that storehouse, that granary, are the wind and the rain and the sun, the good years and bad, the struggle of the seed in rich land or barren, the toil and the hope of the people. A farm and a library are living things. The grain and the books are the nourishment and seed those living things produce to sustain more life.

One hundred years after the founding of the Minneapolis Public Library, this book looks at the people and the environment and the hopes that have sustained that library. This is a story of people and their visions—visions that were sometimes humanitarian and philanthropic, sometimes self-serving. In this story are people who used a

"A popular Government, without popular information, or the means of acquiring it, is but a Prologue to a Farce or a Tragedy; or perhaps both. Knowledge will forever govern ignorance; and a people who mean to be their own Governors, must arm themselves with the power which knowledge gives."

— *James Madison*

collection of books to shape a city; if they hadn't, our city would be different visually, economically, and spiritually. In this story are people who fought for intellectual freedom, people who were leaders in the national library field, and at least two people, Gratia Countryman and T.B. Walker, who deserve part of the thanks for Minneapolis today being a city of unusually literate and well-educated people.

The pioneers who settled Minnesota, many of them, brought along a respect for education and a love of books. Yet it took nearly thirty years after statehood to establish a public library in Minneapolis. And when the library was started, it was begun by people who really didn't need it, who were wealthy enough to afford books and educational resources on their own. Were these founders early examples of the public-spirited business and professional leaders who continue to help worthy causes in the 1980s in Minneapolis? Or did they have some other benefits in mind, some way they thought the library would help them after they'd offered it to the general public?

There are two theories about a public library's role in society; both influenced the development of the library in Minneapolis. The theories are related rather than mutually exclusive, and traces of both will be seen in this history. Each theory looks at how public libraries benefit American society, but one focuses on empowering the individual, while the other focuses on perpetuating the established order of society.

The first theory is democratization—a central theme of America that we all learn in school. Because people rule in a democracy, they have to be educated so they will make intelligent decisions. To make democracy work, education must be widespread; then anyone of talent and determination can rise to whatever level gumption and luck will allow. A public library, the "people's university," is a free tool of education that makes books that are too expensive for the common people available to all.

In the middle of the nineteenth century, the preamble to a proposed law governing the establishment of public libraries in Massachusetts spelled out this idea, saying, "a universal diffusion of knowledge among the people must be highly conducive to the preservation of their freedom, a greater equalization of social advantages, their industrial success, and their physical, intellectual and moral advancement and elevation . . . ."[1] Sidney Ditzion, a historian of the library movement, explained how the notion of democratization tied in with other American ideas before the turn of the century: "With educational opportunity for high and low alike and every inducement for the individual to improve himself by every means within his power, the process of intense competition was producing a race of self-reliant, intelligent, adaptable, enterprising Americans."[2] People could rise to any challenge that a changing world could produce, with the help of education. And, between 1850 and 1900, when the public library movement gathered steam, the world was changing rapidly. The industrial revolution was demanding of nearly everyone new knowledge of science, engineering, and mechanics. Massachusetts statesman Edward Everett (the man who made the other address at Gettysburg, the one little noted nor long remembered), said our public schools trained minds which, after their youthful school years, had nowhere to go but much still to learn about the world. He felt the public library could step in with what we now call "adult education."

There was a missionary side to this benevolent theory of libraries. Public libraries could improve people's moral lives and help them navigate successfully between the shoals of sin and corruption, which were becoming so prevalent in a rapidly urbanizing America. Many of the founders of libraries in New England, where libraries got their best start in this country, were afraid of what would happen as cities grew. They, like Thomas Jefferson, had seen what the factory towns of Europe had become, and wanted no repetition of that in their new world. They were afraid that the young men and women off the farms, and the immigrants off the boats, with their families far away and with a little money earned from city jobs, would fall into vice. A clean, well-lighted reading room might save these innocents from other pastimes. "Let the library be free to all, and then, perhaps, there will be one young man less in the place where intoxicating drinks are found," said an 1865 report of the public library at Lowell, Massachusetts. Continuing, in a sexist tone, the report said, "Make the library free to all and then, perhaps there will be one young woman less to fall from the path of purity and goodness down to that depth of degradation and misery to which only a woman can fall."[3]

This idea was extended from saving individuals to saving society by many idealists in the profession. According to historian Rosemary Ruhig DuMont, "Public libraries endeavored to promote the good life for all. Emphasis was placed on educating the individual to achieve personal happiness and security. Reading in the library would save children from a life of crime and would enable adults to advance economically in their vocation. As a consequence, crime and poverty would be wiped out."[4] This tied in with the rationalist idea, espoused by Jefferson and other founders of America, that humankind was perfectible if the mind was nourished enough through widespread education.

But this democratization ideal had a potentially negative aspect to it, which can be seen in the 1876 report on public libraries by the U.S. Bureau of Education: "As the varied intelligence which books can supply shall be more and more wisely assimilated, the essential elements of every political and social question may be confidently submitted to that instructed common sense upon which the founders of our government relied."[5] This is good democratic doctrine—you should be informed before you cast your vote—but it's possible to detect here a

"I have an unshaken conviction that democracy can never be undermined if we maintain our library resources and a national intelligence capable of utilizing them."

—*Franklin Delano Roosevelt, in a letter honoring Herbert Putnam's fortieth anniversary as Librarian of Congress*

Harrison E. Salisbury grew up in the neighborhood of the Sumner branch library in Minneapolis. As a journalist covering the Soviet Union, he saw that libraries there were closed to the public. A citizen's free access to information in America, Salisbury said, helps preserve our freedom. "The Sumner Library had not cost enough to buy the wheels of a super-bomber today or a thimbleful of nuclear explosive. But to me the contribution of the library to America's security outweighed all the MX's we might build. It had staying power. So did the people who learned to be Americans within its modest walls."

—From **A Journey For Our Times, A Memoir**

hint of fear of the masses, and a sense that participation in government is a permission handed down by an elite after the masses have proven themselves, rather than a right guaranteed by the system.

Melvil Dewey, a patron saint of the library movement and father of the Dewey decimal system of book classification, was quoted in an 1888 government report as saying, "To teach the masses to read and then to turn them out in early youth with this power and no guiding influence, is only to invite catastrophe. . . . The world agrees that it is unwise to give sharp tools and powerful weapons to the masses without some assurance of how they are to be used."[6]

Attaining that assurance is where the second theory, the theory of social control, comes in. This idea says that, although America is a democracy, the country is really controlled by a small percentage of the population. This small, powerful group uses education to explain and rationalize the system to the people who support it. The general public is given democratic power, but, in the social control idea, the elite that guides the country will make sure the public uses the power as the elite would have them do. The best way to assure this is to pass on the elite's value system to the general public, namely through education and through libraries.

Michael H. Harris, a historian and library scholar, advances the idea that the founders of the library movement, men of the Boston Brahmin class, were a social elite that believed in the stratification of society, not in equality. These men were suspicious of the masses, and wanted them to accept the values and the ways of the founders. While these wealthy men believed that humankind was perfectible, or could at least be improved, they felt that there would always be an aristocracy of talent and virtue that would lead the masses. Many of these men saw libraries as a way to educate the masses to follow these natural leaders—the "best and brightest"—rather than follow simplistic demagogues. Libraries could also serve to educate the new "best and brightest" leaders to their role of maintaining the system set up by the founders.

Sidney Ditzion quotes Thomas Russell, president of Princeton University, speaking at the 1871 dedication of the Hingham Public Library in Massachusetts. An educated public, Russell said, is "not so easily led away by agitators; in short, more easily and more cheaply governed."[7] Historian Dee Garrison, considering ideas like this, wrote in 1979 that "if we are to overcome library mythology, it is important to consider that the building of public libraries was motivated by a fear of egalitarianism and upheaval from below as much as by a desire for democratic extension and education."[8] The people in power, according to the social control idea, didn't want their way of life swept away by angry masses. Harris writes of the wealthy philanthropists who helped fund the library movement: "Carnegie and his fellows considered the library a wise investment in order, stability, and sound economic

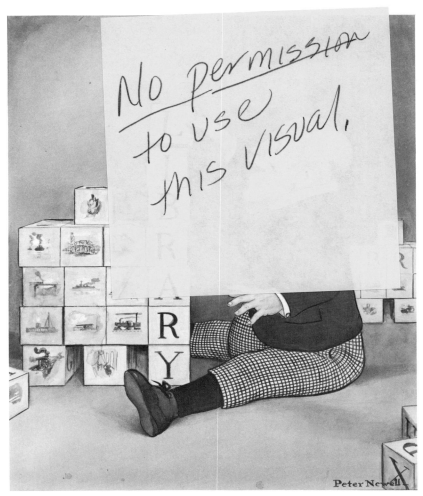

Cartoon by Peter Newell. Used by permission of The Houghton Library, Harvard University, Department of Printing and Graphics, Francis L. Hofer bequest

Andrew Carnegie in a caricature appearing in *Harper's Weekly* in 1903. Carnegie's boyishness is portrayed as he plays with building blocks to make a library. Carnegie gave library buildings to 1,408 communities in America, including four branch buildings to Minneapolis. Some people in Minneapolis thought the steel magnate's money was tainted, and that the city shouldn't accept it, but the library system was glad to have it. According to some critics, Carnegie spent money on libraries as an investment in stability and order, educating American workers into the system that had made Carnegie rich.

This cartoon appeared in *The Minneapolis Star* on September 12, 1966. It expressed the newspaper's support for increasing the city's funding of public libraries after voters in previous years had turned down several measures to increase the library's taxing power. The day after the cartoon appeared, voters approved increasing the library's share of city tax funds. In the year after that, additional funding passed by a two-thirds vote in the primary election; the library purchased fifteen thousand new books as compared to only two thousand the year before.

growth."[9] Harris quotes an 1894 speech by Andrew Carnegie, the steel magnate who spent millions spreading libraries across America (and of whom Mark Twain said, "He has bought fame and paid cash for it"). Carnegie said, "The result of knowledge is to make men not violent revolutionists, but cautious evolutionists; not destroyers, but careful improvers."[10]

Heading off revolutionary change was important. Rosemary DuMont quotes from a 1910 American Library Association publication: "Free corn in old Rome bribed a mob and kept it passive. By free books and what goes in them in modern America we mean to erase the mob from existence."[11] Sidney Ditzion quotes a librarian in 1893, when the national economy was falling apart, as saying, "If society cannot provide work for all, the idle—chronic or temporary—are much safer with a book in the library than elsewhere."[12]

In relation to the social control idea, librarians have been accused by some critics of feeling more affinity for the elite who support the libraries than for the masses who patronize them. Michael Harris asserted in 1978 that "the librarian has shown a clear insensitivity to the needs, hopes, and aspirations of the lower and middle classes in America. Invariably the library profession has defined its role in the context of suggestions directed at it by the social-cultural elite. Too frequently the librarian has exhibited a distaste for the rest of society that goes far beyond social criticism and approximates arrogance. Too frequently they have scorned the things the common man holds dear, and smiled benignly at the things he loves."[13]

Neither of these theories completely fits the development of any library. In the story of the Minneapolis Public Library, we'll see reflections of both. But any good public library, with a broad collection like that in Minneapolis, can be used by individuals for whatever purpose they choose. We'll see the Minneapolis library in the 1960s defending the purchase and circulation of revolutionary material and citing as precedent the inclusion of incendiary writing from the American Revolution in its collection. Works to please the most conservative or the most liberal viewpoints are available in the Minneapolis library, free for all to use.

Of course, although we say the library is free, it really isn't. It takes a great many tax dollars to run it every year, and more tax dollars to buy reading material and to put up the buildings in which that material is made available. Money has always been a major concern of libraries. As J. Harold Kittleson, a longtime friend of the Minneapolis library, wrote to a newspaper in 1955, when a new central library was being put off again and again, "Though all the people of a city benefit by major improvements and perhaps 90 percent would say it was the thing to do if they were polled, nearly everyone wants someone else to pay for these improvements."[14] Although Minneapolis is, as the library's current director, Joseph Kimbrough, says, "a library-friendly town" compared to most, throughout this history we'll see that there have been many times when the people of Minneapolis or their representatives have said, "Enough, no more money—make do."

From the beginning, some people inside the library have complained that the town wasn't supporting it well enough. Many have felt that limited support was a result of the public not really understanding the value of the library. Ervin Gaines, director before Kimbrough, said in 1974, "The public perceives the library as a cultural and largely cosmetic amenity of no crucial importance—hardly on a level of importance with public health, education, safety or transportation. This is a mistaken perception which will require time to adjust."[15] The library is a good thing to have in town, like the Guthrie or Minnehaha Falls, citizens might say, but really, what good does it do us? Those who work in the library, of course, and those who use it consistently, would say we couldn't get along without it, that it affects the daily life of the city and its people.

To the great dismay of many librarians and library supporters, however, there are more people in town who don't use the library than there are people who do. In 1966, Minnesota poet, writer, and historian Betty Bridgman, a familiar face at the Minneapolis library, wrote, "Out of the city population of about a million, 35 percent might eventually visit the library to see what they were getting for their money. This proportion has been the 'ceiling' on use of libraries nationwide for at least 15 years, and the rising literacy rate hasn't increased it. Two-thirds of the population is subsidizing a first class library for the use of the rest of us, and principally me."[16]

It may be a minority of people who use the library, but library Director Joseph Kimbrough says it isn't just those who use the library directly who benefit from it. Information gathered from the library is used by government and business, by newspaper reporters and teachers, by artists and historians and social service agencies. The results of the efforts of these people and groups can affect people who've never set foot inside a library. "We turn on a small number of people who then turn on others," Kimbrough says. Besides, Kimbrough adds, trying to picture a city without a library as part of its cultural and educational landscape, "I think it would be bleak; and if it didn't exist, somebody would be scrambling around to set one up."

The story of the people who scrambled around to set up the Minneapolis Public Library a century ago, and of how that library has changed, and grown, will help answer the question of what good the library does us and what this city might be like without it.

*Minnesota writer and humorist Garrison Keillor mentioned in a conversation with the author of this book one of the dark sides of any library—fines. Once he checked out T. S. Eliot's **The Cocktail Party,** because he felt it was one of those things he should read. He couldn't get into it, he said, and the book burrowed under a pile of other books in his room. He's had it, somewhere, for more than twenty years. "It's a source of great guilt to me," Keillor said. He lives in fear that, like Santa Claus and St. Peter, librarians are keeping tabs on him. "Every day they put another dime against my name." Keillor will have to live a long life to break the record for an overdue fine. A book checked out from the University of Cincinnati Library in 1823 was returned in 1968 by the borrower's great-grandson. The fine, which was waived, was figured at $22,646.*

—Overdue information from Robert Hendrickson, **The Literary Life and Other Curiosities** (Penguin Books, 1982)

Downtown Minneapolis, 1854. Colonel John Stevens's white frame house, barely visible at the right of this photo, was the only permanent dwelling in what would one day be Minneapolis. Winnebago, Sioux, and Chippewa Indians camped frequently around the house. Stevens and his wife Frances passed their time playing the piano and reading from their personal library. The population of all the growing Minnesota territory in 1850 was only 6,077. The following year, the Sioux would sign a treaty with Governor Alexander Ramsey, turning over most of their land in Minnesota to the government, their tepees and hopes drifting westward.

Frontier Readers

The forces that led to the development of a public library in the growing little town of Minneapolis more than a hundred years ago will sound familiar to any present-day observer of the city. The first people who settled next to the falls of St. Anthony were interested in three things: developing a town with all the amenities that would attract and hold a healthy business community; educating their young people so Minneapolis would continue to prosper; and proving to the rest of the country that they weren't just a gang of uncouth barbarians out in the western wilderness.

These motives remain high on the list of those Minneapolis citizens who, in the second half of the twentieth century, have worked to build a Tyrone Guthrie Theater and other cultural institutions, to renovate the city's downtown business district, and to develop a strong system of education. The names have changed from Walker and Lowry to Dayton and Cowles, but the aims are the same.

The role of a library in solidifying Minneapolis's claim to being a city of promise and importance was reflected in the words of the *Minneapolis Journal* when the first stout, stone library building opened in 1889: "The opening of the Public Library Building . . . accentuates the fact that Minneapolis is not only a great manufacturing and business center, but is a liberal and appreciative nurturer of all the multiplied refinements of the highest civilization. The eastern conception of the west as the 'wild west,' uncultured and with grosser tastes, has been rapidly undergoing dissolution of late years, with a riper knowledge

Photograph from the Bromley Collection

Colonel John H. Stevens, the Mexican War veteran who pioneered settlement on the west side of the Mississippi across from St. Anthony where Minneapolis would later rise. Stevens's house became the center of civilization in young Minneapolis, serving as a gathering place for evening talks and for organizing a government on the west side of the river.

of the situation derived from personal and more frequent contact with the people of the great interior."[1]

From the outset, people who settled in America's great interior had (and in many ways still retain) a bit of an inferiority complex when they compared themselves with the more established and cultured East. They continually strove to prove that they, too, could be refined. Yet many of them, especially those who settled in Minneapolis, brought from New England a solid tradition of education and an understanding of the enjoyment and wisdom of the printed word. Besides, they had a lot of long winter nights to get through. Turning to a collection of books and the civility of a reading room was a natural way for them to serve all these needs and traditions.

The first settlers arrived in 1848 at what would become the village of St. Anthony, on the east side of the falls. (The St. Anthony settlement was located where St. Anthony Main and the Winslow House are now: across the Mississippi River from the present downtown Minneapolis. The city of Minneapolis absorbed St. Anthony in 1872.) The first permanent dwelling on the west side of the river, in what would become Minneapolis, was built in 1850. It would be another nine years before the first enduring private library association, the Minneapolis Athenaeum, was founded, and another thirty-nine before the Minneapolis Public Library opened the doors of its first building; but books and the habit of reading, and the sheen of civilization that habit imparted, were with the people of Minneapolis from the beginning.

L. W. Stratton developed the first St. Anthony store that included books and a small circulating library on the corner of Main Street and Third Avenue in 1850, according to *Minnesota Pioneer Sketches* (1904), by Frank O'Brien.[2] Called the Farmer's Exchange, the store stocked popular novels, magazines, and newspapers from the East, and did a lively business. Settlers would come from as far as what are now the towns of Delano and Savage to read and to discuss the issues of the day. The store opened at 6:00 A.M. and closed at 10:00 P.M., except on Saturdays, when the press of business and socializing kept it open sometimes until midnight.

Across the river that same year, 1850, Colonel John H. Stevens built Minneapolis's first house—a small but trim white dwelling overlooking the falls. Stevens, a New England Yankee and Mexican War veteran, came to Minnesota for his health. In the spring of 1851 he planted wheat, corn, and oats on his side of the river and watched them, and eventually a great city, grow. But at first, Stevens and his wife, Frances, lived a pioneer life, surrounded frequently by the tepees of Winnebago and Sioux Indians. It was a lonely time, but, as he wrote later, "Fortunately I had a pretty good library, and Mrs. Stevens had a piano and other musical instruments, which had a tendency to banish from the little house most of the lonesomeness naturally incident to pioneer life so far from neighbors."[3]

Stevens greatly valued reading and the life of the mind. In his book *Personal Recollections*, published in 1890, he listed the habit of reading with the virtues of industry, economy, and church-going as the important characteristics of Minnesota's pioneers. He said of an early library association that was formed in St. Anthony in 1849, "The good results that flowed from the institution seem to have been the commencement of the real tendency of the citizens, which has ever distinguished them, to a high order of mental development."[4]

Stevens recorded that in 1854 John M. Anderson, the first book merchant as well as a bookbinder, opened his doors in the fledgling town of Minneapolis. By 1858, Stevens noted with pride, there were three Minneapolis businessmen, including another New Englander named Thomas Hale Williams, who were supplying "the citizens with choice books and the magazines of the day."

The citizens at the falls were enormously proud of their town and its prospects. They felt they were building a "New England of the West," combining their industriousness with the natural beauty and the water power of the setting to develop a town that would be second to none in the state and able to hold its head up among any in the nation.

Not even the infamous Minnesota winters deterred the spirited pioneers from boosting their new city. A writer in the *St. Anthony Express*, putting forward a charitable opinion of January in Minnesota, wrote, "Let not our distant readers suppose that we suffer any inconveniences from the cold. Far from it, its only effect is to make business more stirring and lively."[5] Thomas Hale Williams was also forgiving in his attitude toward northern winters. In 1857, he wrote that "a general error prevails as to the winters of Minnesota. Judging from the latitude, people regard them (as might be expected) as being *very severe*. This erroneous view is soon eradicated from the mind by residence during a winter or two in the Territory." Williams admitted that the thermometer did often slip below zero in this winter paradise, but said "the dry, pure atmosphere of Minnesota" made this "but pleasant weather." The winter air is not chilling, he continued, but is bracing, strengthening, exhilarating, "a delicious food for lungs. We seldom know of coughs or colds."[6]

Lucile Kane, in her 1966 history *The Waterfall That Built a City*, painted a less idyllic picture of the town's early days: "Sprawled over a lightly wooded prairie sloping gently to the river, St. Anthony at first glance looked like a New England village. Gleaming white houses, surrounded by gardens and cattle grazing in the open land . . . ." But, she soon added, a closer scrutiny of the town revealed less pristine details: sap oozing from houses built with green wood, pigs roaming among

Some things never change in Minneapolis. Colonel John Stevens and his wife, Frances, the first settlers on the Minneapolis side of the river, occasionally missed the "refining influences and conveniences of a well-regulated New York household." But the biggest problem was mosquitoes. "Mosquitoes surrounded the house in such swarms that smoke would not banish them. The windows and doors were barricaded with netting, but that did not suffice to protect us from them." Stevens wrote in 1851, "mosquitoes were more numerous than ever. At sunset the air was filled with them. Everyone, unless protected, was made to suffer from their blood-thirstiness." Stevens, a man of the world, said he'd been well acquainted with this pest in Mexico, Texas, and at the mouth of the Mississippi, "places noted throughout the world for being a great rendezvous of mosquitoes—but I never saw them more numerous than in the neighborhood of the falls during the first few years after the occupation by the whites."

—Quotes from Horace Hudson, *A Half Century of Minneapolis,* and John H. Stevens, *Personal Recollections* tree stumps left in the dirt street, and the constant whining of the sawmills at the falls.[7] And not all the citizens, of course, were scholars eagerly in search of learning and improvement. One early pioneer, James McMullen, recalled St. Anthony in the 1850s as a rollicking place where pranks and a kind of kangaroo court helped blunt the harshness of life. St. Anthony had no sidewalks, but strangers were brought to court for spitting on them, nevertheless, and, as a fine, ordered to buy stogies for the loitering crowd that acted as jury. One visiting attorney was fined apples and cigars for the heinous offense of sporting a stovepipe hat in public.[8]

Not all the pressures of pioneer life were vented so easily. Newspapers in the 1850s and 1860s all too often carried notices of citizens who, desperate and drunk, threw themselves to their deaths in the rushing Mississippi.

But these were the exceptions. For most of its citizens, St. Anthony was a good place, strong and open with the hard-earned optimism of the frontier. Charles Loring, the "father" of the Minneapolis park system, looked back on those pioneer times and said, "The winters were cold, but bright and clear. The few neighbors were hospitable and kind, and I doubt if there has been a time in the history of Minneapolis when its citizens were happier than they were in the pioneer days of the early '60s."[9]

By and large, the people who came to the falls were built of stout stuff. In 1908, historian Horace Hudson looked back on the early days and offered a theory about these pioneers. Because Minnesota was settled during the California gold rush, "the wilder and less stable elements of western emigration at that time naturally gravitated to the coast, while Minnesota attracted the more hard-headed and far-seeing."[10] So while the lawless element headed for the mining camps of the Far West, Minnesota attracted the law-abiding emigrants.

Law-abiding *and* educated. In 1851, a St. Paul newspaper, in an example of a spirited rivalry that persists to this day, had indirectly attacked the intelligence of the settlers of St. Anthony. The *St. Anthony Express*, founded that same year, immediately rose to the defense of its readers: "It is probably speaking within bounds to say, that five-sixths of our native population are from New England and New York. This should be sufficient prima facie evidence of the intelligence of any community. All can read and write, and nine-tenths have enjoyed the advantages of the excellent common schools, which are the pride and glory of New England."[11]

To prove further the mental acuity of the folks at the falls, the newspaper, in a neat piece of self-justification, pointed out that every voter in town took one or more copies of the *Express*, and added that subscriptions to newspapers from other cities and the beginnings of a library further demonstrated the quality of the citizenry.

Photograph from the Bromley Collection

The Winslow House, one of the early landmarks of St. Anthony. This
stately stone hotel was built in 1856 by James M. Winslow, partly to
catch the trade of Southerners who took steamboats up the Mississippi
to the Minnesota Territory to escape the thick summer heat of their
homes. On a rise at Main Street and Central Avenue, the Winslow
House reigned over St. Anthony and overlooked the Mississippi and the
falls. The Civil War stopped the Southern trade, and the Winslow
House fell into decline, the meetings, parties, and balls only a memory.
In 1872, Macalester College rented the building, but left for St. Paul in
1881. The Winslow House was demolished to make way for the
Exposition Building on the same site in 1886. The Exposition Building
came down in 1940, replaced by a Coca-Cola bottling plant. That is
gone now, too, and the site of the old Winslow House is part of the
continuing rejuvenation of St. Anthony Main. In 1980, just across
Central Avenue from the site of the original Winslow House, a new
Winslow House overlooking the river and a bustling St. Anthony was
opened. The least expensive condominium in the new Winslow House
when it opened cost just slightly less than the one hundred sixty
thousand dollars that J.M. Winslow got for his entire hotel when he sold
it in 1858.

A library remained the key to learning and culture for many who were thinking of how the settlement at the falls would develop. Several private libraries and library associations were formed in the 1850s. Although none except the Minneapolis Athenaeum lasted, they showed the determination of those early residents to build an institution that clearly proclaimed the value of learning. The *St. Anthony Express*, which was written as much for Eastern readers who might be convinced to become Western settlers as it was for the population of its own community, described, in an 1852 issue, one of the early libraries in the village: "Among the institutions of our town for the promotion of intelligence and morality, there is none more laudable and deserving of

Photograph by B.F. Upton, the Bromley Collection

The sawmills that helped build the city are seen in this photo of Hennepin Island, St. Anthony Falls, and Minneapolis, taken from the roof of the Winslow House in St. Anthony in 1870. Franklin Steele built the first commercial sawmill at the falls on the St. Anthony side in 1847. The lumber business and the city around the falls boomed, but lumbering hit its peak here in 1899, dropping off precipitously in the next twenty years. In the foreground of this photograph are the St. Anthony sawmills, and on the far side of the river, the Minneapolis mills. The city water works is the four-story white building just to the right of the long, low sheds of the Minneapolis mills. To the left of the Minneapolis sawmills, close by the falls, are several flour mills. Flour milling would not take over dominance in Minneapolis until after the turn of the century. Just above the Minneapolis sawmills is another four-story white building—the Cataract House—a hotel on Washington Avenue.

the liberal patronage of our citizens than the public library. There is, perhaps, nothing which better indicates the character of a community, than the range and quality of the library it maintains. And when it is made accessible to all classes, it is one of the best means for the dissemination of intelligence, and the building up of a sound morality and healthy tone of public sentiment. There is nothing, either, which more promotes the reputation of a town abroad, or in the estimation of substantial and valuable men, constitutes a town a desirable residence. It is to be hoped, therefore, that the constant and zealous interest of our citizens will never cease to be manifested for the maintenance and extension of this important institution. Let the number of its volumes increase with the growth of our town, and St. Anthony will eventually outstrip all her neighbors in the intelligence and morality of her people, as she now does in the classic beauty of her position and her natural resources for business."[12]

St. Anthony was indeed growing, and so was the new community of Minneapolis on the west bank of the Mississippi. In 1855, the year St. Anthony was incorporated as a city, a suspension bridge was opened, linking St. Anthony and Minneapolis and replacing a ferry that Colonel Stevens had operated. That same year, the government began selling land around Stevens's home that had been part of the Fort Snelling military reservation. The bridge and the land sale began a building boom that would enable Minneapolis eventually to absorb its earlier counterpart, St. Anthony. First sawmills, feeding off the vast northern forests of the Mississippi watershed, and then flour mills, processing the fruits of the fertile land to the south and west, fueled the growth of the brash young city at the falls. Still in the future, in 1867, was the organization of Minneapolis as a city with a charter, and farther ahead still, in 1872, the merger of the two cities into one.

The story of the Minneapolis Public Library begins in earnest in 1859, a year that showed a pause in the commercial development of the city, but that would be a landmark in its intellectual development.

Three men were instrumental in the paternity of the Minneapolis Public Library: Bayard Taylor, an author and lecturer whose appearance in Minnesota in 1859 provided the catalyst for the formation of a lasting library association; Thomas Hale Williams, the bookseller and librarian who nurtured that private library association, the Minneapolis Athenaeum, into strength; and Thomas Barlow Walker, the lumberman and art collector who fought to make the Athenaeum more accessible to the public and who eventually led the way to the formation of a public library, which was chartered in 1885.

The years leading up to 1859 had been rough ones. In 1857, crops in Minnesota had been poor, the flow of immigration had slowed, and money was tight, Colonel Stevens wrote. The year 1858 opened gloomily, with trade depressed, currency depreciated, and business and real

Frontier Readers

Bayard Taylor, a man who made his living by traveling and then writing and talking about his experiences. He was a nationally known newspaperman and a best-selling author in the middle 1800s, and his arrival in a town meant diverting tales would be delivered from the lecture stage. His visit to St. Anthony in 1859 was the catalyst for the formation of a private library association, and the profits from his talk helped fund that group, which became the Minneapolis Athenaeum. The Athenaeum, in turn, was the founding organization from which grew the Minneapolis Public Library.

estate sales bad. And the national financial panic in 1857 had made money so scarce in the struggling community by St. Anthony Falls that, according to one pioneer, if it hadn't been for the demand for ginseng, many people wouldn't have made it. Ginseng was a root that grew wild along the Crow River and in many other wooded spots west and south of Minneapolis. It was valued as a medicinal herb and, according to pioneer Frank O'Brien, as a substitute for opium. Farmers and townspeople alike gathered the root and brought it to drying houses in Minneapolis, from where it was shipped to China.

Minneapolis at this time had a population of 5,830. As no railroad lines had yet reached the town from the East, visitors arrived by stagecoach or riverboat. One of those visitors was Bayard Taylor, a thirty-four-year-old adventurer, author, and lecturer. He came to Minneapolis in 1859 with his wife, Marie Hansen Taylor, who later wrote that St. Anthony and "the four-year-old town of Minneapolis across the river, are situated at the end of civilization. North of these two places the only inhabitants are Indians, bears and wolves."[13]

Historian Donald Dale Jackson called Bayard Taylor "a connoisseur of the exotic throughout a peripatetic life."[14] At the age of twenty-one, Taylor had become a literary celebrity for a travel book about Europe. He was the first serious writer to follow the 49ers to the California gold fields and to publish a book about it. He was an adventurer eager to poke his nose into the antiquities of civilization or into the rawest corners of the frontier. He served as a travel correspondent for Horace Greeley's nationally-circulated *New York Tribune,* and to augment his fame and his income he went on the exhausting national lyceum tour. In nine years he gave six hundred talks, including several lectures in Minnesota. Taylor was not, however, universally admired; one contemporary critic said "Taylor has travelled more and seen less than any man alive." But to the frontier town of Minneapolis, Taylor was a glowing light.

He announced in the spring of 1859 that he was making a tour of what was then called "The Northwest," including Minnesota, and would lecture before any literary or library society that would pay his expenses and a small fee, and that the remainder of the income could go to benefit the group that would sponsor him.

There had been earlier lecture and library societies formed around the falls. In an era without radio, television, or motion pictures, a visiting lecturer, imported by these societies on a fairly regular basis, provided education, entertainment, and a social occasion to break the routine of life. These earlier groups had come and gone, but Taylor's visit spawned a lasting organization.

On May 16, 1859, a group of businessmen met in a Minneapolis office to organize a library association to take advantage of Taylor's offer. Two days later the group approved a constitution for the "Young

Red River carts rolling down Main Street in St. Anthony in 1855 or 1856. Before railroads crossed the prairie, the Red River carts were the main overland connections between the towns on the Mississippi and Minnesota rivers and the rich fur country to the north. The carts would travel more than four hundred miles, bringing in furs from Canada and the northwest corner of Minnesota and returning with supplies for the Red River settlements. Caravans of carts lashed together in train would leave from the north as soon as enough spring grass had grown on the prairies to feed the oxen and horses that pulled the carts. The drivers of the caravans were mixtures of French, Scotch, English, Cree, and Chippewa blood, and their colorful demeanor and the shrieking of the ungreased cart wheels made the arrival of the Red River parties an event to be noticed.

Men's Library Association of Minneapolis." On May 25, Taylor, after earlier talks in St. Paul and St. Anthony, crossed the river and delivered his lecture, "Life in the North." The take was $141.75; $58.25 went to the lecturer, $83.50 to the association. Of the association's money $9.00 went to cover incidental expenses, and the remainder became seed money for an organization that was to flower, exactly one hundred years later, into the present Minneapolis Public Library building on something to be called the Nicollet Mall in a city these founders could scarcely have imagined.

The following winter, January 1860, the library association reorganized itself under a new charter and a new name, "The Minneapolis Athenaeum." (The word "Athenaeum" derives from a sanctuary in Athens dedicated to Athena, goddess of wisdom and arts, as well as of industry and prudent warfare. The sanctuary was frequented by men of letters and learning, and during the 1800s gave its name to many institutions dedicated to the nurturing of literacy and ideas.)

Why was this group successful? Why did it last when others had not? It had the same dash of idealism other such groups had possessed, as shown by the preamble to the Athenaeum's constitution: "We, the citizens of Minneapolis, believing that the cause of truth, morality and virtue can be greatly aided and established through the instrumentality of a public library, lectures and debates, do hereby agree to form ourselves into an association."[15]

But it had something more: a man experienced in building a library and dedicated to the educational role a library could play; and several shrewd businessmen members who were dedicated to the development of the city, and who saw a healthy library as an important part of that development.

The original officers of the Athenaeum were: E. J. Jones, president; William F. Russell, vice-president; John S. Young, secretary; and Cyrus Aldrich, David Morgan, and Thomas Hale Williams, directors. This last name is the one that really counts.

Thomas Hale Williams is crucial to the story of books in Minneapolis. He was a bookseller, a director of the Athenaeum, the Athenaeum's first librarian, and the custodian of the books. In fact, the Athenaeum's collection was first housed in the back of Williams's store on Nicollet Avenue near First Street.

But Williams was more than this. In a December 22, 1900, letter congratulating Williams on his fiftieth wedding anniversary, James K. Hosmer, then the librarian of the Minneapolis Public Library, wrote, "In the library history of Minneapolis we know that you are, so to speak, the corner-stone. You are at the foundation of all that has been done in that way. Upon you a great superstructure has been built. When one goes to the bottom of things he comes at last to you—strong, cultivated, scholarly, experienced—the trusted book-man of the little town of forty years ago."[16]

Williams was, in many ways, representative of the kind of people who founded Minneapolis. He had a drive and daring that led him to the frontier and gave him strength when he embraced unpopular causes. He had a wry sense of humor, which was needed to endure the demanding life of the settlements. And he had an idealism, a vision: he believed in the power of the printed word. He believed that books could bring learning, as long as writers were free to write the truth as they saw it. And he balanced all this with a sense of rectitude and dedication to hard work that was reflected in the quality and solidity of the institution he was to help develop.

Thomas Hale Williams was born in Rhode Island in 1813. His family soon moved to New Bedford, Massachusetts, where, at the age of fourteen, Williams became an apprentice printer. He followed the printer's trade in the New England towns of Providence, Salem, and Boston before venturing into what was known in 1837 as "the extreme west." In Alton, Illinois, across the Mississippi River from St. Louis, Williams sought a job on the *Alton Observer*, an abolitionist paper run by Elijah Lovejoy. But before his career there could be launched, Southern mobs smashed into the *Observer's* office, threw the presses into the river, and shot and killed Lovejoy to silence this voice of change. "Four presses have been destroyed in this land of liberty, in little more than a year, because they dared to tell the truth," Williams wrote home.[17]

Williams stood in the rain at Lovejoy's funeral, contemplating bitterly the wreck of the free press over this volatile issue of slavery that was about to tear the country apart. "I wish Gen. [Andrew] Jackson, or Bonaparte, had been mayor of Alton, and then there would have been a different tale to tell," he wrote in another letter.[18] After the disaster at Alton, Williams took a printing job in Jacksonville, Illinois, but returned to the East for his health after a few years.

At the suggestion of his father, Williams entered Harvard Law School. He graduated in 1843 and became associated with several law firms. But he was not enamored of the law, and when friends told him that the Providence Athenaeum was looking for a librarian, he applied. "I was not fit for a lawyer, and should be glad above all things, to have the care of books," he wrote years later.

Williams always loved books and reading. "My father was a minister, a lover of books as well as a buyer. I was born in a house that had a good library in it: and after a ramble in the woods to get a shot of some game, or to pick a basket full of berries, I would return home, lie down on the carpet, and read *The Tempest, The Merchant of Venice, Othello, MacBeth* and other plays of Shakespeare." He said he agreed with the Scottish essayist and historian Thomas Carlyle that "the true University of these days is a collection of books." He later wrote of himself that he had the two qualities essential to being a librarian: a genuine love of books, and "an indomitable passion for order."[19] He also had a passion for watching history happen, and throughout his life kept scrapbooks of clippings that chronicled the development of the towns he lived in. Having found his calling as a librarian, Williams stayed with the Providence Athenaeum, making it one of the best in the nation, until the frontier called him again.

Williams came to Minnesota in 1854. A letter he wrote from St. Paul shows that he was not entirely swept away by his first meetings with the frontiersmen. Almost everybody, he wrote, "smokes, chews,

Minneapolis Public Library photograph

Thomas Hale Williams, the first librarian and founding spirit of the Minneapolis Athenaeum. Although Williams was a stern Yankee who was strict in his administration of the library, he had his lighter side as well. He played the flute at community musical evenings in St. Anthony, and he had a wry sense of humor. On his trip West to Minnesota, he encountered the frontier custom of the "shivaree." He wrote his family back East, "When anybody gets married a mob collect and go to the house, and if you do not treat them, or give them some money, they will make the most horrid noises, by beating kettles, blowing horns, etc. and probably break in the windows." Rather than pay to have the revelers stop, Williams wrote, "I think the best way would be to have two or three of them shot."

drinks, gambles or swears: and some do all together. I have no desire for such company."[20] A move across the river to Minneapolis, and a little time, improved his opinion of what were to become his neighbors. In an 1857 sketch of Minneapolis published by William Wales, Williams wrote, "A more intelligent, industrious, energetic and enterprising class of business men does not exist in the Union."[21] He believed that Minneapolis, with its natural advantages and the quality of its population, would soon eclipse St. Paul and become the most important city in the state. Deciding there was no better place for a man to grow with his country, Williams opened his own book and stationery store and later built a home for himself and his wife, Martha, on the west side of Cedar Lake.

Acting on his belief that Minneapolis would grow to importance, he participated in civic affairs, serving as Minneapolis's town clerk from 1865 to 1867, and as city clerk after incorporation, from 1867 to 1872. But his greatest contribution to Minneapolis was through the Athenaeum. He was chosen to be the group's librarian, and he helped draw up its constitution, modeling it after that of the Providence library. He gave many hours and much energy to the Athenaeum, which for eight years remained housed in his bookstore, and before long saw it grow into a library he was proud of.

During the first year of the Athenaeum's existence, $106.38 was spent to procure sixty-eight books. By April 1860, increased by donations from members, the collection was up to three hundred volumes, and the Athenaeum looked as if it were in Minneapolis to stay.

This was a private library, which meant that one had to pay to make use of it. Shares in the Athenaeum were sold for ten dollars each, and there were slightly more than fifty shareholders at the outset. At their first annual meeting in 1860, members authorized a two-dollar annual tax on shares. The money from shareholders went toward maintaining and expanding the collection, and a small amount went as rent to Williams for the use of his store. Williams took no salary in the early years for serving as librarian.

The by-laws of the Athenaeum allowed a shareholder and his family to take two books from the library for a period of two weeks. At the end of that time, the books had to be returned, unless the librarian extended the period, or a fine of two cents per day was levied. All books were called in one week before the annual meeting so the collection could be inventoried and inspected. And, of course, "no smoking, loud talking, or conduct inconsistent with decorum shall be allowed in the rooms."

People who were not shareholders could also take advantage of the library by paying a user fee. As a historical sketch that accompanied the Athenaeum's annual report of 1876 explained, "While it is not literally a free library, its regulations are such that no lover of good books nor an inquirer in any department of knowledge has been disbarred its use. For ten cents, the price of one good cigar, any person can have the privilege of the library for six days, and by the payment of $1, for three months." A two-dollar deposit was also required, along with the user fee, to assure the books were carefully handled and returned.

The annual report of 1866 mentioned that the library was well patronized by many who were not shareholders: "We doubt not that many an hour has been whiled away in pleasant communion with our 'thousand authors' that might otherwise have hung heavily in the hands of strangers sojourning for a season within our gates." Passing from the altruistic to the pragmatic, the report added that $48.68 came in from user fees the previous year, demonstrating "the wisdom as well as the benevolence of the policy."

Athenaeum members and librarian Williams worked hard from the beginning to improve the collection. The group's 1861 report stated, "We feel much good has been done by this institution in our midst. Many have been made happier, wiser and better prepared for their duties as citizens of our growing city." During 1860, $308.00 had been received from the sale of shares and from fines and lectures; $304.60 of that was spent on books. By 1862, seventy-seven shares had been sold, and the group purchased new books, such as the ten-volume *Works of John Adams*, in an effort to attract new members. The 1864 annual report noted that, for the first time, a book was missing from the collection; but by the 1865 meeting it had found its way back.

A citizen who wrote to *The State Atlas* newspaper in the spring of 1864 praised the library, but bemoaned the fact that there were only ninety-five shareholders. All businessmen, professionals, parents, and "substantial citizens" should support the work of the Athenaeum, the writer stated, adding, "We should take pride in making it worthy of our place, and worthy of the intelligence and enterprise of our citizens."[22]

The year 1865 was one of growth for the Athenaeum. With the private library now past its infant stage, the membership was restless "to enlarge its borders" to keep up with the rapidly growing city. Members envisioned a permanent building to house the now-strong Athenaeum. A public subscription drive was started, and nearly ten thousand dollars was raised from one hundred thirty people in the form of loans, at seven percent interest, to be paid back by rental income from the building. A lot was purchased for one thousand five hundred dollars in the Gateway area, where Hennepin and Nicollet avenues met, then the heart of the downtown business district. By 1866, a two-story building had risen at 215 Hennepin Avenue. The book collection and a reading room were housed in the building, and a bank, a post office, and an "eating house" rented space. In an 1867 letter to his brother

Frontier Readers

"From a little shanty to fine brick and stone." So Thomas Hale Williams described the Athenaeum's move from the back of his bookstore to its first building, completed in 1866. The new building stood at 215 Hennepin Avenue, one block away from the location of the present downtown library built nearly a century later. In this 1913 photo, the Athenaeum Building is the one with the five-globe streetlight in front of it. Next door was the office of a Socialist newspaper, the *New Times*.

Nathan, a proud Thomas Hale Williams wrote, "I think I have done very well the last year. It is not every person who sees a library grow from one book to 1,409—and from a little shanty to fine brick and stone—with plenty of room for the books and renting for over two thousand dollars."[23]

Also proud were the members of the Athenaeum. They must have looked at their building and seen a concrete reflection of their hopes for the intellectual growth of their city. And they saw more: a bit of themselves carried into the future. The 1866 annual report, written in the midst of the building campaign, mentioned members who had died, and said that the Athenaeum is "a record that will not perish; so long as the library shall exist, they will be held in grateful remembrance." Just as books themselves communicate across time and often represent an author's desire for a touch of immortality, so the library would stand for decades as a public confirmation and testimonial of the concerns and values of the men who founded it. The Athenaeum, which took a tangible shape after the Civil War, spoke to the future. The 1866 annual report recalled the men who had met seven years earlier to form the library association: "The silent and unseen influences which they set at work on that evening have been gathering strength through all these years; and the circle will go on widening in all the years there are to come, until it shall be beyond the power of any finite mind to compute its measure."

But the pathway was not always smooth. Athenaeum records for 1869 show a feeling among members that the library was not growing fast enough nor being supported fully enough: "Surely 2,000 volumes is too small a number of books to be upon the shelves as the result of 10 years of growth. It is a reproach upon the intelligence of the community."[24] The group called for more members, and for the beneficence of Minneapolis's wealthier citizens.

That latter call was answered the following year, but from within. Kirby Spencer was a dentist who lived alone in a large white house on Washington Avenue near Third Street, close to the present Milwaukee Depot. An early photograph of Minneapolis shows his house standing there like a monument to civilization on a wandering dirt street. Spencer was a quiet man, very well read, and fascinated by science. He liked to have his patients lean over his microscope and watch the blood circulating in the foot of a frog. He was considered an eccentric—"a very peculiar old gentleman," as the *Minneapolis Tribune* said in his obituary. The newspaper suggested that Spencer had soured at the world and that, although he was known to many people, very few really knew him well. But Spencer was a member of the Minneapolis Athenaeum, a friend of Thomas Hale Williams, and a believer in the benefit of books. When he died March 10, 1870, he left his property to be set aside in trust, with the proceeds to go to the Athenaeum. The property was valued at twenty thousand dollars, and the income it generated each year provided much of the Athenaeum's money to purchase books. Spencer's will stipulated that the money purchase only serious works—

Minneapolis Public Library photograph

Dr. Kirby Spencer, whose bequest to the Minneapolis Athenaeum stipulated that only serious books should be bought with the proceeds of his estate. He didn't want popular fiction purchased with his money nor, since he was an agnostic, books on religion and theology.

Frontier Readers

Photograph by B.F. Upton, the Bromley Collection

Minneapolis in 1857, when Washington Avenue was a muddy track.
The large white house with the porch on two sides, just above and to
the left of center in the photograph, belonged to Dr. Kirby Spencer.
Spencer, a friend of Thomas Hale Williams and a member of the
Athenaeum, left this property to the Athenaeum on his death in 1870.
The proceeds from the Spencer bequest provided new books every year
for the library, and continue to do so today. Also facing Washington
Avenue, from the bottom right of the photo, were a furniture
warehouse, a meat market and harness shop, and a blacksmith shop on
the corner of Third and Washington avenues, this side of Spencer's
house. The large white building at the upper left of the photo was the
new Cataract House, a hotel overlooking St. Anthony Falls. Across
Washington Avenue from the Spencer house, to the left of the house in
this photo, now stands the Milwaukee Depot.

books on science, history, philosophy, art, and only the best of literature. As Spencer was an agnostic, works on religion and theology were left off his list. He also scorned works of popular fiction, and made it clear that his bequest was to help provide a scholary library for Minneapolis.

Aided by the Spencer gift, the Athenaeum grew in strength. In 1872, the year Minneapolis and St. Anthony were consolidated, a suggestion was made at the Athenaeum's annual meeting to have wealthy citizens buy shares that could be put at the disposal of the poor. "Many a young man might be arrested in his course of dissipation and turned to paths of pleasantness and peace by so simple a circumstance as the use of this library for one year."[25] Three years later, in florid language at the end of the annual report, the Athenaeum again called for more members so that it could be "a perennial fountain of waters of knowledge which shall perpetually flow over the arid wastes of ignorance, stimulating into growth the seeds of intellectual vigor that they may ere long blossom into the beauty of art and ripen into the fruitage of wisdom."[26]

But there was a sense of unrest under this tranquil verbal surface. Some members of the Athenaeum were becoming more and more conscious of an inherent contradiction in the group's position. If their goal was to irrigate these wastes of ignorance, and if it was true that their collection of books might be able to turn an unfortunate man away from the paths of unrighteousness, then why were the benefits of this mental and spiritual nourishment made available only to those who could pay for them? Shouldn't the Athenaeum's doors be thrown open, so that more members of the community could pass through them? Here we begin to see the first expressions of the need to extend to the entire populace the advantages a library could afford. These first ripples in the early 1870s would result in the opening of a public library by the end of the 1880s.

In 1873 and 1874, some members of the Athenaeum proposed that shares be sold "on time," with a three-dollar advance payment, and an annual fee of one dollar to be paid for seven years. This would allow people who couldn't muster ten dollars at one time to still have the full benefits of library membership. The proposals were turned down; but they would return.

Concurrent with the arguments about access to the Athenaeum was an argument about the content and atmosphere of the place. The basic philosophy of the organization was called into question. Should the library be a scholarly preserve for serious inquiry or should it be a more popular place that recognized the pleasures as well as the benefits of reading? The question would be debated for ten years before a solution which accommodated both views was reached.

By 1877 Athenaeum officials recognized that their library was not serving all the reading needs of Minneapolis. Noting that the city had

Frontier Readers

a population of more than thirty thousand, the officials suggested in their annual report "that the shareholders appoint a committee to study the legislation of the older States of the Republic upon the subject of libraries, and so cooperate with others in securing the passage of a general act by the legislature of Minnesota, which will enable this city to tax property holders for the support of a free library."

A year earlier, partly at the suggestion of Thomas Hale Williams, librarians from all over the nation had met in Philadelphia to discuss the common problems and possibilities of their organizations. Out of this meeting grew the American Library Association, of which Williams is considered a founder. After hearing Williams's report about what other libraries were doing, some members of the Minneapolis Athenaeum realized that their library could complement a separate, popular library. The Athenaeum could continue as a reference library— as the Spencer bequest seemed to demand. But a free, public library could also be established to satisfy the public's taste for such popular authors as Charles Dickens and Mark Twain. Athenaeum records noted that, with much of the public interested in such popular literature, some recent Athenaeum purchases of serious natural history books had caused "the flippant to talk of fossilization of the Athenaeum."[27]

One man in particular was determined to resist any such fossilization. His name was Thomas Barlow Walker. Isaac Atwater, in his excellent 1893 history of Minneapolis, credits Walker with starting the movement for a free library in 1877. Walker, a long-time member of the Athenaeum, sought to liberalize the library's rules and make it more accessible to all citizens of Minneapolis. A shrewd and resourceful businessman who was used to being able to make things go his way, Walker led a twelve-year struggle against Williams and other traditionalists, a struggle that resulted in the Athenaeum and a new public library becoming partners under a single roof. The fight, occasionally rancorous, was between two factions, each believing it had the best interests of the community in mind. The compromise that ended the fight has endured and prospered for a hundred years.

Thomas Barlow Walker was one of the most fascinating of the men who made Minneapolis. That he was a rich man fighting in the library struggle for the rights of the common people is an irony that illustrates some of the contradictions of his personality. He kept his mansion open to the public so they could see his art collection. He even refused to fence his yard as most people of means did; instead, he provided benches under his trees for the weary to rest upon. Yet he kept a gun under his pillow, a habit left over from the state's early days. The habit was so strong that he taught it to his children; overnight guests at the mansion were provided with loaded pistols, too, as a chambermaid once accidentally discovered while changing a bed. Walker was a firm capitalist who never apologized for making money, yet his work with the library and with his art gallery may have been an attempt to repay the state for all he had taken. In his youth, he had roamed Minnesota's wild northern woods in a dugout canoe, sleeping on the ground and eating camp food. But later, in his Minneapolis mansion, he was cautious about what he ate, banning coffee, tea, tomatoes, grapefruit, and any flour but graham flour from his table. A powerful man in town, Walker was often invited to give after-dinner speeches so people could benefit from his wisdom and learn his secrets for success. But his talks were long, tedious, and pedantic rather than thought-provoking.

Walker had made his fortune from Minnesota's forests, using his muscle, initiative, and wits. A solid Republican, he believed that what was good for business was good for America. To those less well-off, he would point to their bootstraps and their good strong arms, and suggest a hearty application of one to the other. Yet, through the library, he labored to improve the condition of all people; and when the poor lined up at his door, he handed them tickets that were good for a free meal and a bed at a local mission. And, when he had a car, he was known to give strangers a lift. But as his granddaughter, Louise Walker McCannel, later recalled with a laugh, Walker would pick up hitchhikers, and then halfway through the ride say, "So you're in bricklaying. Well, let me tell you the best way to . . . ." Walker knew how to do everything, McCannel said, and wasn't shy about telling people.[28]

An energetic booster of Minneapolis, Walker gave his name, time, or money—and often all three—to almost every new organization or drive that aimed to make the city more prosperous and exciting. He knew that as Minneapolis flourished, so would he, and understood that as Minneapolis increased in cultural importance, he could stand taller among his fellow tycoons of the East.

Walker was born in Xenia, Ohio, in 1840, to a family originally from New York. When Walker was nine, his father died of cholera on the trail to California's gold fields; but that wouldn't deter Walker from later venturing into the frontier. First, however, he worked his way through Baldwin University in Berea, Ohio. Here discipline was strict, completing a lesson Walker's family had started: even minor vices could detour one's career. Here also his dedication to reading showed. He would often walk twelve miles to the Cleveland Public Library for books such as Charles Darwin's *The Origin of Species*. Once out of college, Walker headed west, taking work here as a teacher and there as a salesman. With money earned as a lumberman in Ohio, he bought a supply of grindstones, knowing they would be needed by the mills of the growing west, and set out to sell them. He traveled to Grand Rapids, Chicago, Milwaukee, Madison, Prairie du Chien, and finally up the Mississippi to St. Paul, where he sold the last of his load. A young dock clerk named James J. Hill checked in the grindstones and impressed Walker with his hard-working attitude. The young Hill, who would

Photograph from the *Minneapolis Tribune* and *The Spectator*

Thomas Barlow Walker, 1888. His fortune had been made by this time, but his hard work continued. He was president of the newly formed library board, and would oversee the opening of the library the following year. Walker and his wife, Harriet, who worked on many school, church, and hospital projects, gave their attention and support to dozens of efforts aimed at making Minneapolis a cultured and civilized place. A 1903 newspaper article spoke of Walker's still-youthful vigor and said, "His face has an exceedingly kindly appearance; that of a man who could well be entrusted with anything, and who would faithfully abide by that trust."

Quote from the *Minneapolis Tribune,* October 25, 1903

become a hero to Walker, was just starting a career that would land him in a mansion atop the river bluff on Summit Avenue, where he would reign as Minnesota's foremost railroad magnate. These were boom times, and fortunes were waiting to be made as the region found its strength.

In the summer of 1862, Walker came to Minneapolis. Almost immediately, he went to the north woods, surveying railroad and timber lands for the next several years. Ranging as far north as Lake Pokegama, near Grand Rapids on the Mississippi, he saw the vast timber potential of Minnesota's forests, the plentiful rivers that could float logs to lumber mills, and wealth lying ready.

Photograph from the Bromley Collection

Minnesota loggers standing on what made T.B. Walker his fortune. This 1863 photo was taken on the Rum River and shows part of the great northern forests that were cut and then floated to mills in northern Minnesota and in Minneapolis. The lumber and furniture business helped build Minneapolis, where in 1860, 18 million board feet of lumber were produced. By 1870 that figure had jumped to 118 million, and when the Minneapolis lumber industry peaked in 1899, the city's mills were carving out 594 million board feet. The last Minneapolis lumber mill closed in 1919, but by that time Walker had long been "the Pine King of the West."

He became part of Butler Mills and Walker Lumber Company, and, while surveying for this group near Leech Lake, "went through the temporary, noisy Indian disturbance that came tolerably near ending in our being killed by the Indians."[29] From his experiences among the Chippewa of northern Minnesota, he felt that the socialism practiced by the tribe destroyed individual initiative. This was not a new lesson to a man of Yankee heritage, but it was one Walker would not forget. Although in later life Walker wanted to bring the Chippewa around to his view of the world, he did respect them, and was remembered by family members as treating them well and having several of the Chippewas he'd done business with to his home in Minneapolis for dinner and conversation.

Walker got out of lumbering temporarily around 1873, foreseeing economic troubles. But in 1877, he jumped back in with a new company, Camp and Walker, and built his own mills in Crookston and Grand Forks. A man of solid reputation, Walker sold a large tract of northern timber to Healy C. Akeley of Michigan in 1890. Akeley put his money down without examining the property, saying to Walker, "As you have looked up the timber, I have looked you up, and that satisfies me as to what I am buying."[30] Walker said Akeley didn't even ask for the deed to the land for a dozen years. Out of this partnership came the mills and towns of Akeley and Walker near Leech Lake.

Walker followed his timber interests west to California's forests, and became a transcontinental traveler in pursuit of his business. By this time he was a lumber baron, soon to be called "the Pine King of the West" by a New York newspaper, and was an important figure on the streets of Minneapolis.

Trees turned into money for Walker. He built a spacious home at Eighth Street and Hennepin Avenue on the edge of Minneapolis's business district. There, through the 1870s, the Walker family kept cows to provide the fresh milk that replaced the coffee and tea Walker wouldn't let his children drink. Herd boys drove these cows each morning to a pasture two miles west of town. When Minneapolis passed laws forbidding loose cows in the streets, a hired man hitched Walker's cows to the back of a wagon and drove them to and from the pasture each day. The family always had a winter skating rink, and Walker's sons ran a skate-sharpening business from the blacksmith shop out back. "When strangers touring the town had the T. B. Walker residence pointed out to them as the house of a millionaire lumberman, they were startled to see the sign on the front lawn reading: 'Skates sharpened: 15 cents.'"[31]

Although Walker's formal talks could be dry, Louise McCannel recalled that he was a good storyteller at home, a man with a sense of humor who could turn a clever phrase. He was mild, courteous, and, although opinionated, never swore—yet he did occasionally use the phrase "dirty skunk" for someone who had bested him in a business deal. According to his biographer, Minneapolis school teacher Clara Nelson (whose lengthy manuscript was never published), Walker gave in to one eccentric extravagance of wealth—he kept loose gems in his pocket. He liked to hear them jingle and clink, and he enjoyed taking them out and playing with them in the light. In her manuscript Nelson quotes from a letter Walker wrote to a jeweler. He wanted to exchange a ruby for a diamond, because the ruby was "a little more inclined to get scratched than a diamond would in knocking about in my pocket with other stones."[32]

Walker was also inquisitive. Although a confirmed capitalist, he read socialist papers, as he was eager to understand what the other side was thinking. His own reading ran to philosophy, economics, government—material that dealt with ideas and practicalities, not with people.

About 1874, Walker began turning his omnivorous attention to what he felt was the city's need for a library accessible to all. An avid collector of books, he had been a member of the Minneapolis Athenaeum for years. He wanted to extend the benefits of reading to more people than the Athenaeum then served, and began advocating freer use of the reading room, more evening hours, and the sale of shares on time to bring the price within reach of more citizens.

In 1877, Walker led a revolution. Through politicking and the gathering of proxies, a new board of directors was elected that looked favorably on Walker's ideas for liberalizing the Athenaeum. The new board agreed to sell shares on time. Hours in the public reading room were extended so it closed at 9:00 P.M. rather than 5:00 P.M. And, as Isaac Atwater wrote, "The reading room was also opened on Sundays in order to gather in those who might otherwise be disposed to frequent saloons or other evil places."[33]

When the new directors inspected the Athenaeum more closely, they found the library's six thousand volumes piled two deep on dark shelves in a dark room. They rearranged the room to open and brighten it, laid down a carpet, brought in new chairs, tables, and kerosene lamps. A new philosophy was expressed in the 1878 annual report: "Called to choose between the theories that have been maintained as to the true character of a library, we have thought better to have the books used up, if need be, by readers, than eaten up by moths and mice."

But the struggle between the library's old and new guard continued for another two years. The liberals on the issue said the members of the Athenaeum were "crabbed and selfish," while librarian Williams and his followers felt the new changes violated the original charter.

Williams was what we might call today a "strict constructionist" on the Athenaeum charter. He didn't feel the organization as it was designed should be changed, even for social good. Of selling shares on time, Williams wrote to the *St. Paul Pioneer Press* early in 1880: "It is virtually making the Athenaeum a free library. If one article of the charter can be altered, any other may be; and the charter is not worth a rope of sand."[34] Williams wasn't against the formation of a free public library; he simply didn't think the Athenaeum should be that library: "The inviting of the whole town to use the library is a greater violation of the rights of shareholders than the manner of selling shares," he continued in the same 1880 letter. "In the one case the shareholders derive some benefit from the sale of shares. But in the other they have nothing. They are even prevented from using what belongs to them." Williams said that Dr. Spencer, whose bequest was largely responsible for the growth of the Athenaeum, knew what he was doing when he helped assure the continuance of a serious subscription library. If Spencer had wanted the Athenaeum to be a free library, he would have said so, Williams maintained.

Williams was intransigent on the matter. "I don't see that there is any more reason for having free reading than free soup, especially when the reading has to be stolen from the rightful owners," he wrote. He was afraid that the liberalization policy would end in the destruction of the Athenaeum as it was when Spencer gave it his property. "The object of the Athenaeum was to form a library of good books where the shareholder could obtain information in every branch of useful knowledge," he added. "It was not intended to be a loafing place for tramps to read dime novels."

While Williams was not going to give up easily, his opponent in this contest was also a man who was unwilling, and unaccustomed, to giving ground. Walker would have a public library, or make the Athenaeum into the closest thing to it, if he had to pull every string in town. Why did Walker care so much? A public library was far from the only concern of this busy man, but he put a great deal of time and effort into it for years. His reasons illustrate what he himself called, in a speech in 1904, a "rightly-directed selfishness." This selfishness served his own ends, surely, but just as surely served the city that was his home.

First, Walker himself was interested in reading and learning. His own personal library was once called perhaps the largest private collection of books on literature, science, art, politics, social questions, religion, and education in the Northwest. A 1903 *Minneapolis Tribune* sketch of Walker said his library walls were "lined with bookcases which groan under the weight of books fit to make the heart of a bookworm full of envy."[35]

The article added that, as a salesman, Walker had carried one valise of samples, and one full of books to study in his spare time. Walker said, looking back on his life, that he had devoted more time and attention to studying history and social and political questions than he had to his lumbering and other business concerns.

Walker's collection of art, which was centered around the works

"In T. B.'s opinion, a free library was the best preventative of vice and crime, of labor troubles, of intemperance and riots."

—Clara Nelson, Walker's biographer

of old masters, rare jade and jewelry, and Greek, Egyptian, and Chinese pottery, established him as a man of culture—even though not all the art turned out to be authentic. At a testimonial dinner in 1924, George Dayton said that Walker had "sought to inhale and exhale an atmosphere of broad education, quiet refinement and liberal culture."[36] Walker wanted to share his culture with his fellow citizens; that was why he opened his mansion and his art collection to the public. He was interested in developing the culture of Minneapolis so that it could take its place among the finest cities of the nation. As Horace Hudson wrote in his 1908 history of the city, "In working for a public library, Mr. Walker had in mind that Minneapolis, when she emerged from the frontier stage, must develop taste in fine arts." Walker didn't want his town to be a backwater. A thriving, intellectually active community, Walker realized, would reflect well on its builders. A second speaker at the 1924 testimonial dinner, Dr. C. A. Prosser, mentioned this symbiotic relationship by calling Walker "the man who came here in the pioneer days of Minneapolis to help build a city and let it build him."[37]

Louise McCannel suggested that her grandfather fostered the development of culture in town and kept his private art collection open to the public "partly because he felt guilty." She said he felt "that art was an indulgence," and that he felt less bad about that indulgence if other people could benefit from his collection. Having gained from the development of Minnesota, he wanted to give something back to the people of the state. So his art and library work may have been done to assuage some faint guilt, or at least to salve a social conscience. [38]

Walker himself said that he had a social conscience. In an interview in *American Magazine* late in his life, he repeated a theme he had voiced often before. Business, he said, is "a means to enable me to do everything in my power for the public welfare. I don't expect any special credit for this: it was what I wanted to do."[39]

Working for the public welfare was also something that fit in with Walker's view of capitalism and public improvement. In articles and speeches throughout his life, he talked of a sort of noblesse oblige that required those in the upper ranks of the socioeconomic hierarchy to contribute to public institutions that could help others attain those same ranks. Successful capitalists should, and did, in his view and experience, contribute to the betterment of all. Not through welfare or handouts, but by putting the tools of success at the disposal of the public. The very capitalists who were most subject to public prejudice and antagonism because of their wealth "are found in larger percentage, earnestly contributing time and means to the upbuilding and advancement of educational, religious, civic and charitable work, and show the greatest interest in the advancement of public welfare and have contributed more to the upbuilding of the public institutions that are contributing so vastly to the public welfare than has ever been known in

The interior of the art gallery in T. B. Walker's home at 803 Hennepin Avenue in 1905. Walker's home was open to anyone who wanted to come in and browse through his art collection, with servants at the Walker home instructed to give the public access and guide them through the gallery. Walker's personal interest in art, science, and books helped build Minneapolis as much as did his business interest in lumbering. At a 1924 testimonial dinner it was said that Walker saw Minneapolis grow "from cow paths to asphalt streets," from a "rude civilization" to a "city which is making provision in a big way for all the refinements and arts that go to make a true civilization and a great people."

any time or nation," Walker wrote in a 1915 magazine article, "The Contribution of Capital to the Public Welfare."[40]

In Walker's view, capital, by sponsoring science, learning, and public institutions, had put success within the reach of any person with industrious habits. Responsible businessmen had an obligation to help the public attain "a higher grade of character and citizenship," Walker said.[41] When capitalists helped educate and improve the general public, that public would respond by working diligently within the system that had brought success to Walker and progress to his community on the banks of the Mississippi. Walker wanted, quite naturally, to keep that system and that progress flourishing. What better way could there be than opening the doors of a broad and vigorous public library to a resourceful population eager to advance?

There was something more to Walker's interest in the library, and that was a sense of doing missionary work. He wrote in 1890 that he had always planned that the library "should assume something of the character of a People's University."[42] But it was more than just facts the people would learn at this "University": they would learn how to be good people. Walker wrote to the *St. Paul Pioneer Press* in 1878, "A library will accomplish more towards civilizing, and improving the condition of the people than all the public schools we possess."[43] While some of the other Athenaeum members did not have a "miscellaneous taste for humanity," as Clara Nelson noted, "T. B. Walker, in his self-appointed role of Messiah, had already accepted the fact that the world was made up of the commonplace, the vulgar, the ill-bred. It was his belief that through the Christianizing influence of a free library, the commonplace might sometimes blossom into distinction, vulgarity might be controlled, stupidity tempered and manners improved."[44] In the same 1878 letter to the *Pioneer Press* Walker wrote that the Athenaeum's change in rules "brings into this library some persons who do not wear kid gloves, but I see no reason for the founders to be disturbed by such a lack." Here, Walker the missionary was on the side of the common man against the privileged few. Although he may not have enjoyed the hyperbole, he probably agreed with the spirit of another newspaper letter-writer who, during the Athenaeum controversy, charged that "When any man not a millionaire or an original incorporator comes into the library, the librarian has recourse to his smelling salts to protect himself against the aroma of the intrusion."[45] Walker wanted everyone to have access to a library.

Walker's view of the library's function and his reasons for supporting it are common in library history. The notions of uplifting people, of training them into the American system, of turning them onto the proper paths will be seen again in this history, as well. Walker's thinking combined all these ideas to an unusual degree, and the strength of his position and his personality helped him push for a public library, and helped him leave his mark on that library.

With Walker's force behind it, the Athenaeum's policies became more liberal. The last resistance fell in 1880 when Walker's board of directors cut Williams's pay and hours as a librarian, and Williams resigned. By 1881, fifty-four percent of the books borrowed from the Athenaeum collection were novels, showing the popular reading taste the library was starting to meet. Also by this year, the little private library that started in the back of a bookstore was beginning to outgrow its first permanent building. The 1881 annual report concluded, "The time has now come when a more commodious building, more eligibly situated, is a necessity."

But before that new building would be found, the Athenaeum would change more radically than Williams had feared and Walker had hoped. The struggling forces within the Athenaeum had raised questions which the structure of that private organization couldn't contain. The struggle itself had shown the need, observers said, for an independent public library in Minneapolis, now a city of almost fifty thousand people.

That public library, under the sure guidance of Walker, was about to be born. Its seeds had arrived at the falls of St. Anthony with the first permanent settlers, who, from the earliest hard years, turned to the printed word for comfort, diversion, and enlightenment. It had been nurtured, even in disagreement, by concerned and earnest men like Williams, Walker, and Kirby Spencer. Said Colonel John H. Stevens of these pioneers, "They worked for the good of those who were to follow in their footsteps, inherit this glorious land, and possess the institutions founded in intelligence, and fostered with care. With prophetic eye they viewed with pride the blessings that would be showered upon generations that were to follow."[46]

To ensure those blessings, and to ensure the fruition of those early seeds of culture, all that was needed now was a legal structure. The Athenaeum, which in 1882 rejected the idea of remodeling its own building because such a plan would "meet only temporary needs," became intrigued by talk in the city of establishing a free public library. The Athenaeum members held off on expansion plans of their own to see what would come of this free library idea.

Across the river in the rival city of St. Paul, another private library group like the Athenaeum had been transformed into a public library in 1882. The St. Paul Library Association, created by the merger of two smaller private libraries in 1863, formed the base of the St. Paul Public Library, which was established by the city council in the fall, and then opened its doors on the second day of the new year, 1883. St. Paul had followed the pattern of other libraries around the country: starting with private and mercantile libraries, evolving into a larger subscription library, and finally being changed by democratic governmental action into a public library open to all.

The Minnesota legislature had cleared the way for public libraries in 1879 when it passed a law allowing city and village governments to set up public libraries and to levy a tax of up to half a mill to support them. (A mill is one-tenth of a cent, and it is applied against the property value of a taxpayer's property. If the library levies one mill of taxation, for each dollar a citizen's property is worth, that citizen would

Photograph by Howard in *The Mecca*

Walker, shown here late in life, was a man of firm convictions. He thought novel reading a waste of time, he banned white sugar and white flour from his table, he believed the library could do as much good for people as the churches whose clergymen once complained about the library being open on Sunday, and he was convinced that anyone in America who worked hard could succeed as he had. Walker's biographer, Clara Nelson, wrote, "His judgments were never tentative. Once they were formed, they took their place in the realm of immutability with the tablets handed down on Mt. Sinai."

Frontier Readers

pay one-tenth of a cent in tax to the library. One mill generates one dollar of tax money per one thousand dollars of assessed property value.) Public sentiment in Minneapolis, coupled with Walker's drive and the spur of competition from St. Paul, made the time right for a public library on the west side of the river.

More momentum was gained in 1884, when in November the Minnesota Academy of Natural Sciences suggested to the Athenaeum that the two groups work together with The Minneapolis Society of Fine Arts to construct a new building to house all three institutions. The Society of Fine Arts wanted a home for its collection of paintings and its art school. The Academy of Natural Sciences, a group of scholars

Photograph from the Bromley Collection

That Minneapolis developed a fine Athenaeum and public library shouldn't be a surprise. The residents, many of them emigrants from the New England states, were readers from the beginning. In the early days at St. Anthony, the arrival by mail of a Charles Dickens book was a civic event, and the number of newspaper subscribers was high. Between 1870 and 1900, the number of newspapers published in Minnesota grew from 78 to 537, well ahead of the national rate of increase. Reading in Minneapolis—of newspapers, at least—was made easier by the newsboys, employees of the *Minneapolis Journal* in 1881.
Newspaper information from *Newspapers on the Minnesota Frontier*, by George Hage

"Newspaper row" in Minneapolis around 1897, on Fourth Street
between Nicollet and First Avenue South. Citizens crowd in front of the
Journal Building to see the latest telegraphed news—probably election
returns—posted in the front window.

who studied and presented papers on all branches of natural science,
hoped for a place to meet and display its own collection. When the
academy passed a motion on November 11 suggesting a three-way col-
laboration on a building, the group's president appointed a committee
to look into the matter. On this committee was an academy trustee
named Thomas Barlow Walker, who also happened to be a trustee of
The Society of Fine Arts.

These three cultural institutions proposed to Minneapolis's city
council that they and the city work together to erect a building that
would house a new public library, an art museum, and a science
museum. Representatives of the city, the Athenaeum, The Society of

Photograph by W.H. Illingworth,
the Bromley Collection

In the 1870s and 1880s, Minneapolis decided to become permanent. Stone and brick buildings took over from the earlier wood frame structures. Here, at the corner of Washington Avenue and Marquette (then First Avenue), was the proud new Northwestern National Bank, built of limestone in 1872 for a reported thirty thousand dollars. One block away, at Second and Marquette, was another new limestone building called the Brackett Block, where stores and offices shared the first floor with a pork-packing plant.

Fine Arts, and the Academy of Natural Sciences met in November and December 1884; by December 20, the group had agreed that a fine building could be put up for a cost of one hundred fifty thousand dollars. Funding, the group proposed, could come from one hundred thousand dollars in municipal bond sales, and from a fifty-thousand-dollar private subscription.

An amendment to Minneapolis's city charter authorizing the bond sale, the establishment of a free public library, and a half-mill levy on property values to support the library, was drawn up by E. M. Johnson, John B. Atwater, and Samuel Hill (James J. Hill's son-in-law). Section 10 of the amendment said that "All libraries and museums established under this act . . . shall be forever free to the inhabitants of the city of Minneapolis, always subject, however, to such reasonable rules and regulations as shall be necessary to their effective administration."[47] The amendment also set up a library board to govern the library. On that board were Thomas Lowry, M. B. Koon, John B. Atwater, Sven Oftedal, E. M. Johnson, and T. B. Walker. The mayor of the city, the president of the University of Minnesota, and the president of the Minneapolis Board of Education were ex officio members of the board.

The city council passed the charter amendment, and the new library structure became official when the state legislature approved the charter change on March 2, 1885. For the first time, Minneapolis had—in name if not yet in stone—a public library "forever free" to the residents of the city.

The library board held a brief organizational meeting three weeks later, then adjourned until April 21, when the annual meeting would be held. At that meeting, Walker was elected president of the library board, a position he would hold until his death. E. M. Johnson, who had helped draw up the charter amendment for the library, was elected secretary. By May 1885, the new library board was busy looking for a librarian, and for a building. By the end of the summer, the board had entered into joint agreements with The Society of Fine Arts and the Academy of Natural Sciences to house activities in the new building. And, in a gesture that embraced the new library's forefathers, the board signed a ninety-nine-year agreement with the Athenaeum to pool resources. The Athenaeum would allow its books to be used by the general public, and the library would house, service, and maintain the Athenaeum's collection, as well as its own. It was a partnership that would enrich both sides.

In the summer of 1886, ground was broken for the building that, in three years, would become the Minneapolis Public Library. The vision of learning and civility that dated back to the 1850s was beginning to take solid form.

Photograph by Bishop Brayton

The new library under construction at Tenth Street and Hennepin
Avenue, with the First Baptist Church, which still stands, in the
background. Ground was broken for the library in the summer of 1886,
a year that saw four thousand five hundred new buildings go up in
Minneapolis at a value of $10 million. The growing city laid twenty-
three miles of water main and five miles of sewer line that year, built
sixty miles of sidewalk and graded fifty-two miles of street. The
Minneapolis Exposition Building opened in August of that same year,
three stories of brick and iron with a tower 240 feet tall. The Republican
Party met in 1892 at the Exposition Building, at Main Street Southeast
and Central Avenue, to renominate Benjamin Harrison for a second
term as president. Not all construction in 1886 was successful, however.
In May the Brackett Building at Second Street and First Avenue
collapsed into the hole dug next to it for an addition, killing five
workmen.

Photograph by W.S. Zinn, Minneapolis

The first Minneapolis Public Library, built in 1889 as two wings in an
"L" shape along Tenth Street and Hennepin Avenue. This building was
the centerpiece of what T. B. Walker called "The People's University."
To the library's left in this 1893 photograph is the First Baptist Church,
which still stands. The library itself was torn down, with some difficulty
because it was so solidly built, in 1961, and there is only a parking lot
now on that corner. Minnesota humorist Garrison Keillor, who spent a
great deal of time at the old downtown library as a youth, said, "I still
miss the building. It was a castle, and we certainly were welcome in
there." Keillor has a peculiar memory of the periodical room: "There
were grizzled old men in seedy suits who sat in there reading
newspapers, and a friend of mine told me they were professors at the
University—and that was my first impression of the U."

The People's University

Minneapolis in 1889 was a town of one hundred sixty-five thousand people. Only forty years had passed since the first rude shacks had been built on the banks of the Mississippi around St. Anthony Falls, and only twenty had passed since Minneapolis was incorporated as a city.

This was a time of unprecedented growth in Minneapolis. The national economy was recovering from a bad slump in the 1870s, and European crop failures meant high prices for the bountiful Minnesota harvests. In Minneapolis, the original wooden buildings of the central city were being replaced by stronger structures of brick and stone. The country was striding confidently into the full blaze of the industrial revolution—a revolution that would change America forever.

The past was being left behind. On December 11, 1889, a celebration marking the centennial of the inauguration of George Washington and the opening of the first American Congress was held in Washington, D.C. On December 6, Jefferson Davis, former president of the rebellious Confederate States of America, died in New Orleans, marking the final passing of the great lost cause. And in one year, during a bitter December in South Dakota, would come the massacre of the Sioux at Wounded Knee, the last clash between the once-free spirits of the Plains and the mechanized force that had subdued the American West.

The future belonged to the cities—cities with power to run mills and people to work in them. Minneapolis was one of these cities. The

The People's University

place was booming and brash, but it was about to acquire a mark of civilized distinction that city leaders hoped would help tame things down. At 4:00 P.M. on Monday, December 16, 1889, with very little fanfare, the Minneapolis Public Library opened its doors for the first time.

It was quite an edifice. Thousands of people walked through the library, inspecting the more than thirty thousand books and admiring the oak and mahogany woodwork. Members of the library board received the public and looked quite happy, according to the newspaper reports. Those newspapers praised the new institution, calling it a monument to learning in a community of scholars.

Well, again, they weren't all scholars. The police report for November was just out, showing 284 arrests for drunkenness, 44 for vagrancy, 36 for petty larceny, and 35 for keeping "houses of ill fame." The Reverend D. J. Burrell had, the Sunday before the library opened, decried public corruption and politicians in office who refused to enforce the laws against gambling and prostitution. The Friday night previous, a cockfight had been held in a barn just outside the city limits—Minneapolis birds vanquished Wisconsin birds in four out of five contests. And a problem kept cropping up in trash barrels just south of downtown, where officials said medical students were indiscriminately disposing of the results of their dissections. There were other health problems: a smallpox patient was quarantined in a hospital; the central police station recently had to be fumigated after a man arrested for drunkenness proved to have diphtheria; and scarlet fever was reported in North and Northeast Minneapolis.

Nevertheless, progress and growth continued. Sunday school boards spent the Sabbath making plans for Christmas celebrations and programs, the city council's gas committee had just approved 204 new gas street lamps for the coming year, and the city's first electric streetcar line had begun operations on Saturday. Thomas Lowry, president of the Minneapolis Street Railway Company and chairman of the library board's building committee, had returned from a European trip just in time to take the first ride on the electric car from Twenty-fourth Street to downtown along Fourth Avenue South.

The weather in Minneapolis was unusually mild for winter. After hovering around freezing on Sunday, the temperature for Monday's library opening shot up to forty-two degrees. Temperatures had been so un-Minnesotan that one clothing store, claiming the nice weather had ruined its profits, cut the price of coon overcoats from sixty to forty-five dollars and of goat coats, trimmed with nutria, from eighteen to twelve dollars.

So here, Monday afternoon, December 16, 1889, was the new library building, rising solidly from the southeast corner of Tenth Street and Hennepin Avenue, in what one newspaper called "dreamy seclusion," away from the central business district. The library eventually would take the shape of a square; but on opening day, only the sides along Hennepin Avenue and Tenth Street were constructed, forming an "L" shape. Future additions would complete the square, and eventually cover the open courtyard in the middle.

From *The Public Library Minneapolis, described and illustrated* (New York: Exhibit Publishing Co., 1890)

A line drawing from an 1890 booklet describing the new Minneapolis Public Library. This is the entryway on Hennepin Avenue, with the Jakob Fjelde statue of Minerva in the niche between the windows on the second level.

The People's University

The library had three floors above its basement, which was only half submerged to allow light to reach its reading rooms. The exterior was brown Lake Superior sandstone, cut by Herbert Chalker of Minneapolis. (The same sandstone had been used four years earlier for the Lumber Exchange Building, which, recently renovated, still stands

Photograph by George Miles Ryan Studios, 1946

Minerva, the goddess of wisdom or the muse of history, in her niche above the main entrance of the Minneapolis Public Library. The bronze statue, crafted by Jakob Fjelde, is seven feet high and weighs one thousand seven hundred pounds. Fjelde, born in Norway, also sculpted the statue of Norwegian violinist Ole Bull, which stands in Loring Park, and the statue of Hiawatha carrying Minnehaha across the creek just above Minnehaha Falls.

proudly at Fifth and Hennepin. The Minneapolis architectural firm of Long & Kees designed both buildings.) The library's Hennepin Avenue entrance was decorated with polished granite columns and lintel; and in a niche between the windows above the entrance was a bronze figure of Minerva, goddess of wisdom, sculpted by Jakob Fjelde of Minneapolis, the same man whose monument to the First Minnesota Regiment still looms powerfully over the Gettysburg battlefield. Above Minerva, in large square letters, were carved two words: Public Library.

Visitors who entered the building on opening day went up a few steps, through a set of double doors, and came to a staircase vestibule, open from landing to roof. Danz's Orchestra was playing on the landing to commemorate the library's opening. (The musicians left later in the day for another affair at the West Hotel, a benefit for those who suffered from the fatal fire at the *Minneapolis Tribune* building on November 30.) Downstairs, on the ground floor, or basement, was the newspaper and periodical reading room—out of the way so its traffic wouldn't disturb the rest of the library. Upstairs, on the first floor, was the delivery room, where orders were taken and books handed out. To this room's left was the main reading room, finished in mahogany, with eight-foot wainscoting and fifteen-foot mantels over the fireplace. The furniture was also mahogany; the heaviness of the wood, however, was countered by blue walls above the wainscoting and an airy bay window in the room's northeast corner. To the right of the delivery room was the ladies' reading room, with its carpeted floor, draped windows, leather and mahogany furniture, and large plate glass mirror above the mantel.

On the second floor was the boardroom, where the library board met, and where receptions were occasionally held. This was the most luxurious room in the building—carpeted, the ceiling paneled and frescoed in soft green. The furniture, including easy chairs and lounges, was, again, made of leather and mahogany. The natural history collection of the Academy of Natural Sciences was on the second floor as well, with displays in glass cases. On the top floor, above the museum, was the art gallery, including in its collection six oils donated by James J. Hill. Also on this floor was space for The Society of Fine Arts School.

The building had room for one hundred five thousand books on 10,582 feet of stacks, which were made of 1½-inch gas pipe with adjustable shelving. The ceilings were high—twelve feet on the ground floor, eighteen feet on the first floor, and sixteen on the second and third. Each room had its own thermostat to regulate the hot-water heat. Light was provided by Edison incandescent lamps and, as a backup, gas.

The library was built well, using mostly local workmanship and high-quality materials. The members of the library board were used to things done right, and this project was no exception. The total cost for land and building was $324,893.57.

46

Minneapolis Public Library photograph, 1905

The main entry and stairway inside the new library at Tenth and
Hennepin. This spacious foyer was filled with the music of the popular
Danz's Orchestra on December 16, 1889, as the public wandered
through the building on opening day.

The building was well received by the *Minneapolis Tribune*, which wrote on Sunday, December 15, that the city had gotten its "good money's worth" from the new library. The building, the newspaper said, was beautiful and tasteful, but not lavish, a structure "of dignity and elegance." "The people of the city," it continued with lyrical enthusiasm, "the richest and the poorest alike—may rejoice in the common ownership of this establishment and will meet in it amicably upon the high plane of literature and science."

On Tuesday, the day after the opening, the *Tribune* predicted in another editorial that "the library will prove a true people's university." The paper believed the new building would provide a center for intellectual life and for progress, and, just as important, it would show the rest of the world that Minnesotans weren't all hayseeds. "It is to be wished that Eastern friends who doubt the existence of civilization in a city so new and remote as Minneapolis could have been present last evening in this splendid building," the editorial said. "What city of equal size anywhere could have done better?"

The members of the library board also came in for high praise. On December 17, the *Tribune* editorialized: "Never did a public board better deserve the thanks and praise of constituents." The library these men created would, by its very existence, have a beneficial effect on the town, the *Tribune* said. "In the presence of such a collection of books the wisest man may well be humble, while the ignorant may be hopeful in the presence of rare opportunities. The rich may well remember how poor a thing mere riches are, and the poor may take courage in the thought that there are many compensations in this life, and that the power of knowledge is nobody's exclusive possession. Thus the library should teach the essential unity of men, and should develop true democracy of spirit."

The new Minneapolis library not only served the public interest—it also served the self-interest of those who built it. The men who founded the library were interested in the development of their community and the betterment of its citizens, surely. But there was also a selfish motive for their involvement; a growing community would advance their business and professional interests, as well as their personal interests. The new library was located on the edge of the prestigious southern residential part of the city, on the way to Lowry Hill, Kenwood, and the Lakes. Not entirely by coincidence, seven of the nine library board members had homes in this fashionable part of the city. Four of the board members lived within five blocks of the library. A new main library would surely add to the amenities of the area and enhance surrounding property values.

The new library was also on one of Tom Lowry's streetcar lines. For good access, a public library, of course, should be close to public transportation. But today's sensibilities might see some potential con-

From an 1890 steel engraving

Thomas Lowry, one of the original library board members, and one of eight men who donated five thousand dollars each toward the construction of the first downtown library. Lowry came to Minneapolis in 1867 when it was a town of dirt streets. In 1878 he bought into the Minneapolis Street Railway Company, which operated horse-drawn streetcars, and soon became president of the Twin City Rapid Transit Company, running rails all over the Twin Cities. By the time of Lowry's death, in 1909, the Twin Cities Lines carried 140 million passengers on electric streetcars. In its peak year of 1922, the line carried 226 million. Through the Depression traffic declined, then picked up again during World War II. But the automobile and General Motors buses were forcing the streetcars off the roads, and in 1954 the last of seven hundred streetcars was pulled off the streets of Minneapolis.

Information from Goodrich Lowry, *Streetcar Man*

flict of interest in having the head of the streetcar company also head the committee choosing a site for a new library. In 1889, the benefits to the public of having the library on a streetcar line were clear—as were the benefits to Tom Lowry. And not only to Lowry. When Lowry wanted to expand his streetcar service using electric cars, the city required a performance bond from him of two hundred twenty-five thousand dollars. In a demonstration of the city's "old boy" network, several of those involved in founding the library, including T. B. Walker and Martin B. Koon, signed the bond. If Lowry's venture failed, these men would have to pay. So success for Lowry meant benefits for the others as well.[1]

There was also something symbolic in the location of the new "people's university." As Robert Gordon Freestone wrote in an excellent 1977 graduate thesis for the University of Minnesota on the locational history of the Minneapolis library system, "The location of the library had to symbolically convey the mission of the library. Visitors would not be unimpressed by the link between knowledge to be gained inside, and the prosperous and civilized outcome of personal betterment visible outside."[2] Placing the library in the midst of, as Freestone wrote, "the homes of the class that had made it possible," may have shown a rather mercenary attitude toward education.

The decision on where to locate the new library had its beginning back in 1885, when, at its third meeting, the newly formed library board designated a building committee. On the committee were Martin B. Koon, E. M. Johnson, and Tom Lowry, with Lowry serving as chairman.

Lowry is another example, like Walker, of a civic booster who helped build the city and his own fortune at the same time. He grew up in Illinois under the story-telling influence of his father's lawyer, a man named Abraham Lincoln. In later life Lowry often used anecdotes and parables to make his points, as Lincoln had. Lowry came to Minneapolis in 1867 at the age of twenty-four, when the oldest house in town had been standing for only sixteen years. He was trained as a lawyer, but played heavily in real estate during the 1860s and 1870s. In 1874 he built a mansion, stuffed with heavy picture frames, dark mahogany, and ponderous fringed furniture, on the corner of Hennepin and Groveland, on what is still called Lowry Hill. In 1878, three years after the first horse-drawn streetcars started rolling through downtown, Lowry and several partners bought the streetcar company, partly to spur development of the then-remote Lake Calhoun and Lake Harriet areas. Lowry was a tireless promoter of Minneapolis, and was involved in many ventures that he hoped would make the city grow.

Lowry's grandson, Goodrich, told a wonderful story about Tom Lowry in a 1979 biography. Tom was in New York, trying to raise capital for a Minneapolis project. A beggar woman approached him on Wall Street and asked for a handout. Lowry gave the woman a quarter, pointed across the way, and said, "Yes, yes, but you go and work that side of the street; I'm working this side."[3]

Lowry's committee in 1885 was charged with finding a suitable location for a new library building. There was no coherent plan, except to get the library away from the bustle, noise, and soot that plagued the Athenaeum in its central downtown location. Libraries across the country at this time were still regarded as cultural retreats, and it was thought they should be located in a contemplative setting.

The committee opened the site-selection process for suggestions and bids, and received enough to keep it busy for six months. Most of the preferred sites were on the southern fringe of downtown where the stylish residential section began. Board members wanted a spacious site that would enable the library to be set back from the street (an idea that was abandoned), to be naturally lighted from all sides, and to expand, if the need arose. The committee and the board eventually agreed on the corner of Tenth and Hennepin, a piece of property owned by Joseph Dean, one of the earliest members of the Minneapolis Athenaeum. Dean discounted the purchase price of fifty-two thousand eight hundred dollars by five thousand dollars as a contribution to the building fund.

When the state legislature set up the library board in 1885, it also empowered the city of Minneapolis to issue one hundred thousand dollars in bonds for construction of a library building—on the condition that an additional fifty thousand dollars be raised from the citizens of Minneapolis. That second fifty thousand dollars wasn't hard to come by. Twelve men or groups kicked in a total of fifty-four thousand dollars, including the Minneapolis Athenaeum, which contributed eight thousand dollars. T. B. Walker and Tom Lowry each gave five thousand, as did Joseph Dean (through his discount on the property), William S. King (Lowry's associate who developed the areas around Lakes Calhoun and Harriet), William D. Washburn, and C. A. Pillsbury and Company. The library fund soon became oversubscribed, raising a total of $61,665. The small number of contributors showed the power of the group interested in building a public library.

The man charged with running the library, Herbert Putnam, may have felt some trepidation when the library doors were first thrown open on December 16, 1889. He later wrote that the library was not prepared to handle the demands the public almost immediately placed on it. There was no complete, printed catalog of the books in the library, there weren't enough of the books themselves, or enough attendants and checkout facilities. But by the end of the first year, except for the library staff's insatiable desire for more, more, and more books, Putnam had the problems partially or completely solved.

It was not surprising. Minneapolis's fledgling library was in the hands of a man who would later become Librarian of Congress. Put-

The People's University

Photograph by Walter L. Colls

Herbert Putnam, the Minneapolis Public Library's first director. Putnam came West to be librarian for the Athenaeum in 1884, and in 1888 was named librarian for the new public library as well. He got the library on solid footing before returning East in 1892. Putnam served as president of the American Library Association, and then served four decades as the Librarian of Congress.

nam's leadership of the Minneapolis Public Library set a scholarly tone that Kirby Spencer and Thomas Hale Williams would have approved, and that Putman's successor, James Kendall Hosmer, would continue. But Putnam also believed that the library should be accessible and useful to all citizens, not just scholars, and he took the first careful steps to assure that the library reached out to its public. One step that most assured that outreach was his hiring of a young woman named Gratia Countryman, who, in another fifteen years, would become head librarian and take the library to the people in ways that must have dazzled her more conservative mentor.

Herbert Putnam was born in New York City on September 20, 1861, the son of George Putnam, founder of the Putnam Publishing House. Herbert graduated from Harvard University in 1883, and from Columbia University in 1884 with a law degree. Samuel Hill, a son-in-law of James J. Hill who had gone to Harvard with Putnam, invited the new graduate to Minneapolis to practice law and to look into the job of librarian of the Minneapolis Athenaeum. In 1884, Putnam came West and was appointed to the post. The Athenaeum was changing when Putnam took over—looking for a new building, entertaining thoughts of combining with a proposed free public library, and just getting over a battle that would make its book collection more accessible and more appealing to popular tastes. By 1885, the legislature had approved a public library for Minneapolis, and by that summer an agreement had been reached merging the Athenaeum and the new public library. In 1888, the library board hired Putnam to be its librarian, and allowed him to continue in the same capacity at the Athenaeum. His salary was set at two thousand dollars.

Putnam, like most people involved, saw the combination of the Athenaeum and the public library as beneficial to both parties and detrimental to neither. He immediately set about making the new venture a success. He pruned the Athenaeum collection by about one-fourth, selecting twelve thousand of the best volumes to be transferred to the new public library. In the summer of 1888, he went on a European tour, purchasing eight thousand books for the library that were either unavailable or more expensive in the United States. With money from both the Athenaeum and the new library, he purchased another ten thousand books in this country, and opened the Minneapolis Public Library with an impressive collection of thirty thousand volumes.

Putnam's philosophy about libraries was a dynamic one. He wanted the library actively to engage the minds of the city's people. He had stated his goals when first coming to the Athenaeum. "A library must contribute to the discussion and solution of contemporary problems. The library, to be involved in the life of its community and in the life of mankind, must provide people with information about social, economic and international issues." Books, he wrote, "that are only milestones marking the progress of ideas, make a library a cemetery of dead letters." But, he added, a library that contributes to public discussion of current issues by offering resources that "strike the interests of the community as they come hot from their everyday events," a library that "shall bring forth the experience of yesterday to mould the principles of today," is a "living organism, itself a factor in the future."[4] This is an eloquent philosophy that still gives inspiration today.

Putnam considered the library movement in the United States an arm of education, a way both to help serious scholars and to reach the common citizen who hungered for knowledge. He didn't feel libraries should sit back and be passive, waiting for people to come in. He once

Minneapolis Public Library photograph, 1905

The stacks, the heart of the library. Here were the books stored, waiting for patrons to call for them. The shelves were made of gas pipe and wrought iron, and could hold one hundred five thousand books. The new library, designed as a hollow square, eventually outgrew its book storage space and the central court area was roofed over and filled with shelves.

The main reading room in the new public library. The ceiling was eighteen feet high, the mahogany wainscoting reached eight feet up the walls, and the mantel and furniture were also of mahogany. In language as genteel as the ambiance, an 1890 publication described the room's appointments this way: "There are tables and chairs of such designs as secure the largest amount of comfort to all who have occasion to use them. These are conveniently disposed and, as the floor is laid in linoleum, they can be moved easily and noiselessly."

said, "There are two great problems in library management, one to get the books to the readers, the other to get the readers to the books."[5] In order to get readers and books together, Putnam was cautiously willing to try new approaches.

One of these approaches was a fairly open policy about letting the public wander among the stacks. In many libraries, people weren't allowed to browse among the shelved books. An order would be placed, and the book brought to the patron by a library aide. This was often the case at the Minneapolis Public Library: if a person wanted a specific book, she or he asked for it by name and a library employee brought the book out. However, if a person needed to browse through several books in an area, she or he could get a permit to go back among the stacks. And if a library aide couldn't satisfy the patron's request, the aide would often take the patron back into the stacks, point out the areas where the kinds of books the patron was interested in were kept, and let the patron browse. This system of controlled access worked well. T. B. Walker, the library board's president, said in his first annual report that the loss of books from the library was very small, although "probably a freer access to books has been permitted here than in any similar library." That this library, with "a very exceptionally free and liberal management," had a smaller loss rate than many other libraries with "the most stringent regulations" Walker attributed to the good character of the people of Minneapolis.[6]

Another approach involved taking the books to the public. The library system's first three branches opened within two years of the central library. At first Putnam wasn't sold on the branch idea; but once the branches were established it didn't take long for him to see their usefulness.

Even before the new building was completed downtown, the North Minneapolis Improvement Association had asked the library board to open a branch on the North Side. Once the new North High School was completed, at Eighteenth and Emerson avenues North, the pleas were renewed with more vigor. John Green, the first principal at North, asked Putnam if a collection of books could be housed in his school. Putnam is said to have replied, "The library cannot go out in the woods to deliver its books."[7] Checking his records, Putnam claimed that only six books had gone "north of the tracks" in the past month. Green wouldn't give up, and decided that Putnam was insufficiently aware of the glories of the North Side (a prejudice of South Minneapolitans toward the North Side that has become a city tradition). So Green took Putnam for a horse-and-buggy tour, and ended up standing on the roof of the new high school with the librarian, pointing out the growth of the area. Putnam was impressed, the library board eventually agreed, and the first branch of the Minneapolis Public Library was opened on February 27, 1890, in the basement of North High School. About fifty leading periodicals and several hundred books were placed in the school, and books ordered at the branch in the morning could be delivered there from the central library that same afternoon. By 1891, gas lights had been installed at the branch, and the *Northside Chronicle* called it "a great educator in our midst."[8] So many books were circulated through what was essentially a delivery station at North High that, in another

The People's University

three years, a separate library building was opened on the North Side and became the first true branch.

On April 23, 1890, two months after the North High branch opened, a branch was inaugurated for the south side of town, at Seventeenth and Franklin avenues. The rent for two rooms in a store was provided by South Side residents. At the time, the South Side was the heart of the city's Scandinavian community, and the branch soon specialized in ethnic material. By 1904, all Scandinavian books in the system were shelved at this branch. A third branch, this time for the East Side, opened on November 1, 1891, in the old Winthrop School Building at 22 University Avenue Southeast.

This beginning of an outreach program represented a potential conflict in library philosophy, one which had its roots in the old Athenaeum struggle. Should the library expend its resources to build up a strong and scholarly collection at the central building, where those interested in learning could come and explore? Or should money be spent on branches and branch collections in an effort to reach people who might not be motivated or able to come to the library downtown? The first two directors of the library, Herbert Putnam and James Hosmer, leaned toward the idea that a solid reference collection downtown was a credit to the city and would stimulate intellectual growth in serious students, whatever their age. These men would not turn their backs on people interested in easier access or lighter material; but because they, themselves, particularly Hosmer, were scholars, their sympathy lay with amassing a serious body of information in the central library. Their colleague and student, Gratia Countryman, the third director of the library, would shift the emphasis from scholarship to outreach, following her own interest in people, which resembled that of a social worker. But the basis for her expansion of the library system out into the communities was laid down by Herbert Putnam within the first year of the new library's operation. Countryman later said that Putnam foreshadowed the major developments of the library, and that he was "one of the leaders who shaped the intellectual mold of Minneapolis."[9] The staff he trained, including Countryman, stayed with the library for many years.

Putnam was a stern man, with an authoritarian personality. He seemed to some a bureaucrat who resisted change. In later years he was said to have overstayed his welcome as Librarian of Congress, not allowing the necessary growth and change that institution would enjoy under his successor, Archibald MacLeish. But this slight man with bushy eyebrows and a drooping mustache may have been exactly what the new Minneapolis Public Library needed to help it become established. His conservative attitude helped the library maintain a focus and develop a firm foundation in scholarship before other programs were started. His serious approach was exactly what many of those who founded the library wanted because it made the library grow in prestige and national reputation. That had been one of the goals from the earliest meetings of the men of the Athenaeum—to prove that Minneapolis was not a barbarous outpost in the Wild West. Putnam felt the library's collection should concentrate on the solid and scholarly, eschewing the most popular and ephemeral books, which the public could obtain from other sources in the city. He thought that Minneapolis would develop a "literary class, a scholarly class; a class demanding products of continental scholarship at first hand. It will be the effort to meet this demand that may uplift the Minneapolis library to the scholarly ranks of the great libraries of the East."[10]

At the end of his first year as the head of the library, Putnam reviewed the collection he had helped build. He said it had an above-average reference department (thanks largely to the Athenaeum). The Shakespeare collection was adequate, with workable editions for students rather than rare and costly editions. The medical collection was just getting started, and history was good, although lacking in Americana. There were some "sumptuous works" in natural science (Kirby Spencer's legacy showing through), but political science and political economy needed help. Dogmatic religious works were omitted, for fear of offending anyone whose viewpoints were left out. (Again, Spencer's atheism had precluded his money being spent on religious proselytizing.) Comparative and historical works on religion, however, were included in good number. Biography and travel were adequate. With care, Putnam said, a little more light fiction and travel could be included, and there was a definite need for more works on foreign scholarship in history, philology, sociology, and arts and science.

In his 1891 annual report, Putnam listed the tasks that lay before the library. He wanted to complete a card catalog, with entries listed by author, title, and subject, so people could readily find out what the library contained. He wanted to establish more delivery stations, and to increase the circulating collections at the branches. And he encouraged more cooperation with the public schools.

With those suggestions, and with much of the groundwork laid to achieve them, Putnam left Minneapolis in 1892. His mother-in-law was ill, and he returned with his family to Boston. He practiced law there until 1895, when he became head librarian of the prestigious Boston Public Library. In 1899 he was appointed by President William McKinley to head the Library of Congress, which had moved into its new building only two years earlier. The appointment was a tribute to Putnam, and reflected well on the library that had given him his start. Putnam retired from the Library of Congress in 1939, the same year he won the Joseph W. Lippincott award for outstanding contributions to librarianship, awarded at the American Library Association's sixty-first annual conference. Putnam died at age ninety-three, in 1955.

A World Wide photograph, 1929

Herbert Putnam in his later years. The man was a less dashing figure now than in his youth, but as Librarian of Congress he had become nationally known and respected. Putnam was appointed to the Library of Congress post in 1899 by President William McKinley, and retired in 1939 with plaudits from President Franklin Roosevelt.

The Minneapolis library Putnam left in 1892 was a healthy one, settled in a handsome new building with a solid collection of books. It had begun a system of expansion into the community before the shine was worn off the floors of the central library, and it was busy. Putnam reported that, in 1891, the library had circulated 279,193 volumes, which ranked it sixth in the nation, behind libraries in Chicago, Boston, Baltimore, Newark, and Cleveland. The Minneapolis Public Library had made an impressive start, thanks in part to Herbert Putnam.

The library didn't let any moss grow on its new brown sandstone. It was open seven days a week, offering knowledge to the people of the city. It opened at 8:30 A.M. and closed at 10:00 P.M. each weekday, which then included Saturdays. On Sundays and holidays the reading rooms and reference department were open from 2:00 P.M. to 10:00 P.M. Part of the idea was to help keep people on the straight and narrow, to stay open on Sunday so that people who didn't have work to occupy them wouldn't fall prey to some of the less uplifting activities the city had to offer. Library cards were made available to people who didn't live in Minneapolis—if they had a regular place of business in town. Again, the idea was to be as accessible as possible.

The other two institutions housed in the library building were developing as well, although T. B. Walker reported that the art collection was sadly reduced when members of the Lowry family upon returning from a stay in Europe took back some paintings they had previously loaned to the collection. But the art school was building up a reputation, Walker said, and the Academy of Science was becoming an important resource.

The library was even becoming a community center. In its first year it had served as a meeting place for many civic groups, including the Hennepin County Medical Society, the Association of Collegiate Alumnae, the Engineers' Club, and the Minnesota State Dental Association. Walker wanted the library to keep growing. He wanted more books—more good books, the highest grade of books that would still attract readers. He called light fiction a confection, but said it might get people reading, and then they might become interested in more useful books. But even if they didn't, he said, the people would still be reading, and that was better than a lot of other ways they could be passing their time.

Walker was the first to give his voice to a kind of Greek chorus chant that would be repeated through all the years of the Minneapolis Public Library's history: "More room, more room." He said in his 1891 report that the central library needed to be enlarged by as early as 1893. This new building, the pride of Minneapolis, was already reaching its capacity.

Something else the library needed, now that Putnam was back in Boston, was a new librarian. Thirty serious applications for the post

**The art gallery on the top floor of the new central library building. The
pictures in the collection included paintings donated or loaned by James
J. Hill, T.B. Walker, and Thomas Lowry. This gallery, along with the
art school also housed on this floor, demonstrated the way the new
library building provided facilities for the pooled resources of the public
library, the Athenaeum, The Society of Fine Arts, and the Academy of
Natural Sciences.**

were received from all over the country—a measure of the library's
growing national reputation.

Quality draws quality. The man the library board hired would
bring credit to the city and the institution, and would help the library
develop along both its chosen paths—serious scholarship and popular
appeal. The new librarian wrote in a letter to the board, "The [Min-
neapolis] library I know very well, and regard as an institution of much
promise."[11] James Kendall Hosmer would help develop that promise.

James Kendall Hosmer, the second director of the Minneapolis Public Library. Hosmer was a sweet and gentle man, a scholar, an author, a man who had seen and absorbed life from the drawing rooms of Boston to the trenches of the Civil War. While Hosmer wrote history of such quality that it is still compelling reading today, his assistant Gratia Countryman did much of the work of running the library.

Of all the historical figures in the saga of the Minneapolis Public Library, James Hosmer is perhaps the person who would be most interesting to meet today. Hosmer, librarian from 1892 to 1904, would not seem terribly out of date now. He would be eager to learn about the world of the 1980s, and would not be shy about commenting on it. He would be a delightful talker, as well as a good listener and observer. He would be very little surprised by the course the world has taken since his death in 1927. And even if he returned as an aged man, he would probably outwalk most of us soft moderns, and outthink all but a few.

Hosmer was a Yankee of impeccable pedigree—his great-grandfather fought the British at the Battle of Concord. Born in 1834 in Northfield, Massachusetts, Hosmer brought to his entire career the faith in books and learning that the best of the Yankees carried West with them, and acted upon that faith to the last of his days. He was a noted historian who looked at his country with a vision unobscured by the excessive romanticism so prevalent in the nineteenth century. The histories that he wrote in the late 1800s and early 1900s are still very readable today, and might be included by some in the revisionist school. A graceful writer of fiction as well as history, he commented jokingly about his career as a poet. In 1857 he sent a poem to the editor of the *Atlantic Monthly*, James Russell Lowell. The rejection slip came back inscribed, "Hardly good enough, but the writer deserves encouragement."[12] Hosmer said that nipped his poetic drive in the bud. "I hung my modest harp on the willows and have almost never since twanged the strings." Yet in later years, when asked, he would recite his own poems. If a listener requested a copy, Hosmer would tell her or him to take it down as it was spoken, for Hosmer held the piece only in his head and had never written it down.

Hosmer learned to smoke cigars when he was almost seventy. He would sit for long evenings with his friend, William Folwell, lion of the University of Minnesota, who smoked an ancient pipe, and they would discuss history, politics, literature, and life. Folwell wrote, in a tribute after Hosmer's death, "He was one of the most versatile men I knew. Just at the point where I thought I knew the man, he had something new for me. At Harvard, he was the class poet; then, he became interested in a host of subjects, none of which he forgot, and all of which he had ready for discussion."[13]

Hosmer encountered the greats of American politics and letters—Daniel Webster, Stephen Douglas, James Russell Lowell, Henry Wadsworth Longfellow, Oliver Wendell Holmes—and, while he was respectful and interested, he was not overawed. Though a Harvard-educated Unitarian minister, he seems never to have become a snob. Having served in the ranks and the trenches in the Civil War, Hosmer wrote, "One does not learn to think less of human nature from contact with 'rough men,' however it may be from contact with those at the opposite social extreme."[14]

Hosmer was not a professional librarian, but rather a scholar. When Herbert Putnam, Hosmer's predecessor, heard Hosmer had applied for the librarianship at Minneapolis, Putnam wrote, "His appointment would certainly confer credit on the library abroad." Hosmer, at the time he applied for the Minneapolis job, had been for eighteen years professor of English and German literature at Washington University in St. Louis, Missouri. He had earlier taught at the State University of Missouri and at Ohio's Antioch College, where he had also been college librarian. While in St. Louis, he had been a director of the St. Louis Public Library, working extensively on acquisitions. "I have all my life been a bookish man, and am familiar with the best libraries in America," he wrote the Minneapolis board.[15] Much of his summer literary work had been done in the alcoves of the Harvard library, the Boston Public Library, and the Boston Athenaeum. "Books and magazines are scarcely less necessary than bread," he would write later, and by the time he stepped down from his Minneapolis post he was able to say, "we furnish [books] so fully, that in Minneapolis, the private citizen hardly needs to buy them. If his home is roomy and permanent, he may have his private library; but it is a luxury, not a necessity."[16]

While steward of the Minneapolis library, Hosmer wrote and published continuously. He believed that, because he was surrounded by such a wealth of knowledge, it was his responsibility to put something back into the stream. Hosmer also wrote because he shared with Thomas Jefferson the idea that self-government would succeed only if the population was educated, if people were aware of their world and their history. Peace and justice, Hosmer believed, could best be secured among men through self-rule, but only if those men were self-controlled, which to Hosmer included being educated. Given that qualification, he was a staunch democrat. "The masses of mankind can trust no one but themselves to afford to their welfare a proper oversight. No one will claim for democratic government that it is not beset by embarrassments and dangers. Its course is always through tumults; its frictions under the most favorable circumstances cause often painful jarring and obstruction. But when all is said against it that can be said, it remains true that, for Anglo-Saxon man, no other government is in the long run so safe and efficient."[17]

For Hosmer, as for the people who founded the Minneapolis Public Library, a library served as a haven for reading, writing, and learning, and so was a shrine of democracy. More than a shrine: a tool.

Hosmer's writing demonstrated the high quality of the reference collection at the Minneapolis library, due largely to the efforts of the Athenaeum. In 1902, Hosmer published a popular history of the Louisiana Purchase, written for the centennial celebration of that event.

Hosmer presented the thesis that Jefferson's acquisition of the West had more to do with internal French politics and with French-British diplomacy than it did with shrewd American maneuvering. He said the purchase gave Napoleon cash for land he thought would end up in British hands anyway. Hosmer backed up his position by using information from the library's set of the official French government journal *Moniteur.*

Hosmer's histories were written with a tone and style that would stand up today. Like a good Yankee's, his outlook mixed idealism and pragmatism. In an 1890 book, *A Short History of Anglo-Saxon Freedom,* he pointed out that the settlement of America began in 1607 in Jamestown for "no higher purpose than the establishment of a trading enterprise that might be lucrative." In the Jamestown company were "few or none actuated by any high principles." Many were idlers and convicts dumped out of England involuntarily. The better class of early settlers, Hosmer wrote, came not because of disagreements over politics or religion in England, but because "they desired simply to make money."

He also took a straight look at the American Revolution, which he said was brought about by a very vocal minority dragging along an apathetic majority who would have preferred some small adjustments in the status quo. If the trouble with England had been over politics alone, Hosmer said, the Revolution never would have happened. Religion, of course, entered into it, but, in Hosmer's view, the catalytic factor was a series of restrictions on commerce that "poured profit into pockets at home [England], at the expense of the population living in the dependencies."[18]

Although Hosmer was a scholar, he didn't seem to be stuffy. Nor did he expect everyone else to be interested in the same things he was. In the library's running debate over how much emphasis should be placed on fiction, Hosmer came down frequently in defense of reading novels.

Ever since the Athenaeum had been founded to raise the tastes and consciousness of the settlers of Minnesota, there had been tension between those who wanted to provide serious books on history, sciences, and the affairs of mankind, and those who wanted to recognize that it was all right, occasionally, to read for pleasure and diversion. The debate began in the ranks of the Athenaeum—where fiction eventually constituted a large proportion of what people checked out—and continued among the leaders of the Minneapolis Public Library. Some looked at fiction, particularly popular novels, as a waste of time, or worse. Hosmer didn't agree. He bowed to public taste, but also put a philosophical framework around the reading of fiction. In 1893, the library circulated 368,090 books; forty-seven percent were novels. Copies of Thomas Hardy's moody, atmospheric romance, *Tess of the D'Urbervilles,* were checked out 759 times that year by Minneapolis readers. Hosmer defended those readers of novels against the notion that they were reading trash, saying, "Much of the most effective teaching of the present day in science, philosophy and religion has been done through novels."[19] Three years later, with economic hard times pushing up library circulation (a pattern that has recurred throughout the library's history, for when times have been tough and depressing, and unemployment high, people have turned to the library for solace, escape, and training in new fields), Hosmer returned to the defense of fiction in his annual report. Circulation for 1896 was 559,053 books, forty-eight percent fiction. Hosmer quoted Andrew Carnegie, the "patron saint" of libraries, who said popular fiction can do more to "raise the standard of conduct by setting before men true pictures of healthy, worthy, kindly human life among the humblest—more to draw them closer together in loving sympathy—than a thousand dull, prosaic homilies"on the virtues of helping one's fellow man.

Carnegie added that novels can inspire generosity, self-abnegation, purity, and devotion to duty and to country. Hosmer agreed with Carnegie, although he cautioned that too much novel reading, if it resulted in turning away from more serious literature, could be bad for people. Therefore Hosmer had all novels screened, and only the best were retained.

Carnegie's defense of fiction may sound self-serving, as if this titan of industry were instructing the lower classes to read the kind of moralistic novels that would make them happy with their lot and keep them quiet in the factories and tenement houses. It is doubtful that Carnegie would have been thrilled to have the novels of Theodore Dreiser or other American realists circulating too freely among library patrons. But, as America and Minneapolis continued in an economic depression, readers in increasing numbers were turning toward fiction for relief for the soul and mind. In the 1897 annual report Hosmer continued his defense of novels with this statement: "If it were the case that the novel serves merely to amuse, that alone would be reason enough for its existence. The bow must be from time to time unbent in order that it may retain strength to speed the arrow." Hosmer, of course, felt that novels did do more than merely amuse, but the image of unbending the bow was one that many of his weary countrymen would surely have appreciated, as would fiction readers today.

Also, early in 1897, Hosmer doubled the spending on magazines for the library. Of popular magazines, like *McClure's, Munsey's, Harper's,* and *Scribner's,* which carried fiction as well as factual journalism, between thirty and forty copies were purchased. Hosmer said this move was very well received.

At the same time, Hosmer wasn't giving up his advocacy of scholarship. In 1897, he put into effect a new rule that allowed adults to check out two books at a time from the library; but only one of those could

The People's University

From *The Public Library Minneapolis, described and illustrated* (New York: Exhibit Publishing Co., 1890)

From the booklet proudly describing the new library at Tenth and Hennepin, a drawing of the ladies' reading room. Women could read in Minnesota, but at the time of the library's opening they were denied the full use, through voting, of the knowledge they gained. However, Minnesota was ahead of much of the country in allowing women to vote on questions regarding schools and libraries. By act of the state legislature in 1876, women were allowed to vote and seek office in school elections. That right was secured and enlarged slightly by an amendment of the state constitution, approved in 1898, which extended the 1876 act to include public library elections. It was not until 1890, one year after the opening of the Minneapolis Public Library, that any American women were granted full suffrage—that by the constitution of the newly admitted state of Wyoming. Finally, in September of 1919, as the first order of business at a special session, the Minnesota Legislature ratified the Nineteenth Amendment to the United States Constitution, recognizing women's right to vote in all elections. That amendment became part of the Constitution the following year, 1920.

Suffrage information from William Watts Folwell, *A History of Minnesota* be a novel. In this way he hoped to spur the reading of more serious books. He had said several years earlier that it would be a credit to the city if the public's taste for poetry, history, philosophy, and science improved.

This debate over fiction had been around as long as there had been public libraries in America. When the supporters of tax-based libraries argued that those libraries would make democracy work by educating the public, and would spur economic development by providing more highly trained workers, it was embarrassing for library leaders to see the public checking out so many books for so prosaic a purpose as entertainment. Perceiving an example of library philosophy not quite jibing with the practices of the people who actually read the books, Hosmer, in defending fiction, may have been tailoring that philosophy to better fit the practice. But it seems more likely that he believed in fiction, at least good fiction. Indeed, Hosmer himself wrote fiction, mixed in with his histories and biographies. Although he was an Eastern patrician, he did have an appreciation of the ordinary citizen, perhaps because Hosmer had served in the Civil War with so many of them. Whatever the reasons, he helped develop a library that tried to serve the needs of "the common man."

Serving these needs wasn't easy. One year after Hosmer took over as librarian, the financial panic of 1893 hit, sending Minneapolis into a five-year depression. Resources dropped, demands on the library climbed, and maintaining a quality institution became difficult. The depression caught Minneapolis after a period of expansion. There had been wild inflation of real estate values during the boom, but now, with business slowing down, housing developments around town had empty homes with weeds growing where children should have been playing. Vacant shops, especially along Riverside and Central avenues, also testified to the hard times. By the turn of the century, the city bounced back, taking its place as the commercial and banking center of the Upper Midwest; but in the meantime, a new spirit of caution and conservatism took over in business and government. The expansion of the library system slowed, and Hosmer was hard-pressed to maintain the services that had already begun.

These hard times demonstrated the value of the cooperation between the Minneapolis Athenaeum and the Minneapolis Public Library. The merger had proceeded smoothly from its beginning in 1885, as shown by the report of the Athenaeum's board of directors for 1890. "The union of the Athenaeum with the City Library has so far worked to the great satisfaction of our stockholders, who have been relieved of all the burden of assessments. The library has been better taken care of; it is equally accessible; and its usefulness to the public is greatly increased. So far we have not heard a single complaint or regret that this union has been effected." The Athenaeum books purchased under the

Spencer bequest that year had averaged $3.50 per volume, while the books purchased by the Minneapolis Public Library averaged $1.25, showing the relative quality. The following year, that disparity grew with Putnam returning to Europe to buy books, including a fine arts collection. But by 1893, the city budget was reduced, and book purchases by the public library were curtailed. The Athenaeum began supplementing the general library collection, buying more popular books than it would normally have acquired following Spencer's guidelines. By 1894, "owing to the financial embarrassment of the City Board," the Athenaeum spent three thousand dollars on current nonfiction books, "thus meeting the immediate demands of the reading public in all departments except [popular] fiction."[20] Current fiction the Athenaeum passed over, considering it too ephemeral and too subject to loss by wear and theft. That same year the Athenaeum purchased full sets of the official publications of the British and American Ornithological Unions, the complete recorded transactions of the Royal Society of London, the oldest scientific society in existence, and a set of French mining and metallurgical periodicals dating back to 1818.

Hosmer credited the Athenaeum with helping the city library through these hard times by buying general circulation books while the city spent its money on administration, maintenance, and on a few popular books and periodicals. By joining resources with the Minneapolis Public Library, Hosmer concluded, the Spencer fund accomplished far more for Athenaeum members than it would have had it stood alone. By the same token, said Hosmer, the city library "would have been indeed a poor and maimed affair without the Athenaeum's support."[21] The association with the Athenaeum had another benefit. During hard times, T. B. Walker said, the library shouldn't be buying expensive, specialized books. What money there was should be spent for books that would be widely used. It was easier for the public library board president to say this when he knew that the Athenaeum was still making purchases that could help the library maintain a reputation as a scholarly reference center.

In 1896, in the midst of problems, the first woman joined the library board. She was Jennie C. Crays, president of the Minneapolis school board, the first woman to hold that post as well. This was a year of continuing financial trouble for the library. Walker warned all departments to keep expenses down, and Hosmer responded in his annual report that the library had done so. Hosmer said that, since 1891, the work load at the library had doubled (including what he called a "phenomenal increase" in circulation for 1896), while the library's payroll had increased less than eight thousand dollars, from $15,011 in 1891 to $22,743 in 1896. In fact, individual salaries had actually been cut in 1896, although no jobs had been lost. But the hard-pressed staff was falling behind in its work—the cataloging efforts were behind, and no

A group of library staff members in 1892. At the top of the pyramid is
Gratia Countryman at age twenty-six, when her career and the new
library were three years old. In a dozen years she would be at the top of
all the staff, starting a reign as head librarian that would push library
services into nearly every nook and cranny of the city. This photograph
was taken in the art gallery of the downtown library.

inventory had been taken in three years. Exacerbating the problem, Hosmer said at the end of the decade, was the fact that, during the 1890s, the valuation of city property had fallen steadily. Yet the mill rate had remained constant at .40, so the library's income actually dropped twenty-five percent while business tripled during the decade. Halfway through 1899, the library cut off new purchases, cut in half the salaries of people manning delivery stations, and shortened its hours. These cost-saving measures—and an increase in the mill rate to .47—enabled the library to weather the year.

It wasn't a totally depressing decade for the Minneapolis library. Some strides were made. With the books Herbert Putnam purchased in Europe, a special art collection opened in 1893 in what originally had been the ladies' reading room. This was the first special department in the library. (By 1904, it would move up to the third floor where more shelf space was available and where sloping tables were put in for reading the oversize volumes.) Also in 1893, a makeshift children's room came into its own. When the library opened, children's books had been mixed in with the regular collection. In 1892, several hundred children's volumes were grouped in a corridor in the basement as an experiment, to get the crowding and commotion away from the adult area. By 1893, all children's books were grouped in this spacious corridor, and what Gratia Countryman called the first children's room in the country was ready for business. Children's rooms and collections had existed in other libraries, but this was said to be the first with a special attendant and with open shelves from which books could be checked out for home use. In March 1906, when a new wing was added to the library, the children's collection moved into a newly decorated room on the ground floor, finally finding a true home.

Another form of outreach was begun in 1893, with the first collections loaned out to schools. Lowell and Longfellow schools were the first recipients, and Hosmer said the children "caught at the books with enthusiasm." Parents were interested as well, and the librarian said, "Households to which the Library had been utterly strange felt for the first time an influence from it."[22] When the Lowell school burned that year, taking with it about half of the library books, the library board cooled to this "radical departure" and said no more school collections should be started. Still, by 1895, eight schools had books from the Minneapolis Public Library.

The year 1893 also saw the construction of a separate library building for the North Side branch, which had started so successfully under Putnam in the basement of North High. The land, near Eighteenth and Emerson, was donated by library board member Samuel C. Gale and by Judge Charles E. Vanderburgh, and part of the $10,708 building cost was donated by members of the community. Community meeting rooms were included on the second floor and in the basement, and the new building opened for business January 26, 1894.

Books were going farther than just the city as well. In the late 1890s, a horse-and-buggy delivery of books to Bloomington Ferry on the Minnesota River was the first effort toward reaching out to rural readers. This delivery service was the progenitor of the rural book truck that would later flower in Gratia Countryman's reign.

Economic troubles were beginning to abate by the turn of the century, and the Minneapolis Public Library looked forward to the 1900s with some promise. Ten years after opening, the library had stretched

Minneapolis Public Library photograph

The first branch in the Minneapolis library system, at 1834 Emerson Avenue North. The building opened in 1894 and this photograph was taken shortly after. The North Branch, as it was called, had originally opened in the basement of North High School in 1890, one year after the main library was completed downtown. This branch was the first tangible evidence of an outreach program that would take library service to people all over the city.

Photograph by Sweet, Minneapolis

The falls of St. Anthony powered the growth of Minneapolis, and flour milling was the second economic force fostered by the falls. After the building of the first commercial flour mill at the falls in 1854, and the first export of flour (125 barrels to Boston from a Minneapolis mill in 1858), flour production boomed in the city during the 1870s and 1880s. Developments in technology, allowing for the fine grinding of spring wheat, and the business acumen of local millers, allowed Minneapolis to boast of itself as the flour-milling capital of the world in the 1890s. Minneapolis flour production peaked in 1915 at 20 million barrels, and then the flour milling business moved on to the more convenient cities of Kansas City and Buffalo, New York. Remaining in Minneapolis, however, were the still-growing companies the mills at the falls had produced—General Mills Inc. (formerly Washburn-Crosby), The Pillsbury Company, and International Multifoods (formerly International Milling). This photograph, taken between 1905 and 1910, shows the Washburn-Crosby mill, with the Stone Arch Bridge across the Mississippi visible just above and to the left of center, and St. Anthony beyond.

and grown. When it opened in 1889, the collection had stood at thirty thousand books, and the first year's circulation was one hundred twelve thousand volumes. In 1899, the collection had grown to two hundred two thousand books, and circulation to five hundred ninety-six thousand.

The year 1899 provided another landmark for libraries in the area—a state library commission had been formed by the legislature, with the power to establish and aid libraries in cities around Minnesota. This commission, and the expansion of the library movement throughout the state, was largely the work of Gratia Countryman, Hosmer's assistant at the Minneapolis Public Library. She had agitated for years for a state commission, traveling like a missionary across Minnesota, discussing libraries in small towns, appearing before the legislature to lobby for a statewide library bill, and working to establish a similar commission in the neighboring state of Wisconsin. Her work brought her national attention, and demonstrated her dedication to bringing books to all the people. She was named the first secretary of the commission.

The new century dawned bright for the Minneapolis Public Library. Circulation actually dropped in 1900, partly because branches were now closed in the mornings, but also because an economic recovery had begun, which put people back to work and took away some of their time for reading. Renewed prosperity helped the city get back on its financial tracks, and by 1901 the library budget grew a little bit. By 1902, ten thousand dollars was set aside toward building the new wing of the library that T. B. Walker had been harping about for years. In 1902 and 1903, the public's access to the library's collection was improved, thanks to the cataloging efforts of Gratia Countryman. And in 1901, art reproductions from the art collection were first circulated, helping to beautify Minneapolis homes. The medical library, which had been supported by doctors in town, was moved out of the central library in 1901 and maintained independently by the profession, a practice that the library had suggested several years earlier. But the rest of the library's collection was growing again—the periodical room, for example, had 354 magazines and sixty newspapers. Three newspapers from each of the cities of Minneapolis, St. Paul, and New York were collected daily and bound as part of the library's permanent collection.

In 1904, with the Minneapolis Public Library returned to health, James Hosmer took his leave. At the age of seventy he still had things to do. He went to Washington, D.C., to be close to the records he needed for his latest project—a two-volume history of the Civil War. Later he returned to Boston to live, and finally to Minneapolis, where every Sunday he took a front seat at the Unitarian Society. He walked a great deal, enjoyed his after-dinner cigars, and continued his life of letters. This firm but soft-spoken man began losing his sight at the end, but

The People's University

Photograph from the Bromley Collection

A scene along Fourth Street in Minneapolis near the turn of the century. This was the era of gas street lamps, a time when a haircut cost two bits and a shave a dime, when porterhouse steak went for thirty-five cents a pound, and when you could have a home telephone for a dollar a month. The Spanish-American War was on, with Minnesota sending four regiments. The state's population had grown to 1.7 million. The new state capitol was under construction in St. Paul, and within a few years, in 1903, the Minneapolis Symphony Orchestra would give its first concert. This scene shows Fourth Street between Hennepin and Nicollet avenues, and is shot looking northwest toward Hennepin. The Hotel Vendome, its sign visible behind the woman with the parasol, would be razed in 1960 to make way for a parking ramp across from the new downtown library, which would take over the block at the right of this picture.

that only slowed, rather than stopped, him. He received an honorary Doctor of Law degree from Harvard, and then a more local honor. In 1926, the staff of the Minneapolis library branch at Thirty-sixth Street and Fourth Avenue petitioned the library board, "with a desire to honor Dr. Hosmer and ourselves," to change the branch's name to Hosmer, which was done. A library publication noted that Hosmer, then ninety-two, "still walked every day to the Central Library and did an amazing amount of reading."[23]

Hosmer had written about old age in 1912, in a book called *The Last Leaf.* "Standing on the threshold of my eightieth year, stumbling badly, moreover, through the mutiny, well justified, of a pair of worn-out eyes, I, a veteran maker of books, must look forward to the closing of an over-long series." He said he hoped he didn't turn into a doddering old storyteller, the kind of old man whom young men see as last leaves, "capable in the green possibly of a pleasant murmur, but in the dry with no voice but a rattle prophetic of winter."[24]

James Hosmer's voice never became that dry rattle. After his death in May 1927, a memorial carried in the library publication *Community Bookshelf* read: "He had reached the ripe age of ninety-three, but he was so young in spirit, so vitally interested in people and events, so mentally vigorous that we did not think of him as an old man."[25]

So Hosmer passed from the scene. He and Herbert Putnam had deliberately and carefully built a library that served two constituencies: the leading citizens who wanted a scholarly showcase, and the ordinary citizens who simply wanted something to read. The Minneapolis Public Library was a success, brought into the twentieth century by two respected, thoughtful scholars. Now, in 1904, it was about to be turned over to a dynamo.

Minneapolis Tribune photograph, November 26, 1922

Gratia Alta Countryman. No individual had a more dynamic and positive effect on the library system of Minneapolis, and few played such a significant role in the cultural development of this city. Her father named her Gratia (pronounced GRAY-shah) out of his thankfulness at her arrival on Thanksgiving Day, 1866. She became a missionary in what she sometimes felt was the intellectual and social wilderness of Minneapolis. Her gospel was books and human concern, and she would have it preached to every soul, the low and the high, in Minneapolis and Hennepin County.

Countryman's Vision

When Gratia Countryman was head librarian in Minneapolis, one of her staff members resigned, saying he was tired of doing "missionary work." At first Countryman was disturbed, but then she realized that missionary work described, about as well as anything, what she was up to. What was meant as a criticism of her, and the institution that was a part of her, she accepted with pride.

Educated as a teacher, with the instincts of a social worker, Gratia Countryman, during years of war and boom and bust, sent the Minneapolis Public Library out to save the world.

Gratia Alta Countryman was born on Thanksgiving Day, November 29, 1866, in Hastings, Minnesota. Her father, a Latin scholar, gave her the name of Gratia to express his thanks at her birth. The Countryman family homesteaded in a log cabin in Hastings in the mid-1850s. The father was a farmer, a schoolteacher, and, after serving in the army during the Civil War, went into the agricultural machinery business. Gratia finished high school at the age of fifteen. At her graduation she presented an essay on women's vocations, arguing that women's capabilities should not be thwarted because of their sex, and that they should have their choice of careers depending only upon their abilities and interests.

After her graduation, the family moved to Minneapolis, where Gratia attended the University of Minnesota. There she studied music and literature, as well as education, under the guidance of Maria San-ford, an outstanding educator and one of the first female professors in the United States. In college, Countryman was a pioneer. She was the first woman to appear in an oratorical contest at the University of Minnesota, and at one point was the only woman in a surveying class. "She thought the carrying of stakes and chains about campus on spring days quite a lark."[1] Although later she would become a peace activist, while in school she insisted that women be allowed to participate in military drill, for she felt this was an excellent form of exercise. She graduated Phi Beta Kappa in the spring of 1889, after losing some time to an illness. Some forty years later she would return to the university, this time to accept an honorary master's degree for public service both on and off the job. She was the first woman to be granted this degree by the University of Minnesota.

Throughout Countryman's career she fought for women's social, economic, and political equality. Speaking in 1917 to the Intercollegiate Prohibition Society at Hamline University, she told her listeners that womankind's "campaign for freedom" was as important a moral crusade as the banishment of alcohol. Her arguments were clear, and her words, as always, sharp and firm. She mentioned the traditional arguments against letting women vote and take part in the people's government, and then shattered those arguments. "You say that public life will destroy men's chivalry toward woman . . . may I ask how much chivalry is being shown the 10,000,000 wage-earning self-supporting women in this country who must depend upon the kindness and chivalry of men? Do you think the records of the sweated industries, the white slave traffic, show any chivalry toward women? What would the laboring man do without the ballot to protect himself? What are these 10,000,000 laboring women doing without it? Chivalry isn't protecting them." Another tired complaint Countryman defeated was that "public life unsexes a woman. Unsex her—how could you, her sex isn't like an old glove that she might accidentally lose or throw away."[2]

Countryman was the first president of the Women's Welfare League, which helped find decent housing for working women, delinquent girls, and women with tuberculosis. She helped organize and was first president of the Business Women's Club, an organization providing fellowship and a network of contacts for professional women. She also joined in organizing the Woman's Club of Minneapolis, and she continually tried to improve the working, living, and recreational conditions of young women, and to encourage the older women of Minneapolis to take some responsibility for and interest in the younger women in their midst. Through all of her outreach work with the library, Countryman always had in mind educating young people, female and male, and providing them with something to fill their time and thoughts other than the more sordid pastimes the city offered.

As an outstanding and energetic student at the university, she came to the attention of its president, Cyrus Northrop, who was an ex-officio member of the Minneapolis Public Library's board of trustees. Northrop encouraged Countryman to apply for a job with the library, which was just moving into its new building at Tenth and Hennepin. Library work was one of the few careers open to women at the time, and because Countryman was interested in literature and learning, she took Northrop's advice. On her application form, she gave as references "any professor at the university, especially Dr. William Watts Folwell and President Northrop." One question asked what her motive was for engaging in library work—was it to make libraries her profession, or to gratify an inclination to work with books? She responded: "Partly both. Intend to make it a profession *because* of desire to work with books." The next question asked if the applicant meant to make this a life's work. "Cannot answer—probably a life work." That would become one of Gratia Countryman's few understatements.

On October 1, 1889, the library hired her. She helped in the rush to open the building, and did so well that within a year librarian Herbert Putnam appointed her head of the cataloging department. In 1892, Countryman was appointed assistant city librarian, working under James Hosmer. Since Hosmer was an active writer, and was very much interested in the research aspect of the public library, a great deal of the day-to-day responsibility for administration fell to Countryman. She learned her job well, and worked with diligence and zeal. Already a charter member of the Minnesota Library Association, in 1892 she was elected its secretary. She began her advocacy for state help for cities wishing to start libraries, which culminated successfully in the 1899 establishment of the state library commission; there she served as recording secretary for nearly twenty years. In 1902, her capabilities were recognized when she was elected to a five-year term on the national council of the American Library Association, an organization she would later serve as president.

In 1904, when Hosmer gave up the head librarian's job to devote full time to writing, Countryman applied to succeed him. Herbert Putnam, by now Librarian of Congress, highly recommended Countryman, saying that her sex should play no role in the library board's decision. Hosmer also recommended her, writing, "Well-endowed by nature, thoroughly equipped by education, specially trained and vouched for by the most skillful master of our profession [Putnam], minutely familiar with this institution, which indeed her care and counsel have done very much to shape, what can be expected for her but the best success."[3] The local press supported her as well, and by a six-to-three vote, the library board appointed Countryman head librarian.

But there was controversy. The board hired her at an annual salary of two thousand dollars, which was one thousand dollars less than Hosmer had been paid. In addition, the job of assistant librarian, which

Photograph by the Miller Studios

This photograph of Gratia Countryman appeared in the *Minneapolis Tribune* July 7, 1925. A noted figure in Minneapolis life, Countryman was the subject of both local and national attention for her views on the library's role in society.

Countryman had held, was eliminated, so Countryman herself would have no designated assistant. Arguments flared, with some members of the public saying that, because Countryman was a woman, she was being asked to do more work for less pay than the man who had held the job previously. Even Putnam, in his letter of recommendation, had said it would be "unfair to accept from a woman a man's service and not give her the salary and the title which go with that service."[4] Many librarians from around America wrote to Countryman, saying that reducing the librarian's salary at the time of her appointment was an injustice. Letters to the editor in local papers also decried the board's discriminatory practice. T. B. Walker felt obliged to answer these criticisms by pointing out that the board had, in essence, kept her work the same as it had been, and in actuality had given her a seven-hundred-dollar-per-year raise over what she had made as an assistant librarian. He said there was no discrimination involved.

Wherever the truth lay, the debate subsided, and Gratia Countryman took over the library. She was thirty-seven years old, the first Minnesotan to head the library, and, in 1904, the only woman in America to be in charge of a library the size of the Minneapolis Public Library.

Outspoken and forthright, Countryman sparked anger in her staff, as well as deep loyalty. One librarian who worked under Countryman called her, years later, "a little Hitler." Others called her a dear friend. With her energy and dedication, with her almost endless drive, she did more than anyone in the library's hundred-year history to bring the library and its services to the people of Minneapolis. If, after Gratia Countryman was done with her work, a citizen of Minneapolis hadn't heard of the public library, that citizen just hadn't been paying attention. She cast books and their magic across the city and the neighboring countryside the way Johnny Appleseed scattered seeds across the land. She was a zealot, a missionary who would bring learning to the multitudes.

Neither Countryman nor her staff was ever confused about who was the boss. She was something of a benevolent dictator, enormously cooperative with those who cooperated with her, and sharp with those who violated her ideals about the library or about personal or professional decorum. In the days before unions and pay scales, she was perceived as arbitrary about money. "She looked at you and decided what your salary would be," said Jane Gamble, a former staff member.[5] There was no recourse beyond Countryman. What she said stood. She was demanding of her employees, especially when the library was short of resources. But she was as quick to recognize and praise good work as she was to correct bad. She inspired a tremendous amount of loyalty in those who shared her vision of what a library should be. Many thought of her as honest and fair. Clerks as well as department heads were invited to her house for picnics in the summer. She sometimes helped her staff with personal problems, and helped many to advance in their careers. George Goodacre, who started as a page at the library in 1915, was sent by Countryman to Dunwoody Industrial Institute to learn a new trade, typesetting and printing, so he could work on the library's publicity. Goodacre never forgot her.[6]

A 1935 article about Countryman in *Woman's Home Companion* said, "The library is her workshop, her profession, her recreation, her hobby." Her total interest was consumed by library work and by professional and women's groups she belonged to. Her diaries and daybooks occasionally comment on weather, health, or travel, but mostly reflect her professional life and the amount of time and energy she devoted to her causes. This librarian, described by a Minneapolis newspaper as "a stocky little woman with keen blue eyes and slow, meaning smile," was a tireless worker because she believed so deeply in what a library could do for people of her city, and in what all libraries could do for the people of her country. She believed education was crucial to the success of democracy. When she was twenty-three years old, Countryman argued in a speech that an ignorant electorate was the gravest danger this nation faced. She proposed educational, economic, and moral qualifications for voting. People must be able to read and write, support themselves, and must obey the laws before they should be allowed to cast a ballot, she thought. This would keep tramps, troublemakers, and vote-buyers from having "a voice in this government of order."[7] At first this seems inconsistent for a person who would later champion the downtrodden of the city; but it wasn't. For Countryman saw education—and the library—as a way to uplift the cast-offs of society, develop their character, improve their morals and minds, and turn them into the bright raw material of democracy. A mission glowed in her eyes, and she would see it succeed. She said a librarian should be a "propagandist for education," and that's just what she was. And she would fight. When the city, in financial straits, cut the library budget, she fought for recognition and funding, mobilizing citizen support to make her case. She would not let her vision of a library slip away.

When Countryman took over the Minneapolis Public Library in 1904, a staff of forty-three people worked at its central library, three branch libraries, and ten delivery stations. When she left the library in 1936, the staff had grown to two hundred and fifty; books were distributed through 353 points in the city, including fifteen branches; the budget had quadrupled; the book collection had grown by a half-million volumes; and the number of books circulating each year had risen from five hundred thousand to 3.6 million. Of course, the first part of the twentieth century was a time of general growth for the city and the country, and not all this increase can be attributed to a single person. This library would have developed no matter who ran it. But

"Woman suffrage is imminent and will bring a great body of uninformed voters into the political world. The Library will certainly be requisitioned to help in the necessary education of this new force. Women are likely to take this new duty very seriously and are already preparing themselves to assume a grave obligation."

—Gratia Countryman in Annual Report for 1917 and 1918 (together in one volume)

the driving force behind this explosive growth was, indeed, Gratia Countryman.

The librarian laid down her philosophy in her first annual report, written in 1905. Countryman wrote that the public library was "the one great civic institution" supported by the people that was "designed for the instruction and pleasure of all the people." She said that the only limit on the library's function would be financial, and that the library should be all things to all people in the world of thought, serving both the leaders of the community and the ordinary citizens. "This will mean many forms of activity which in the past were not connected with the idea of a library," she wrote. "Perhaps still in the minds of many a library is only a place where books are stored, or distributed under many objectionable restrictions. But in the larger sense, the library should be a wide-awake institution for the dissemination of ideas, where books are easily accessible and readily obtainable. It should be the center of all the activities of a city that lead to social growth, municipal reform, civic pride and good citizenship. It should have its finger on the pulse of the people, ready to second and forward any good movement." She continued by admitting that most of the people in Minneapolis were indifferent to books and learning, but said she hoped to change that. "It is obvious that if a library is to perform its functions of elevating the people, it will need to adopt methods other than buying a fine collection of books and housing them in an attractive building and then waiting in a dignified way for people to come. The scholarly and studious will come as surely as the needle turns to the north, but the others will wait until the library goes to them."

This was an activist's manifesto. She put the library board and, she hoped, the public, on notice that although the library might look the same, it was in fact a different animal in the hands of a new keeper. Countryman's philosophy had roots in the statements of her predecessor Putnam, but her manifesto crossed a boundary that Putnam never breached. It stated that the library was more than just an intellectual warehouse; it would be a social force that would intervene in people's lives to improve their welfare. Countryman was making explicit something that had been unspoken in library philosophy: improving people's lives through reading would help ensure stability and strength in the community and the country. So Countryman put her emphasis not on books, but on the people who used them. And, showing a zeal typical of all reformers and social engineers, she decided that if people weren't going to come into the library to see the light, she would bring the light to them.

As the years went on, and especially as the years darkened with war and economic depression, Countryman began to sound more and more like a social worker involved in the lives of her cases. For example, in 1910 a reading room was opened on Bridge Square at Second

Gratia Countryman's "door of opportunity" for unemployed men.
Bridge Square reading room in the old City Hall at Second and
Hennepin was in the heart of the district of cheap hotels and flophouses
where the unemployed, many of them immigrants, congregated in
despair. The men were forced out of the boarding houses during the
day, and Countryman opened this reading room in 1910 so the men
would have some place to go other than the saloons. Here readers could
search for news of home or advertisements for jobs in Swedish and
English newspapers. This photograph was taken in the early 1900s.

and Hennepin, near the employment bureaus and cheap hotels where
unemployed men, many of them immigrants, lived in despair. At any
hour throughout the day, one hundred fifty to two hundred men were
in the room, reading papers in English and Swedish, finding a haven
they might otherwise have secured in a saloon. As Countryman said,
"They have no homes, they have not even the privilege of a chair in
many of the lodging houses; where shall they go in the daytime?"[8]
Sounding more like an angel of social welfare than a librarian, Countryman said the library should be "the door of opportunity for all such
as these." Schools, she added, don't reach the majority of foreigners,
"but the library, because it is more informal and more inviting, and

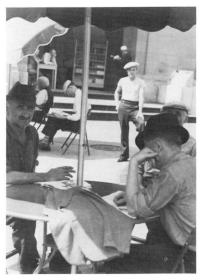

Minneapolis Public Library photograph

**The reading room tradition
begun by Gratia Countryman in
1910 continued in Bridge Square,
at the junction of Hennepin and
Nicollet avenues, with an open-
air reading area in the Gateway
Information Center. This
photograph shows men using the
reading room in the 1940s.**

because it makes less strenuous demands upon tired men and women, can come into a more genial relation with them."[9] As Minneapolis became more industrialized before World War II, and thousands of women came into the city to join the work force, Countryman's library began putting book collections in factories and telephone exchanges, not just to enlighten the workers' minds, but to keep the young women from "going wrong." Seeing children and young adults with time on their hands, the library staff opened their buildings for social clubs and for kids needing recreation. "The library is not primarily a recreational agency," Countryman wrote, "but it is a social agency as well as an educational one, with the avowed purpose of making and developing good citizens."[10]

Countryman wanted her staff not just to serve the public, but to enter into the lives of the people who came through the library's doors. She told a newspaper reporter that librarians should have a "real love, not only for books, but for people," and added that "human sympathy is the greatest gift a library can possibly give people."[11] Her social concern came through in a 1932 piece she wrote for the American Library Association: "We deal with books, but the profoundest learning is only effective in our human life if it be joined to an understanding heart, able to enter sympathetically into other people's problems."[12] That same year, with the Great Depression gathering its terrible strength, Countryman said in her annual report, "The library is accustomed to ally itself and rightly so with the educational agencies. But we belong just as much with the social agencies and with all the movements for social betterment and social righteousness."

One wonders how all this talk of a social and recreational agency dispensing human sympathy and understanding would have sat with Kirby Spencer and Thomas Williams, those original guardians of the scholarly tradition of the Minneapolis Athenaeum. They would certainly have flinched at the change, for the quiet, intellectual seeds they had planted were growing into a dynamic organism that was reaching out to engage life all over the city.

A crucial element in Countryman's vision of a library involved with people was the notion of actively bringing the library to those people. She wouldn't wait for the people to come to the library. She often said, "This isn't the century when Abraham Lincoln walks twelve miles for a book." Her social concern made her think of those people who weren't foremost in the thinking of the Athenaeum's founders. "We have to consider the old people, the shut-ins, the poor people, men in shops, clerks, telephone operators, the little children, women too busy to go far from home for a library book, farm folks on back roads in Hennepin County. All want books."[13]

Countryman wasn't content simply to expand the library's service through traditional branches. The library would take books not just to where people lived, but to where people worked. In 1905, two small library collections were set up in the Twin Cities Telephone Building and in the Cream of Wheat Factory, and what would become known as the "Business House" department was underway. The following year, the board authorized setting up libraries in firehouses, where the men had plenty of leisure time between calls. By 1911, there were libraries in twenty factories and companies. At Northwestern Knitting Company, where most of the one thousand employees were women, a small collection of three hundred books turned over almost twice each

Theodore Dreiser had captured for American readers the tragedies women could face when they came to the cities to work. From the beginning, a library in Minneapolis had been seen as a way to give young people a clean and decent alternative way to spend their time, and in the early twentieth century that idea was expanded. Public library book collections were put into the factories and telephone exchanges, where the women just in from the farm or just over from the old country worked. This outreach program started in 1905, and by 1936, fifty-three businesses and factories in Minneapolis had books from the public library right at their workers' fingertips. This photo shows women in one of the factory stations in the early 1900s.

month. A reading room was opened at the Twin Cities Rapid Transit Company's station at Lake Street and Twenty-third Avenue South with one hundred volumes. In 1913, libraries were placed in eight telephone exchanges in Minneapolis. The women handling the calls took fifteen-minute breaks every two hours, and could read the books then or take them home. In two years, these women read more than nine thousand library books. By 1924, thirty-one factories and businesses had library collections, including Western Union offices, where telegraph messenger boys followed special reading programs between runs. These "young uniformed businessmen . . . are often obliged to enter the commercial world before they acquire the habit of reading," a library publication said.[14] The larger concerns involved in the Business House outreach included Dayton's, Northwestern National Life, the Federal Reserve Bank, the Donaldson Company, Power's Mercantile Company, and the Soo Line Railroad. By 1936, fifty-three businesses and factories were part of this program.

Photograph by C. J. Hibbard, Minneapolis

Gratia Countryman's outreach philosophy would move the books to the readers, wherever they might be found. Here, in the early 1900s, a library collection in a Minneapolis fire hall gives the men something to do between calls.

The librarian in charge of the Business House libraries explained in 1920 why the libraries were popular. "The science of business demands that every worker know his particular line as well as a college professor. Salesmen are not satisfied with passing goods over the counter—they want to know all about it, where made, how made, and why made in the manner it is."[15] If the salesman couldn't go to the factory, he could learn what he needed to know in a library, and therefore become a better salesman. As the nation boomed after World War I, business became a cultural passion, and every up-and-coming young man had visions of an executive desk. To be sure, much of the reading done through these business libraries was recreational, but a great deal of it was serious, too. To facilitate this kind of serious education, a business and municipal branch library was opened in 1916 in the business district, at 508 Second Avenue South. Here, reference material about government and public policy issues was combined with information on banking, finance, manufacturing, sales, advertising, and distribution. The branch did a steady business up through the Great Depression.

Library historians have pointed out that educating workers was crucial to the development of America as it industrialized early in the twentieth century. "Mental development went arm in arm with industrial development and, with the new methods of manufacture, was prerequisite to it," wrote historian Sidney Ditzion.[16] Industry and business were becoming more complicated, science was stepping into the marketplace, and workers had to be educated and trained if they were to perform well. The pattern was set early in the nineteenth century in Massachusetts, where several factories created libraries for their employees, either paid for by management or by a small deduction from the workers' pay. Ditzion pointed out that another stimulus for educating workers was the competition among cities to attract business, a competition Minneapolis had felt keenly since the first founders stared with an appraising eye at the power of the falls of St. Anthony. "It was generally understood that a town which failed to educate its population would fall behind in the race for business supremacy."[17] Workers wouldn't be as talented and productive, and companies might decide to settle in richer pastures.

And then, historians and social observers suggest, there was another reason for educating the workers, for providing them with amenities like libraries. The industrialization of America was a time of turmoil, of rapid change and dislocation. Social patterns were shifting, wealth was being accumulated by the few, and some of the many weren't altogether thrilled about it. Labor was organizing, with pain and bloodshed, and frightening words like *populism, socialism,* and *bolshevism* were on the lips of many workers. Many business leaders, including those across the country who served on library boards and had helped to found the cultural institutions of America, felt that only

Countryman's Vision

Minneapolis Public Library photograph, 1916

When business became an American passion early in the twentieth century, the library reached out to embrace it. Along with putting small collections in offices and factories, the Minneapolis library reached a branch into the middle of the downtown business district, at 508 Second Avenue South. This branch's staff and collection provided government information and advice for rising young workers hungry for success.

ignorance could lead to such violent challenges to the system. If workers could be educated, could be shown a way to better their lot gradually, they might spurn the violent change of revolution. "Thus," historian Rosemary Ruhig DuMont wrote, "conservative spokesmen consciously preached self-help as the most virtuous, patriotic and intelligent way to improve one's position. They hoped to convince workingmen that they had more to gain from honest study and self improvement than from vague projects of social reform."[18] Following World War I, and into the unemployment trauma of the Great Depression, some of the most popular books in the Minneapolis library system were those that told the reader how to qualify for a new job or how to get better at the one she or he already had. This, of course, was beneficial to the workers, but it also may have served the purposes of those community leaders who founded and oversaw the library. DuMont talks about the motives of business tycoon Andrew Carnegie, who gave library buildings to 1,408 communities in America, including Minneapolis. She says Carnegie felt that libraries could help labor and management understand one another better, communicate better, and work together more harmoniously. "Obviously, then, Carnegie envisioned the library as a supporter of the status quo. Once men had read of economic laws and conditions, they would understand why things had to be as they were."[19]

The reach into the working place by the Minneapolis Public Library was quite successful, in terms of circulation and of quality. In 1930, the library's house organ reported that "the working man and woman is reading many more and much better books than 10 years, or even five years ago." There were hitches, however. Beginning in 1928, the Business House department lamented the loss of circulation as two Northwestern Bell telephone exchanges became automated. Machines might be able to switch calls, but they couldn't read. Wrote librarian Alice Jones, "Inventions have continued to reorganize industry and to reduce the demand for labor until one has wondered what the fate of the coming generations will be."[20] A year later, a decrease in circulation in the music department was at least partially blamed on the fact that many musicians had been thrown out of work when sound movies made organ and piano players in theaters superfluous. The music librarian reported that unemployed musicians across the country were waiting for the day when the public would rise up against this "canned music." It's been a long wait. Humorist Will Rogers, of course, had a comment on this mechanization. "We originated mass production, and mass production produced everybody out of a job with our boasted labor-saving machinery. It saved labor, the very thing we are now appropriating money to get a job for."

Another target for Countryman's outreach was the children, and school libraries expanded dramatically during her tenure. After the first few school collections were sent out under Hosmer, books were sent to grade schools, junior highs, and, finally, a high school in Countryman's era. The library provided the books and the attendants, and, after some haggling, the schools provided the space rent-free. In many grade schools, the books were divided up among the individual classrooms, with teachers ordering specific books to complement their course of instruction. By the time Countryman retired in 1936, there were 243 small classroom libraries in thirty-six elementary schools around the city. As Countryman was herself trained as an educator, she was particularly eager to cooperate with teachers. From her first years as head librarian, she crusaded to get children to take out library cards, and to have teachers bring their classes to the library. As education nationally turned toward encouraging children to read more and to explore sources of information beyond their classroom texts, the public library pitched in to help. There were, as always, both selfish and selfless motives in this drive. Reading would clearly help the children to learn, and, just as clearly, early involvement with the library would help assure that when those children grew up they would be regular patrons.

The school libraries, especially the nine that were in junior high schools by 1936, were supposed to serve the community as well as the students. These libraries were opened around the city with an eye to bringing library service as close to each citizen's doorstep as possible. But they were never very successful at attracting adult patrons, largely because adults apparently weren't eager to go inside a school building to check out a book. Some children did check out and carry home books for their parents, often asking the librarian to choose something for their folks along the line of romance or adventure. But a branch that opened in Roosevelt High School in 1922 greatly increased its adult circulation when, five years later, it moved into its own building across the street from the school and became a true community branch.

The library reached beyond the schools, too. In 1915, books were first sent out to correctional facilities, to the workhouse and the boys' detention home, to city and county jails, orphanages, and the poor farm. During times of unemployment, small collections, often of books too worn for the main libraries, were sent to relief agencies, shelters, and flophouses. No one was going to elude Countryman's grasp.

You couldn't even avoid her if you were sick. Beginning in February 1923, the Minneapolis Public Library delivered books on Tuesdays and Fridays to patients at Minneapolis General Hospital. In May, Swedish Hospital was added to the rounds, and by fall three more were included. An attendant would wheel books through the wards for the patients, and a reading room with a rotating collection was set up for the hospital staff. A book drive that year netted four thousand books for the hospital service. These books were greatly appreciated by patients on their backs

Students at Bremer School, at Emerson and Lowry avenues North, cram for book reports for their Library Club meeting. The Minneapolis Public Library sent its first small collection to a public school in 1893, and greatly expanded the school library program under Gratia Countryman. This outreach would result in serious trouble when the library wanted to get out of the school business in the 1940s and 1950s, and many parents felt the public library was abandoning young people. This photo was taken in the 1920s.

Countryman's Vision

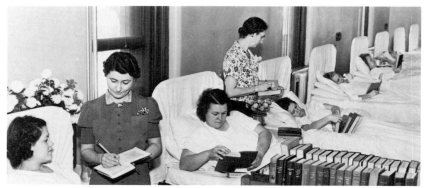

Minneapolis Public Library photograph

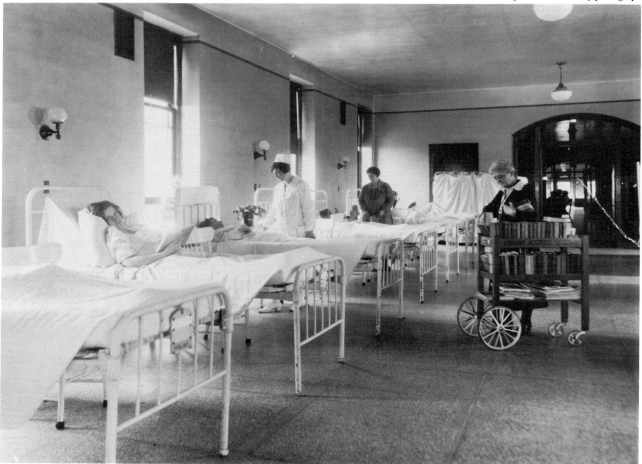

Photograph by A. H. Kairies, Minneapolis

The hospital service of the Minneapolis Public Library in 1928 at General Hospital. In the days before it was eclipsed by television, the library's hospital outreach program brought needed relief and entertainment to patients in more than a dozen hospitals around the city.

with time on their hands. An article in the April 1924 issue of *Community Bookshelf*, the library's monthly publication, reported, "Nor is reading just a matter of idling the time away. One little foreign woman said, 'Without the books I go crazy. I have no home, no money, no job. I am sick. I read and I forget. And then I go to sleep.' 'Please, lady,' said the youth with the broken hip to the attendant, 'Give me a regular hellchaser of a book so I can forget these darn leg arches.' "

Most read fiction, although the doctors and nurses read more non-fiction, and at the maternity hospital, child-care and health books were hot items.

In fact, unmarried mothers at Maternity Hospital in Minneapolis, where women stayed for several months, were required by the directors to work through a reading list of child-care books, inspirational biographies, and civics and vocational books.

By 1927, service had been extended to fourteen hospitals in the city. At General Hospital alone, each visit took one part-time and two full-time librarians to meet the demand and find the right book for each person. In 1923, forty-eight thousand books were read by hospital patients and staff; by 1936, with fifteen hospitals in the service, circulation rose to 212,777—although the Depression had caused a drop in hospital stays as people decided to live with health problems rather than pay for medical care.

Countryman saw another rich field of service beckoning beyond the Minneapolis city limits. Originally, library cards were granted only to city residents. Then, borrowing privileges were extended to people who lived outside the city, but who worked in Minneapolis. Finally, in 1915, the library was opened up to all residents of Hennepin County, and the county board was prevailed upon to appropriate one thousand dollars to cover administrative expenses. County residents could come into town to get books, or they could order them through parcel post. Countryman felt this extension was a natural growth: "The public library is an institution so pliable that it bends to every growing need of community life; so susceptible to the social needs, so eager to render all possible service, that it must by virtue of its own nature reach out beyond the city borders."[21] Enlightenment was needed beyond these borders, Countryman thought. In many speeches she stressed that "The improvement of rural life is one of the major problems before our country." She saw a need for education here, both among adults and children. In many ways country life was joyous and fine, she said in 1932, and electricity and good roads had helped upgrade rural opportunities. But still, she said, far down the back roads there was darkness. "Drive out farther and see the families where no newspapers or magazines are ever received in the rural mail, where the children have little background, short schooling, and lots of hard work, with little leisure."[22] To these people she wanted to bring the crusading light of her books, and so the library began leaving little collections of books in general stores around the county, where rural folk could easily get to them.

The library tapped a rich vein in the hinterlands. By 1916, there were forty delivery stations established around Hennepin County, and 15,209 books circulated. Business was so good that the expenses were high, and in 1921 the county board agreed to place a one-mill levy on county residents, beginning the following year, to support the library work. In 1922, the Hennepin County Library was officially organized, with headquarters in the Minneapolis Public Library and a woman named Gratia Countryman as head librarian. Thus began a long, symbiotic relationship between the county and city library systems.

In June 1922, the Hennepin County book truck, called a "traveling bookcase" with covered shelves built onto its outside, began making regular rounds. Countryman went on the maiden voyage, taking two hundred books to the outpost of Excelsior. The truck made 115 monthly stops, and would also stop at any farmhouse along the way if the residents notified the library ahead of time. The truck visited more than eighty elementary schools each month, "roads and weather permitting." Entire classes would pile out of the schools to pore over the five-hundred-book collection. Teachers could order special books to be delivered, or they could go to the city library on weekends and check out as many books for their classes as they wanted. In the first year of full county service, more than ninety-two thousand books circulated, or three for each of the thirty-one thousand rural county residents. The library truck was generally welcomed in the rural areas, although a few farmers complained that books kept their kids from doing the chores.

In 1923, the county library saw a fifty percent increase in circulation. Countryman was delighted. "County children do not, as a rule, go to school as many years as city children, but now that books come directly to their doors, their mental growth and education need not cease."[23] By 1935, a new book truck—with inside shelves for less frigid winter browsing—was making 508 stops every month. By the time Countryman retired, twenty-three communities had created branch libraries under county auspices, taking advantage of funding from the state library commission. These branches, from Champlin to Eden Prairie and from Osseo to St. Bonifacius, were complemented by fourteen smaller county stations, the whole system circulating more than five hundred thousand books. Countryman, who had worked at spreading libraries all over the state, called the county library the most promising of all extension systems.

Countryman was asked to speak all across the country on how school libraries had been set up, and on how the county system worked. The cooperation in the Minneapolis area was a revelation to some other cities, and Countryman explained how it came about. She also recognized that Minneapolis's business and government leaders liked the county outreach program partly for commercial reasons. Minneapolis was encouraging trade with the people of the countryside, and the library served as one way to connect rural people with the city. If country people got used to having library books, they might some day visit the main library downtown—and even stay to spend money at downtown stores and businesses.

The most impressive extension effort during the Countryman era was the city branch system. During her tenure, library branches mushroomed around Minneapolis the way fast-food restaurants do today. Gratia Countryman wanted libraries to be part of people's lives, and library buildings to be part of their neighborhoods. She wanted

The county book truck was part of Gratia Countryman's program to bring books to the people. This 1922 version of the book truck was a popular sight on rural roads outside Minneapolis, stopping at schools and farms to deliver enlightenment. The Hennepin County Library at this time was still part of the Minneapolis library system.

them all over town, so people of all classes and ages would be within reach of the library's benefits. "The free distribution of books . . . gives a chance for that thing which is so dear to the American heart—equality of opportunity," she said. People who disliked going downtown or who were put off by the imposing central building might be enticed into a small, comfortable branch library near their homes. A magazine article said of Countryman's outreach philosophy: "She sees it as carrying help, pleasure, enrichment into the lives of citizens who would never ask for it because they know nothing about it."[24] In 1905, Countryman noted that Minneapolis was a city of 267,000 people, yet only 44,218 residents held library cards—not nearly enough. More outreach, and branches, were needed to bring in more people.

Minneapolis Public Library photograph

The Seven Corners branch, 300 Fifteenth Avenue South. This building opened in 1912 and became a haven for the immigrants of the neighborhood. The branch was closed in 1964 and later razed for highway construction.

Countryman saw the city expanding outward, and she wanted to follow the people with books. In 1906, when the Minneapolis Public Library had sixteen branches and delivery stations, she noted that the Grand Rapids, Michigan, library had thirty-six stations, "and I believe they are on the right road." In 1908, with the branch system already growing, she wanted more. "At least ten new branch buildings should be erected as soon as money can be obtained for the purpose," she insisted.[25] Countryman had a solid backer in library board president T. B. Walker, who was constantly pushing the city for more money for libraries. In 1908, he complained that there were only two decent branches, the rest being housed in poor facilities that were dimly lighted, cramped, and poorly ventilated—"a discredit to the city." Walker felt that libraries should be looked at the same way neighborhood schools were; everyone in the city should have equal facilities and access. Since libraries were an integral part of education, Walker added, there should be as many branch libraries as there were schools.

Library branches were an innovation that started, like most other library matters, in Boston. The Minneapolis library board started experimenting cautiously with branches under Herbert Putnam. Branches opened when a neighborhood organization agitated for a library, when land was donated, or when the library itself saw a need for reaching out to a part of the community that wasn't being served. Many branches started as delivery stations, often in drugstores, and then progressed to reading rooms—small collections in rented space. When these reading rooms did a good business, they were often advanced to full branches, and efforts were made to secure separate buildings for them.

Countryman, however, carefully planned and watched over her branches. She had a large map on her office wall that showed branches and stations and their "spheres of influence" and circulation, as well as the population and ethnic makeup of the neighborhoods. Under her direction, branches were no longer a cautious experiment. They became a major strategy in her campaign to win the minds of Minneapolis.

In 1904, ten years after the opening of the North Side branch building, the library got its second branch, a gift from John S. Pillsbury, governor of Minnesota from 1876 to 1882. In 1901, Pillsbury offered to build a branch library at the corner of University and Central avenues in old St. Anthony. The location was a few blocks from the seat of the family fortune, the Pillsbury "A" Mill on the Mississippi, and not far from the governor's own home. Pillsbury died before the library was opened in April 1904, but the family carried out his wishes and completed the gift. The library was built of white marble, befitting the donor, and furnished with mahogany. The cost of the land and building was seventy thousand dollars, the largest gift the library had received to date. Into this new Pillsbury branch moved what had been the East Side library.

From an 1890 steel engraving

John Sargent Pillsbury, Minnesota's eighth governor, who donated the Pillsbury library at Central and University avenues to the Minneapolis library system. Born a New Hampshire Yankee, Pillsbury came to St. Anthony in 1855, engaged in the hardware business, and moved into lumber and flour milling, founding C. A. Pillsbury & Company with his nephew Charles. He became a member of the St. Anthony city council, the Minnesota Senate, a regent of the university and was elected a Republican governor, beginning his term in 1876. This was the year of the nation's centennial, the year of the fight at the Little Big Horn, the year of the disastrously unsuccessful raid of the James-Younger brothers gang on the Northfield bank. One of Pillsbury's first responsibilities as governor was to help secure relief for the stricken farmers whose crops had been devoured for the fourth straight year by Rocky Mountain locusts.

Photograph by Sweet, 1920

The Pillsbury branch of the Minneapolis Public Library, which opened in 1904. The city's second branch library was located within a few blocks of the mill district in old St. Anthony, where the city and Pillsbury's fortune got their starts.

In 1906, another branch was established at 231 Cedar Avenue, replacing a successful delivery station. The branch was in a rented room facing Seven Corners, on the West Bank of the Mississippi across from the university, in an area that was poor and heavily populated by immigrants. The library was busy, as one staff member speculated, partly because it was close to the "slums" and people preferred to read at the library "rather than to take books to their cheerless homes."[26] A permanent Seven Corners branch building was erected at 300 Fifteenth Avenue South in 1912 to house this bustling branch, at a cost of thirty-two thousand dollars.

The New Boston branch opened in January 1907 in a large rented room (thirty by seventy feet) in a new building on Twenty-fourth and Central avenues Northeast. The building's owner, a man of the community, agreed to wait one year for the rent, and the neighborhood raised one hundred and fifty dollars for tables, chairs, and shelves. Circulation was high at this branch, so when Carnegie money became available for four branch libraries, Countryman decided to give the branch a permanent home in a newly-constructed building at Twenty-second and Central. Renamed the Central Avenue branch, it reopened

The Central Avenue branch, provided by Carnegie money, opened at
Twenty-second and Central avenues Northeast in 1915. When it first
opened in rented quarters in the neighborhood, the library was called
the New Boston branch. This photo was taken in 1954.

in this building in November 1915. In 1908, two branch reading rooms
were opened, at Lake Street and Lyndale Avenue, and on Twenty-fourth
Avenue South, just off Franklin Avenue.

Another drugstore station was replaced by a branch building in
1910. On the north edge of Minneapolis, Charles and Mary Webber
were building a field house in Camden Park (now Webber Park) in
memory of their late son John. The city's park board accepted the gift
of the field house, complete with dressing rooms and swimming pools,

Countryman's Vision

This park board field house also housed the Camden branch, which opened in 1910 at 4380 Webber Parkway. The building was built and donated to the city by Charles and Mary Webber in memory of their son John. The library remained in the field house until 1979, when the park board razed the building to make way for a swimming pool. The park board then deeded land for a new library building to be constructed in the park, now called Webber Park. The new Webber Park Library opened in 1980.

and the library board accepted use of the second floor (a sixty-by-thirty-foot room with Flemish oak trim and a beamed ceiling) as a library. The Webbers' gift stipulated that the library should be operated continuously until better quarters could be found not more than six blocks from Camden Park. The branch was opened, without fanfare, on January 1, 1910.

T. B. Walker, in his annual report for 1910, said the city needed more branch libraries and reading rooms, not only to train people for better citizenship, but "to offset these temptations and demoralizing influences which to an ever-increasing extent afflict society." A year earlier, Walker had acted on this desire to compete with the gambling house and saloon trade by donating land at Twenty-ninth and Hennepin for a new branch library. The Walker branch, which opened in June 1911, was one block from the new West High School, in the middle of a good residential district (and just across the street from the present, underground Walker Community Library). The two-story brick building, which cost forty-five thousand dollars, was neoclassic in style, had an Ionic facade with two sandstone pillars guarding the door, and, in the words of long-time *Minneapolis Star* columnist Don Morrison, "It looked like a library."

South Minneapolis got another branch in 1911, this one in the Linden Hills neighborhood west of Lake Harriet. Ground floor space was rented for the branch in the Lake Harriet Commercial Club Building

Minneapolis Public Library photograph

The Linden Hills Community Library, at 2900 West Forty-third Street. Having done a good business in rented quarters, the branch finally earned its own building in 1931. The branch looks the same today as it did in this 1954 photo.

at 2720 West Forty-third Street. Circulation boomed in this residential part of town until 1928, when the library lost its lease on the ground floor and had to move upstairs. Many older people and women with children had trouble hiking up to the library's new location. "A very touching story was told of seeing an old lady looking into the old room," wrote one of the branch's librarians. "She was shown the removal sign, for she was deaf, shook her head and moved away."[27] The library board asked the city's board of estimate and taxation for fifty thousand dollars for a new branch building. Citizens from the area appeared at a city meeting, but the request was turned down. Not until 1931, after a fifty-thousand-dollar bond issue was passed, did Linden Hills get its own branch building. Located at the corner of Forty-third Street and Vincent Avenue South, the colonial-style brick edifice opened on February 4, 1931.

In 1912, Walker was proud to point out that Minneapolis had the highest per capita circulation of books of any major city in the country. Walker used figures supplied by Richard Lavell, who the year before had been named Countryman's assistant, and who may have been acting rather like a home-town official scorer at a baseball game. But there was no doubt that the Minneapolis library system was in high gear. In 1911, circulation had broken the one-million mark for the first time, with about seventy percent of the books going out through the branches.

A year later, the library and its branches got another boost. Andrew Carnegie, known in library lore as "Saint Andrew" or "The Patron Saint of Libraries," was not at first keen on the idea of giving money to support branch libraries. He believed a large central collection would best serve a city's needs. Minneapolis, along with several other cities, pointed out to Carnegie the advantages of branches and the need for outreach. Eventually they succeeded in changing his mind. Beginning in 1909, Minneapolis submitted requests for money to build branch libraries, and in 1912 the efforts paid off. The Minneapolis Public Library was granted one hundred twenty-five thousand dollars for the construction of four branches. Gratia Countryman said later that the day she received the letter notifying her of the grant was one of the best days of her long career, equalled only by the day she received her honorary degree from the University of Minnesota.

Not everyone in town was so swept away. Some labor leaders said Carnegie's money was earned through the cruel abuse of workers, and that the city should reject it. Even several city aldermen called Carnegie's wealth "tainted money, coined from human blood." The controversy raged in the newspapers, but finally the city council, with only two dissensions, voted to accept the gift. As usual with Carnegie's grants, the money was for a building only, with the library system to provide the books, maintenance, and staff. And, the Carnegie Corporation had to approve the plans for the library buildings.

On June 20, 1912, the four sites chosen for Carnegie libraries were announced. Franklin and Seventeenth avenues South; Central Avenue between Twenty-sixth and Twenty-seventh avenues Northeast; Lyndale and Sixth avenues North; and Thirty-sixth Street and Fourth Avenue South. But before libraries would grow at these places, land had to be provided (the Central Avenue site was later changed to Twenty-second Avenue). So in January 1914, the city sold forty thousand dollars in bonds to purchase the sites.

While the Carnegie libraries were gestating, the library board launched its second joint venture with the city's park board, this time in Logan Park in northeast Minneapolis. The library paid eight thousand dollars for a one-fourth interest in the park's field house, where it established a small reading room on June 23, 1913. Recreation and craft classes were held at the field house by the park board, and some of these classes, such as china-painting groups, would check out books from the library to help them in their efforts. Alice Dietz, recreation director at the park, praised this cooperative venture ten years later, using language that warmed Gratia Countryman's heart: "As a matter of fact, I never feel that the library is a separate institution. We are all one up here, serving the same people to the same end."[28] This was a very ethnic part of town, with Scandinavians, Russians, Italians, Syrians, and Slavs all using the park together, and the library hoped to help them enter the melting pot. The library room was generally hopping. "There is a liveliness about the place which distinguishes it from a dignified reading room. The characteristic aroma of crowded children's rooms smites the nostrils. The usual unconscious grind and shuffling of feet harasses the nerves. Two desk assistants, blotted from sight by a wall of borrowers, charge books. The librarian circulates through the jam finding books here, looking up questions there, subduing arguments on that side and in general making an active effort to please his public."[29] This vivid 1923 description comes from the library's own publication—obviously this sort of social hurricane was right in line with Countryman's philosophy of involvement.

The first Carnegie branch to open was the Franklin branch, which got a head start when Sumner T. McKnight and his family donated the land for it. The land was valued at thirteen thousand dollars, and the building went up at a cost of forty-one thousand dollars. Located at 1314 Franklin Avenue East, the library was a solid two-story brick affair that became the busiest branch in the system throughout the 1920s. The library opened in August 1914, and had a formal dedication ceremony on January 29, 1915. The Scandinavian books and magazines collected here drew readers from all over the city; a 1927 report said strangers to Minnesota and America were "delighted to obtain books in their native tongue."

The second Carnegie library to open was the Central branch, on

International News Service photograph in the
Minneapolis Tribune, Oct. 14, 1934

Andrew Carnegie struck it rich in America, his steel empire booming in time with the Industrial Revolution. Born of a Scottish family with a heritage of support for populist and labor causes, Carnegie at first feared the effects great wealth might have on him. Although somewhat of a social Darwinist, Carnegie thought America was the perfect land of opportunity for those who wanted to work. His "gospel of wealth" held that people like himself had a social responsibility to provide aid for people who were willing to struggle but needed a hand. His philanthropy spread $300 million across Scotland, the United States, and Canada, and put library buildings in so many American towns that his name became forever linked with "library."

The architect's drawing of the Franklin branch at 1314 East Franklin Avenue, the first Carnegie branch to open in Minneapolis, in August 1914. The library soon became a center for the Scandinavian Collection, as the neighborhood was heavily populated with immigrants. Still in use today, the library was remodeled in 1979 to provide better access for handicapped people.

November 15, 1915, replacing the New Boston branch. And the third result of Carnegie's largesse developed into one of the most active and interesting spots in the entire Minneapolis system.

"People never came to the Sumner Branch of the Minneapolis Public Library just to take out a book. They met their friends there, studied there, sometimes brought home-baked bread to the staff. One couple became engaged at Sumner, and now their children and grandchildren use the branch," a Minneapolis newspaper said during Sumner's fiftieth anniversary celebration in 1962.[30] This North Side library, considered a friend and a vital part of neighborhood life by many residents, perhaps came closer to living out the ideals of Gratia Countryman than any other branch in the city.

The Sumner branch was started, after a request from the community, in a rented room in 1912, at 901 Sixth Avenue North, in the most heavily Jewish part of the city. On December 16, 1915, the library moved into the new Carnegie building at Sixth and Emerson. The building cost twenty-five thousand dollars, the land eight thousand dollars. It may have been some of the best money the steel magnate and the city ever spent. The brick, L-shaped building was two stories tall, with steeply pitched roofs and an entryway that looked like a tower from an English castle. The library soon became the first stop for many immigrants and native-born Americans who wanted a part in the American dream. The place was rowdy and often vandalized. It was a distribution center for clothes and food during the Depression. It was a teacher of English, a social-service center, and a haven for those whose homes were cramped and poor.

The library's neighborhood was at first stately and Anglo-Saxon. As the city grew beyond it the neighborhood became home to immigrants and blacks. It would become an occasionally troubled part of Minneapolis, but the flavor of the area remained varied and cosmopolitan. Its story would be, in microcosm, the story of America.

Minneapolis Public Library photograph

The Sumner branch library, opened in 1915 and moved one hundred feet in 1938 for the expansion of Olson Memorial Highway. Harrison Salisbury, in his memoirs, *A Journey For Our Times,* said this library was the immigrant's university. "Here they learned English in special classes and read the papers, both English and Yiddish. Here they learned to be Americans. A small building. It cost the Carnegie people $25,000." An excellent investment, Salisbury said.

One of the Sumner library's most distinguished children, Pulitzer Prize winning journalist and author Harrison Salisbury, said he wouldn't have traded his youth in this neighborhood for anything. Growing up in the Sumner neighborhood helped give Salisbury a deep understanding of America and of the other parts of the world that had made America. Salisbury's boyhood home was a rambling Victorian house at 107 Royalston Avenue North, loaded with gingerbread trim, verandas, balconies, and more than enough nooks and crannies to delight a boy. He watched the neighborhood tumble toward a slum, the large houses split into smaller apartments. The Jewish flavor charmed him— Yiddish was the "lingua Franca," and "I was about the only goy in the neighborhood," he later recalled. Many in the neighborhood were Russian immigrants, and Salisbury credited them with his abiding interest in the Soviet Union, where he later served as a correspondent. He haunted the Sumner library, saying later, "I just thought it was the greatest place on earth." Sharing the library with him were immigrants engaged in "Americanization," learning English and the history and customs of the United States. "It was their university," Salisbury said. He returned with pride to his old neighborhood for the library's fiftieth anniversary, giving a talk on the Soviet Union and renewing old friendships.

From the beginning the Sumner library had a huge circulation of children's books. The librarians attributed this to the Jewish people's eagerness to learn, but many of those children's books were also borrowed by adults of various nationalities learning to read English. "The [Sumner] Library is the first resort of the immigrant who has come to his own people in the neighborhood and who wants to make his adjustments to American ways, first by learning English, then by taking out citizenship papers," declared a *Community Bookshelf* article in the spring of 1929. "Books in his own language as well as guides in simple English are there to help him. The librarian gives him these and puts him in touch with other agencies which Minneapolis has organized for his particular benefit. His children, who learn English very quickly, become regular library patrons within six months."

Those regular library patrons, the children, became so numerous that within a year they were squeezing the adults out of the main reading room. So Sumner converted its basement auditorium into a children's room in 1916. Ten years later a librarian reported, "We have, during a decade of Sumner Branch, seen the youngsters who used to try to read all the fairy books in the world develop into students of law or medicine at the University of Minnesota. We have seen former newsboys who have been able to start a little business of their own out of their childhood earnings. We have watched the strivings and admired the successes. We know what deprivation and sacrifice on the part of the adult goes into these achievements of the young people."[31] Youth groups formed with the library as their meeting place, and in 1927, a girls' library club was organized whose members helped with the younger children and with shelving books and other library chores.

Photograph by C. J. Hibbard, Minneapolis

The Sumner branch library children's room in full swing around 1920. Here many immigrant children learned a new language that they then helped teach their parents. Here some helped develop the skills that would make them successful businesspeople and professionals. Here some escaped the noise and depression of their homes. And here more than a little hell was raised. The children's section was originally on the main floor of the building, but the young charges became so rambunctious that they were moved to the basement. The librarian occasionally thought of closing the place down when the fun got a little too free, and did sometimes call in area principals to stretch the heavy hand of order out to their students after school hours. Through it all, Sumner remained one of the most interesting, and perhaps most useful, of the city branches.

Not all the kids were so constructive, of course. Some gangs were barred from the library, and one night a particularly rambunctious band locked the staff inside the library with an iron bar and padlock. Vandalism was a neighborhood sport for some, and a policeman became a regular feature at the Sumner branch. The year 1931 was marked down as being calm because only two windows were broken—one by a rock and one by a bullet.

The neighborhood continued to run downhill, although one librarian reported that during Prohibition the area experienced a burst of prosperity—from bootlegging, to the librarian's chagrin. By 1930, things were quite bad. "Other years we have felt that people were bad, but prosperous. This year we have pitiful cases all about us of people in terrible need. (The very bad still seem to flourish and to be well fed.)"[32] In 1932, Adelaide Rood, who was the Sumner branch librarian from 1916 to 1953 and who seemed to be both amused and saddened by the character of her library's neighborhood, wrote, "Beyond our fences, in every direction, we note no improvement. The neighborhood goes more or less gaily on in its interestingly wicked way. For us it is enough that within the walls of the library, there exists for those who want it and who need it, a different atmosphere."[33] To help those in need, the library staff collected donations and distributed goods to the neighborhood. Rood wrote in 1936, "We have, quietly as always, furnished much clothing for children who obviously needed it. Snow suits, shoes, overshoes, coats, dresses, and underwear have been brought to the library by those who know intimately the neighborhood conditions."[34] Area residents got more than material help from Rood. Beth Lawrence, once a children's librarian at Sumner, recalled in 1962 that Rood "played a part in the lives of four generations. She knew the people in the community so well and was so interested in them that they came to her for advice about personal problems—and they followed it."[35] Even social workers came to Rood and her staff for information about the condition in the area. The librarians were glad to see someone coming in to help, but, Rood wrote, "When it comes to ferreting out personal information, however, the librarian and staff are obliged to draw the line sharply. Our very great usefulness to this most cosmopolitan community would cease to exist if we relinquished in any degree our policy that this library shall be a place that treats alike the very rich and the very poor, the good and the bad, the teacher and the bootlegger, the rabbi and the IWW [Industrial Workers of the World, an early labor organization], regardless of race, creed or color."[36]

Here was a dynamic library, working quietly for change in the midst of turmoil and tension. If that tension in the neighborhood was creative for many, it was due in large part to the Sumner library, Adelaide Rood, and her mentor, Gratia Countryman.

The fourth Carnegie branch opened in March 1916, at Fourth

Avenue and Thirty-sixth Street, on a streetcar line and near the new Central High School. It was another large, two-story brick building with an entrance arched and guarded by double turrets. It was called the Thirty-sixth Street branch until 1926, when it was renamed for James Kendall Hosmer. The former librarian celebrated his last birthday, in 1927, at the fireside of the Hosmer branch library.

T. B. Walker, always a little crusty when talking about what he considered the niggardliness of the city tax board's library levy limit, said about branch construction in 1915, "Our progress along this line for the past year has been owing more to the helpfulness of Mr. Carnegie's contribution than to any extra helpfulness from the city's appropriation."[37] And, indeed, when the last of the Carnegie branches was built, the boom times for branch construction ended. More branches would come, but not in such a flurry.

Minneapolis Public Library photograph

The Hosmer branch, built with Carnegie money, still serves its community at 347 East Thirty-sixth Street today. Opened in 1916 as the Thirty-sixth Street branch, its name was changed in 1926 to honor Minneapolis's second librarian, James Kendall Hosmer. In 1980, the building received a new ground-level entrance and interior elevator for handicapped accessibility.

106

Countryman's Vision

A branch largely dealing with the "practical arts" was opened in 1916 at the Dunwoody Industrial Institute across from The Parade downtown, complementing that school's vocational-technical approach. The Business and Municipal branch opened in a rented downtown room at 508 Second Avenue South that same year, and only five more branches were inaugurated during the next twenty years. After the Longfellow branch opened at 4001 East Minnehaha Parkway in 1937, it would be another thirty years before a new branch appeared.

The East Lake branch, at 2916 East Lake Street, began service in February 1924. With a business and manufacturing boom going on in the area, the new branch was vaunted as a "reading factory," its architecture making it appear more like a store than a traditional library. On February 15, 1927, the Roosevelt branch moved from Roosevelt High into a new building at 4026 Twenty-eighth Avenue South. This branch was modeled after the East Lake branch, a simple one-story brick building with a "saw-toothed skylight, like a factory, which floods the room with light."[38] The lot, building, and furnishings cost twenty-eight thousand dollars. Also in 1927, showing the library's concern with the country's worsening social and economic conditions, a Social Service

Minneapolis Public Library photograph

The original East Lake branch, at 2916 East Lake Street, opened in 1924. With its simple architecture and skylight this building was called a "reading factory." East Lake was replaced by a new branch of the same name in 1976.

Minneapolis Public Library photograph

The Roosevelt Community Library, 4026 Twenty-eighth Avenue South, started its life in Roosevelt High School. In 1927 it moved into its own building, where it still operates today.

branch was opened in the Citizen's Aid Building downtown. This library had a special collection dealing with issues that concerned social workers, such as child welfare, psychology, labor, public health, and crime. Although the circulation at this branch was never enormous, it was used and appreciated by those trying to keep the social fabric from becoming too tattered as the Depression clamped down.

Then came a lovely, if slightly unusual, addition to the library system. In 1936, the library acquired what became the Longfellow branch, near the intersection of Minnehaha Parkway and Hiawatha Avenue. The land was flat and wooded, and Minnehaha Creek curved here as its water rolled toward the falls a few hundred yards away. In this setting was a stately, trim house, made as a replica of Henry Wadsworth Longfellow's home in Cambridge, Massachusetts. The home was built by Robert Fremont Jones, one of the most colorful characters in the history of the city. Jones was a New Yorker who heeded the call of the West and arrived in Minneapolis in 1876. He opened a fish market downtown, first a stall on Bridge Square and then his own place at Third and Hennepin. He was said to be the first merchant to offer oysters to Minneapolitans, and once, to spur interest in his business,

Countryman's Vision

Photograph from the *Minneapolis Tribune,* 1937

This replica of Henry Wadsworth Longfellow's Massachusetts home was built near Minnehaha Falls in Minneapolis by Robert "Fish" Jones. The house was given to the city when Jones died, and the Longfellow branch library operated there from 1937 to 1968. The Longfellow House, at 4001 East Minnehaha Parkway, still stands.

he added a seal to the staff of his fish market. He became known to the city as "Fish" Jones—whether because of his products or their lingering smell was a matter of debate. Decked out in a Prince Albert suit, a Van Dyke beard, and a natty silk top hat, Jones's five-foot-five-inch frame was a landmark in town. He was accompanied in most of his meanderings by a pack of graceful Russian wolfhounds claimed to be descendants of the Czar's dogs, and he bought a carriage once owned by Grand Duke Alexis of Russia. In this carriage, pulled by a matched team of two black and two grey horses set diagonally in the traces, Jones proudly drove Generals Ulysses S. Grant and William T. Sherman up Nicollet Avenue during their postwar tours. A good judge of horses, it was Jones who saw the pacer Dan Patch on the racing circuit and purchased him in 1902 for Marion Will Savage, a business tycoon who had an estate on the Bloomington side of the Minnesota River and a horse-training ranch across the river in what is now called Savage. Dan Patch went on to become a national legend as the greatest harness-racing horse of all time, setting fourteen world records, including a 1:55¼ mile in 1905, a mark which stood for sixty years.

In 1885, Jones's interest in animals prompted him to sell his fish business and buy a farm at the bend of Hennepin Avenue where St. Mary's Basilica now stands. Here he collected animals until the menagerie outgrew, or perhaps outgrazed, the premises, and in 1906, he moved south to the Minnehaha Falls area, where he developed the Longfellow Gardens Zoo. A fan of the poet, Jones used photos of Longfellow's residence to build a replica that was the centerpiece of the gardens. For nearly three decades the people of the Twin Cities came to Jones's zoo to visit lions and tigers and bears, seals and elephants, exotic birds, and much more. Not all the neighbors in the area were thrilled with the odors and noises generated by his unusual business, and, after receiving numerous complaints, Jones agreed to turn his private zoo over to the city. He died in 1930, before that transaction was completed. In 1934, the zoo closed, and the property was deeded to the park board, which then asked the library if it would like to set up a branch in the Longfellow House. The library board bought the building for one thousand five hundred dollars, five hundred of which was raised by area residents, who may have been relieved to see something quiet and normal added to the neighborhood. The branch library, in its beautiful park setting, opened in 1937, after Gratia Countryman retired.

Back downtown, there were problems. Even though the new main library building, when it opened in 1889, was the pride of the library board and the city and, by the tone of the newspaper reports, all of western civilization, it didn't take long for it to become inadequate. By 1904, construction had begun on a new wing, the third side of the square. The annex would be one hundred thirty feet long, thirty-five feet wide, and four stories tall. By 1905, the lower floors were completed, and the children's room and receiving departments moved in. The following year the new wing was nearly done, and the Natural History Museum, which had been stored during construction, moved onto the third floor, while the art gallery took over the fourth. New Year's Eve receptions were held in the library in 1905 and 1906, so the public could see and celebrate the changes.

But even with this new space, Countryman complained that conditions at this library location were bad, and that expensive books would be damaged "so long as the surrounding churches, laundries and apartment buildings are allowed to pour volumes of black smoke and cinders down upon us."[39] By 1909, Countryman was looking for new territory to rule over. "A new building in a different location, with sufficient reading room space, is absolutely inevitable," she said in that year's annual report, adding that the new building must come within the next five to ten years. In 1910, she wrote, "It is not too soon to be considering the necessity of a new Central Library Building." The library had become crowded, even with the new wing, and the art department's best works, for example, were stored away from public view for lack of display space. "The present building is out of date and entirely inadequate," Countryman continued, "and some action should be taken looking toward a building which shall do credit to the new Minneapolis, developing so rapidly and so splendidly."[40]

The space crunch was eased some in 1915 when The Society of Fine Arts moved its collection and its school to the stately new Art Institute in South Minneapolis. The society, along with the Academy of Natural Sciences, had been partners with the library since the new building opened in 1889. Both the art and science museums had been very popular. In 1909, the society's art collection had added works by Van Dyke, Turner, Correggio, Corot, Murillo, Botticelli, and Constable. That year, about sixteen thousand people browsed through the science and art museums. During the art society's last year at the library, the paintings had been viewed by more than fifty thousand people. The move to the Art Institute opened up more room for library work, but in 1918 a more tantalizing prospect came into view.

T. B. Walker, a man who wanted to be remembered, had a vision of his private art collection being joined with the library he helped create in a single magnificent building, a tribute to culture on the prairie and to the rewards of good hard work. In August 1918, he offered the library his art collection, as well as three-and-a-half acres of land on Lowry Hill for the site of a new central library building. His gift stipulated that authorization and funding for the new building would have to be obtained within a year, and that the new building, housing both the library and the art collection, would have to be built within a reasonable time once the country recovered from World War I.

Minneapolis Public Library photograph

Nicollet Avenue early in the twentieth century, looking north from
Eighth Street. The intersection of Seventh Street and Nicollet, where
Dayton's is located in this photo, was considered the center of
downtown, the corner that handled the most traffic of people working
and shopping in the central city. When the library began thinking of
either expanding the present building or constructing a new one, the
question of how close to be to this intersection was soon raised. Some
thought the library should be away from the main downtown bustle,
others thought the closer to the center the better. When the new library
location was finally decided upon in the mid-1940s, it was something of
a compromise—three blocks north of this intersection, but still on
Nicollet, Minneapolis's main street. Across Nicollet from Dayton's is
now the IDS Center, and north of those two are the new City Center
complex and the planned Norwest Bank tower, scheduled for 1987
completion, all of which reinforce the point that Seventh and Nicollet
remains the most important corner downtown.

The land Walker offered was a block bounded by Groveland, Bryant, Vineland, and Hennepin, where the Walker Art Center is located today. Walker himself had moved into a mansion, formerly owned by Tom Lowry, on the hill above this lot. Walker envisioned this location, close to Loring Park, The Parade (an open park area where Parade Stadium is now located), and the Dunwoody Institute, as a new cultural center for Minneapolis.

Gratia Countryman was ecstatic. She thought the site was beautiful and heartily recommended that Walker's gift be accepted. The location, she pointed out to the library board, was "on the highway from the East Side to the lakes and Minnetonka. It is very close to the William Hood Dunwoody Industrial Institute. It's a stone's throw from The Parade and Loring Park, each of which lures thousands of people for winter and summer sports. The site is at present far enough out to escape the dust and noise of downtown traffic and the smoke from the big buildings."[41] In a letter, she added, "I think the Lowry site could not be improved . . . . We should build for the next 50 years, and I should think that long before that time, the Lowry Hill site . . . will be very central and easily accessible."[42] Meeting objections that the site was too far from the central business district, she pointed out that the library's extension system had brought books within reach of most of the city, and that the central library was "the heart of a large circulatory system." In 1917, she said, only seventeen percent of the books for home use were borrowed from the central library; therefore, its location in the center of downtown was no longer such a crucial factor. To critics who asked "Why do we need a new library building?" she retorted: "The question reminds us of father's 'Why do you need a new dress?' when mother's old alpaca is out at the elbows."[43] She noted that in the past thirty years, Minneapolis had outgrown most of its public buildings, and that hotels, churches, stores, and city hall were all housed in new establishments. Her tone suggested that the library would not be considered progressive, would perhaps lose some of its prestige, if it didn't follow suit.

Soon objections were raised about the site's location at the *bottom* of Lowry Hill. Some Hennepin County politicians, and the Minnesota chapter of the American Institute of Architects, suggested that a site on the crown of the hill would be more appropriate, so Walker added two-and-a-half acres to the gift, including the top of the hill, which meant he would have to move his mansion a few hundred feet to the south.

Still, not everyone viewed the proposed gift with Countryman's enthusiasm. The Working People's Non-Partisan Political League of Minnesota objected that there was not enough public money available for a building to house both Walker's art collection and the library. They argued that the library's needs should be met first, and suggested that Walker's collection go to the new art institute. Some Minneapolis aldermen, skeptical of Walker's motives and fearful that a new library would favor the central city over the outlying wards, blocked a bond sale that would have helped finance the new building. Some funding through state bond sales was arranged, but not enough, and the deal was never finalized. Alderman John Peterson, deeply suspicious of the powerful people behind the proposed library, complained that "there is a secret, invisible subsidiary government in this city. . . . The aldermen should realize that this Lowry Hill gang and other similar sinister organizations can't control a few of us who are not weak milk sops."[44] Walker had extended his deadline for the gift's acceptance, but, stung by the criticism, he finally withdrew his offer in 1923 and ceased all negotiations with the city. He wrote, "I think the attitude of the persons who have shown hostility to my proposed gift has been greatly influenced by certain officious persons in the community, and I cannot feel that the future of my gift could be properly safeguarded."[45] Walker wasn't eager to see his art collection "tucked away in some isolated room" at the Art Institute, which was itself in a location Walker wasn't happy with. So he built his own art gallery on a portion of the site he had offered to the city; it opened in 1927.

With the sinking of the Walker plan, it was clear there would be no new library—yet. As something of a consolation prize, the library board authorized the completion of the fourth wing—the back side— of the old building and the construction of a roof over the open central court. By 1925, the move into the new wing was completed, and some two hundred and fifty thousand books were vacuumed and moved into new stacks in the center of the building. All departments reported an increase in space, the outside of the building was sandblasted, and the *Community Bookshelf* reported, with what had to be gritted teeth, that "the old building now seems roomy and attractive. The remodeled plan makes it an up-to-date library building. There will probably be space enough to accommodate our Central Library activities for some years to come."[46]

But a new building wasn't the only financial concern the library had during Gratia Countryman's days. A world war and then a nationwide depression brought people into the library by the thousands, and reduced the institution's resources to serve them.

The library, under Walker and Countryman, was always looking for more money. The legislation setting up the library allowed a half-mill tax levy, but the city's board of estimate and taxation set the actual levy for each year. It seldom reached the maximum, and Walker thought the library was being shortchanged. As early as 1906 he said, "The policy of shearing off just enough from our appropriation each year to so cripple and limit our work seems inappropriate and impolitic and quite unsatisfactory to me."[47] He and Countryman both said the

114

Minneapolis Public Library photograph

Grace Wiley with two members of her menagerie that enlivened the
fourth floor of the Minneapolis Public Library from 1922 to 1933.
Wiley's collection included mammals and birds, but her favorites, and
the most chilling exhibits, were reptiles like this gila monster and
rattlesnake. The museum, of which Wiley was curator, originally
belonged to the Minnesota Academy of Science, a partner in the library
building on Tenth and Hennepin. In 1928 the Academy of Science
disbanded and gave the museum, including the beasts, to the library.
That same year, Grace Wiley was bitten by one of her exhibits and
spent several days in General Hospital, with the library board picking
up the medical bill. Wiley and the reptiles moved on to the Chicago
Zoological Park in Brookfield, Illinois, in 1933. Wiley lost her job in
Chicago when she left the cobra cage open once after cleaning it, and
then she moved to Long Beach, California. There she kept hundreds of
animals, doing serious work in the study of reptiles and amphibians,
and loaning fifteen-foot king cobras to the Hollywood movie studios. In
1948, while showing her charges to a photographer from *True
Magazine,* Wiley was trying to get a new cobra to spread its hood in
attack position for a picture. The cobra obliged, then bit Wiley on the
finger. Ninety minutes later she was dead.

library did its utmost to keep expenses down, and Walker thought that the library board itself, as a body of civic-minded people, ought to be able to set its own appropriation. There was some empire-building, and at least a little pipe-dreaming in this. Walker won a point in 1907, when the legislature increased the levy limit to one mill; but the actual level allowed by the city stood at .6 mill for that year. Another bill to authorize one hundred thousand dollars in bond sales for expansion was defeated in 1907.

World War I brought an increase in use of the library, along with a crimping of the budget. Readers were interested in Europe and Russia, in diplomacy and history, and in books and poetry by soldiers. (Rupert Brooke, Alan Seeger, and John McCrae stood at the head of the poetry list.) Many women came looking for information about jobs they were filling—such as elevator, lathe, and telegraph operators—while the men were away at war. But throughout the war and into the twenties, library services were cut back and hours reduced for lack of funding. In 1921, book purchases were stopped, staff was cut, and many of those remaining were put on half-time or on extended vacation leave. That year, Countryman took her case to the people as part of a "Save the Schools and the Libraries" campaign. Library advocates spoke in the schools and to community groups, and school children wrote essays on "What the Library Means to Me." The battle was successful, the levy was raised again, and by the following year hours were back to normal. Patrons who had been confused by the sporadic hours of operation began to come back. In 1922, forty thousand new books were purchased, the largest number for any one year so far and almost twice the previous year's total.

By the end of the twenties and the end of prosperity, money became scarce again while library business boomed. More adults were seen throughout the library system, reading about new trades as the old ones evaporated. The year 1930 saw a jump in circulation of two hundred seventeen thousand, to 3,363,379. "Whether this large increase of 217,000 is due to unemployment cannot be proven. We do know that unemployment is having a very decided effect upon our reading room," a library publication recounted. Women, and a great many more men than usual, were filling the library, "harassed in mind, unsettled and depressed. They need relief of mind as well as body. It is the great privilege of the library to furnish just this kind of relief work."[48] The technical department was particularly busy. Trade papers with help wanted ads were called for constantly, and carpenters and plumbers nearly consumed the construction journals, searching for news of jobs. People wanted books on making money at home by raising rabbits, or making candy, rugs, or furniture. Bartering services for goods came back into practice, and as services and repairs became too expensive for unemployed people, they came to the library to learn how to fix

A Christmas card drawn by Grace Olive Wiley, the "snake lady" of the Minneapolis Public Library museum. Huckleberry Finn was the name of one of the rattlesnakes that lived at the library. There was an irony to Wiley's death by snakebite. The cobra that killed her had a natural, but clearly marked, capital "G" on the back of its hood, and Grace, because of that initial, called it "my snake."

116

Countryman's Vision

things themselves. In 1931, gold fever even sprang up again, as reports of unemployed men striking gold in Montana sent many hopeful people to the library to study mining methods to try to beat the hard times.

In 1932, the library's budget request was reduced four times by the city, hours were cut again, and staff reduced by attrition. The summer schedule, with the libraries closed Saturday afternoons, all day Sunday, and every evening except Monday, was held over into fall and winter. "Just the time when we are most needed, the work has been curtailed," Countryman complained. In an eighteen-month period during 1931 and 1932, forty-five thousand new borrowers were registered in the Minneapolis libraries, at a time when the budget was falling apart. The book-buying budget was slashed, while circulation peaked at 3.9 million books. But at least Minneapolis was not alone. A 1934 study showed that between 1929 and 1933, the libraries of seventy-seven cities with populations of more than one hundred thousand jumped in circulation by twenty-three percent, "while total expenditures dropped by an identical percentage."[49]

Not all of this rise in circulation was from people reading serious books to prepare themselves for a changing world. Fiction was doing a good business, as were books about hobbies, particularly those on checkers and chess. There was a lot of interest in books and articles on neon gas, the snazzy new tool of advertisers and designers. And there was an increase in the circulation of religious books, and of college-level books as students who could no longer afford school sought to keep up with their education. And, when the Eighteenth Amendment was repealed, ending prohibition in 1933, there was a great demand for information about making wine and beer at home and on the art of mixing drinks. It was at this time that librarians throughout the system reported a strange phenomenon: all information about alcohol had quietly disappeared from the library collection. Back when prohibition started, apparently, "books [about alcohol] were stolen and whole sections of encyclopedias were cut out."[50] This was true across the country, and whether it was due to prohibition zealots, or to resourceful people wanting to keep busy at home, is anybody's guess.

Things were grim for the library in 1933. The budget, which had been five hundred and seven thousand dollars in 1930, was down to three hundred and thirty-nine thousand dollars. For 1934, it was projected to drop to two hundred sixty-four thousand dollars, "a drop which no institution can long survive and give any kind of adequate service," wrote Countryman. "We are not using too strong a term when we say that the library has been nearly wrecked in its downward fall. Roads and bridges, sewers and paving have loomed larger in importance in fixing tax levies than the values of human life, the passing years of youth, the re-adjustment of older men and women to perplexing and overwhelming experiences."[51] Shortened hours continued, and after July

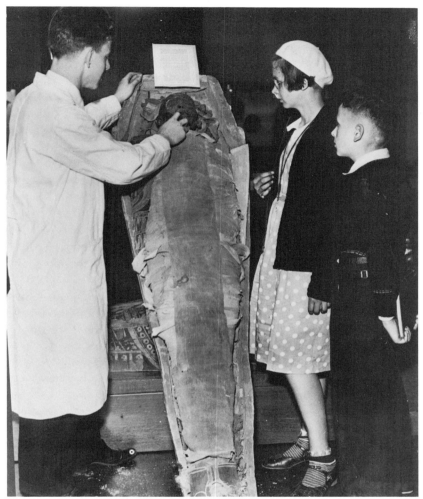

Photograph from the *Minneapolis Sunday Tribune,* June 2, 1935

This 1935 photo shows one of Minneapolis's most well-known citizens, an Egyptian priest from the Fifteenth Dynasty, 712 B.C. to 663 B.C., entertaining students at the old downtown library. Nearly everyone who grew up in Minneapolis remembers the mummies at the library. Thomas Lowry, the streetcar magnate, presented the mummies to the Academy of Science, which put them on display in their museum in the library when the building opened. Lowry purchased them in 1886 in Egypt, writing from Luxor on the Nile to a friend in Minneapolis, "My little boy has been very anxious since our arrival in Egypt to see a live mummy. I consoled him by saying that his father was as near an approach to it as he was likely to find." That didn't satisfy his son, so Lowry sent back two mummies to delight all the "equally curious" children of Minnesota. The mummies were displayed in the museum area of the new library from 1961 to 1980 and were transferred to the Minneapolis Institute of Arts in 1983.

Quote from *Streetcar Man,* Goodrich Lowry

all libraries closed entirely on Wednesdays. Some help came when twenty-five librarians were added to the staff through the Civil Works Administration, and the next year other workers from the Emergency Relief Administration chipped in with maintenance and repair help.

But Countryman looked elsewhere for reinforcement in her fight to keep her institution healthy; she aimed to mobilize the public to speak up for its library. The library board added a little shock treatment by announcing in 1934 that budget cuts would force all the libraries to close for the coming summer. A publicity campaign brought the library's case to public attention, and many citizens turned out to argue for the library before the city's board of estimate and taxation. Part of the publicity drive was a community-use survey that demonstrated how important the library was to the city. Taken on March 12, 1934, it showed that on that one day, 27,789 people came to the various outposts of the Minneapolis Public Library, checking out 21,867 books and magazines.

The publicity campaign worked. Countryman and the library won two rounds with the board of estimate and taxation. First, the tax board agreed to loan the library enough money to get the 1934 budget up to the previous year's level; second, it guaranteed that the full levy limit, which now was two mills, would be allocated for the following year. In 1935, with a full two-mill levy and a budget of $434,026, book purchases more than tripled and regular hours were restored. The library was back in business, as the two-mill levy held for 1936 as well.

More than reading was going on at the central library. In 1934, a psychologist loaned from the board of education spent two afternoons a week counseling people about how to prepare for, find, and adjust to new jobs—and how to deal with the loss of old ones. This was typical of the social-work orientation of Countryman's library. She felt people might go to the library for this kind of help more easily than to a professional's office. Besides, the library's service was free. By 1935, the psychologist was working full time at the library, paid by federal funds.

Throughout Countryman's tenure as head librarian, a concern was shown not only for quantity of circulation but for the quality of what people were reading. There was the question of "subversive" material during World War I when Countryman reported, "All books suspected of German propaganda, many of which were donated while the United States was a neutral state, all books which might weaken our unity of action during the war, or awaken antagonism toward any of our allies, were removed from the shelf."[52] This cut a pretty broad swath through some material that was no doubt relatively harmless. Once the war was over, the question of propaganda died down—except for a fear of socialism.

The librarians had a more overriding concern with books that they felt might undermine the morals of their readers. Fiction, they felt, was a frequent culprit. A 1922 report from the circulation department said that, while some novels could deal intelligently and well with tough sexual issues, too many were trash. "If the code of morals adopted by [the author's] characters goes contrary to that accepted by law and society," said the report, "and family ties and sacred obligations of life are treated with contempt—and all with the approval of the author— the book is undesirable."[53] This has always been a hard call. Does a book that shows something outside of society's accepted codes corrupt the reader, or does it help the reader question, examine, and perhaps reaffirm those codes? Countryman addressed this question in a 1931 magazine article. "As for the censorship of books which are, say, well-written but sordid or unusually frank in matters of sex, we have to remember that the books on our shelves are free to young and old, to those who have read little and those who have read much. A book of this kind may please one reader for the good of it and offend another for the bad, and the library is more apt to hear the blame than the praise. So we can only continue to use our best judgment and try to consider as many of our readers as possible."[54] Novels were ordered on approval, and read by staff members throughout the system. Books that were found offensive weren't added to the collection, although Minneapolis was more broadminded than many libraries. For example, Theodore Dreiser's *An American Tragedy*, which was banned in several locations, was stocked and heavily circulated in Minneapolis. But a single librarian who reviewed a book could keep it off the shelves. One Minneapolis librarian was quoted in a 1934 article in the *Journal of the American Association of University Women* as saying that questionable material shouldn't be put on the shelf at all lest it lead astray "a comparatively untrained mind." While some might profit from "the strong meat," and miss it if it was omitted from the library collection, that was preferable to having "the untrue or the too-sensational offered to undiscriminating minds."[55] This attitude was at least a little patronizing, but the librarian's concern was genuine. Lois M. Jordan of the library's order department was rather upset at what she considered the low quality of fiction published in the early 1930s. "In selecting fiction," she wrote, "one is forced to choose between the nice clean romantic story which young girls and many women simply adore but which in no way taxes one's mentality to read, and the excellently written realistic novel which more or less melodramatically drags its reader through the depths of squalor and iniquity, or the weird and repellant forms of mental aberration or perversion or manifestations of unbridled passions of one kind or another."[56] Jordan offered some informal guidelines for choosing good fiction. If fiction is well written and presents a good cross section of life, if it reflects "the behavior and customs of the times," the book can be good even if its characters aren't moral, she said. But

One million immigrants have changed the face of Minnesota during its history. In Minneapolis, the arrival of immigrants meant increased traffic in the libraries as the foreign-born studied the language, history, and customs of their new country to pass citizenship tests. Although the bulk of the immigrants arrived in the Twin Cities before 1900, the first decade of the twentieth century saw nearly a fifty percent increase in the foreign-born population of Minneapolis—from just above sixty thousand to nearly ninety thousand. Poles, Romanians, Italians, Swedes, Norwegians, and Danes accounted for much of this growth. In response to this increase, between 1906 and 1914, the Minneapolis library opened four facilities that catered largely to immigrants—Seven Corners near Cedar-Riverside, across the river from the university, Logan Park in Northeast Minneapolis, Sumner in North Minneapolis, and Franklin just south of downtown. By 1915, Seven Corners, Sumner, and Franklin had their own buildings and were lively examples of the American melting pot ideal.

*—Immigration information from **They Chose Minnesota: A Survey of the State's Ethnic Groups**, June Drenning Holmquist, ed.*

if the writer takes the reader into a wide range of immorality and uses filth or obscenity just to boost sales, then the book is "unfit for general reading." Jordan, too, seemed to look down a little on Minneapolis readers. She felt a "truly adult" reader could handle questionable books, but "the average reader at the public library is far from being a mental adult."[57] In 1932, Jordan added, "probably the works of William Faulkner are the most outstanding examples of power and strength and excellence of diction, although the characters in his books and the incidents described are rather overwhelmingly sordid."[58]

The reading public didn't always agree with the librarians' tastes. Since the beginning of the Athenaeum, one of the library's purposes was to elevate the people of Minneapolis, but things didn't always work out that way. During the uncertain times of the twenties and thirties, the library offered much popular fiction on a rental basis. A patron could check out a book for five cents a week (later raised to ten cents, and then to two cents per day). When the book paid for itself, it was then offered to borrowers for free. This kept the library from having to pay for what were considered light or frivolous books, and may also have helped discourage some readers, which the librarians didn't mind. In 1932, Jordan wrote, the library had planned to buy only three hundred fiction books, but had to increase the supply because of the demand, "finding that some books which we felt should be in the library were not as satisfactory renters as some of the lighter novels."[59]

The library was especially concerned with what immigrants read and how they thought. In helping foreign people new to this country become assimilated into the main channels of society, the library was serving two interests: the interest of the immigrants themselves, who wanted to be able to know at least enough about America and its language to land jobs and be able to live here peacefully; and the interest of mainstream society, which in some ways feared the immigrants and wanted them to play by mainstream rules.

Even though America is a nation of immigrants, the ones most recently off the boats are often treated with suspicion. They are different in language, dress, and customs. They seem fumbling and foolish because they're not accustomed to life in the new world. Their ideas and their background are, quite literally, foreign. Americans who have become part of the mainstream society often forget their own origins and turn away from or take advantage of the most recent "new Americans." The established Americans are afraid the new arrivals will either take their place or do something to disrupt the system that the established ones have by now learned to work. So the task of getting the newest immigrants to understand and buy into that system is crucial to the well-being of the established society and to the success of the immigrant. This work is called Americanization, and the library took to it avidly in the first third of the twentieth century.

Between 1820 and 1975, some forty-seven million immigrants came to the United States. About one million of those came to Minnesota. The boom period for immigration to Minnesota was from 1850 to 1920. The largest groups, of course, came from Germany and Scandinavia, but ethnic groups from all over the world settled here. In the view of the established society, if the immigrants were going to enjoy the benefits of living here, they would have to share the values of those who had come before. During World War I, Carol Aronovici, an immigrant who chaired Minnesota's state committee on Americanization, wrote, "It is almost the fashion now to talk, write or organize in the interest of Americanization work . . . and folks who used to be just human beings are being classified into American and unAmerican, according to their willingness to agree or disagree with the Americanizers as to what their social, economic and political ideals should be."[60] It was feared that some of these immigrants brought frightening political and social ideas with them from the turmoil of the old world. Late in World War I, after the revolution in Russia, Countryman wrote about the new sense of liberty that was sweeping the world: "Can we foresee what is coming with the whole world throwing off the iron hands of age-long tyranny, with a new-born consciousness of power growing in the minds of those who have long resented oppression?" This new "power to the people" ideal might be exciting, but Countryman also found it rather frightening. "Yet this very consciousness of power is a terribly dangerous force in the hands of ignorant people," she said. The wind of change may blow too hard and carry away with it all restraints. The "ignorant people" must be enlightened so that the change spares what is good. "This new consciousness of 'we, the people,' must be an educated consciousness," Countryman stressed. "The great rank and file must learn to think clearly and to act thoughtfully." In Minneapolis, as across America, the public library would be the great democratic school that would train the masses to use their power wisely. "The rich and well-to-do use the library only occasionally and for emergency calls. The middle classes and the poorer classes form the great body of borrowers; they are the beneficiaries," Countryman wrote.[61] The rich didn't need to be educated about the American system; they understood it quite well already. But the middle and lower classes did need to be brought into the fold.

Library scholar Michael H. Harris wrote about this subject in a 1975 essay. "Librarians, like all educators, rose to this new challenge, and programs designed to Americanize the immigrant, thus rendering him harmless to the American way, sprang up in all major libraries in the country." The ostensible purpose was to open the immigrant's mind and increase his potential, but Harris quotes Countryman in 1903 as giving the real purpose. "Discontent with surroundings and ignorance are the causes of rebellion and disloyalty to one's country, and both

Countryman's Vision

Scavenging was a way of life at Bohemian Flats in the early part of the twentieth century. Czechs, Irish, Swedes, and other immigrants lived in shanties on the West Bank of the Mississippi just across from the university. Below the Washington Avenue Bridge, where Bohemian Flats used to be, is now a coal-loading yard. In this photograph, resourceful women strip down a stray log at the river's edge. The Seven Corners branch drew from this area many immigrants who hoped education could get them out of the flats.

of these the library may help to dispel from the foreigner."[62]

The library had a large task to Americanize the immigrants of Minneapolis and Hennepin County. In 1912, Countryman reported that of the city's three hundred and one thousand people, eighty-six thousand were foreign-born, and another ninety thousand were born in this country to foreign-born parents. The librarians realized that the best way to get immigrants into the library was to have books, periodicals, and newspapers available in their own language. These materials could act as bait to get readers through the doors. Once there, the immigrants could start learning English at adult classes offered in the evenings, and then start reading about American history and customs. By 1914, the library had books in twenty foreign languages, and Countryman was asking for more. These foreign collections helped keep Americanization from being a one-way process. Keeping in touch with their native lands through their own language and literature helped the immigrants maintain a certain amount of their own cultural identity and interest. Countryman also advocated that native-born Americans study the foreigners' countries, through the resources of the library, so as to be more neighborly to and informed about the immigrants.

By 1916, library assistants went to court when immigrants were taking out naturalization papers. When the judges advised the immigrants to go to the library and learn about the country so they could pass their citizenship tests, the library assistants were right there to take the new registrations for library cards. A 1919 report from the county library department said that some parts of Hennepin County were almost entirely German. "To these districts we send books on patriotism, easy American histories and lives of great Americans," said the report. "Sometimes we enclose a few German books for the parents, and a book on crocheting or knitting is often an entering wedge where they are suspicious of library books."[63]

In the branches patronized by immigrants, children's story hours mixed history with Mother Goose. Sumner branch librarian Adelaide Rood said, "Sumner library keeps continually before its patrons examples of that which is worthwhile in American history and American life." There were pictures of great Americans on the walls, and biographies, sketches, and pamphlets about American life always at hand. Rood called Sumner "the one thoroughly American agency in a thoroughly foreign neighborhood," and felt it should be supported well. "The anti-American agencies are sparing no money or time in their effort to instill into the minds of these new Americans a distrust and hatred of America and its institutions. The American libraries cannot afford to make less of an effort to support and carry on real American ideals."[64] The branches also reached out to the adults who were taking English and history classes in night school. Said Rood: "In the interpretation of our national life to our newest neighbors, the library has its maximum opportunity. To these grown-ups, long past the assimilation years of childhood, the library perhaps more than any other institution could help them to get ahead, mentally, emotionally, commercially and spiritually."[65]

Many of Minneapolis's librarians were pleased when someone from the community came in with her or his newly-awarded citizenship papers and thanked the staff for their help toward this milestone. By 1928, both the Sumner and Franklin branches reported that fewer foreign-language books were being checked out. This was due partly to the fact that Americanization efforts were working and people were reading in their new language, partly to a decrease in immigration, and partly because many immigrants were moving to other parts of the city as their situations improved. Not everyone shared in this success, of course, and some librarians reported distress at how many immigrants remained illiterate.

Faces at the Seven Corners branch in the 1920s. This part of town showed both the tattered and hopeful side of the American dream. The Seven Corners area, across the Mississippi from the University of Minnesota, provided cheap housing for the immigrants from Northern and Eastern Europe who came to work in the mills and businesses by St. Anthony Falls. Bohemians, Swedes, Norwegians, Irish, and Germans lived in everything from shanties on the riverflats to tenements along Cedar Avenue. In 1890, almost two-thirds of the residents of the area were foreign-born, and Cedar and Riverside avenues were a cosmopolitan parade accompanied by a welter of languages. Beginning in the 1920s, when quotas slowed the flow of immigration to America, blacks joined the mix of people in the neighborhood. Some from the Seven Corners area followed the upwardly mobile pattern of success and moved into more prosperous neighborhoods, while for others Seven Corners became a permanent home. The branch library was in the middle of it all, providing education and entertainment. Shown here are some regular customers at the Seven Corners library.

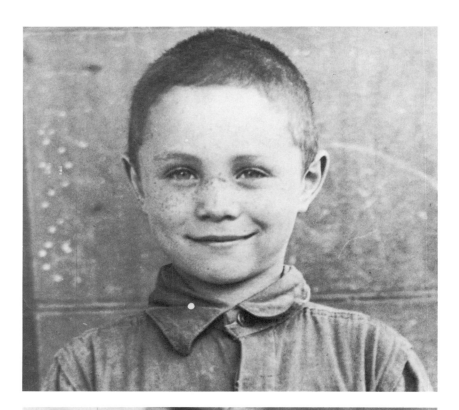

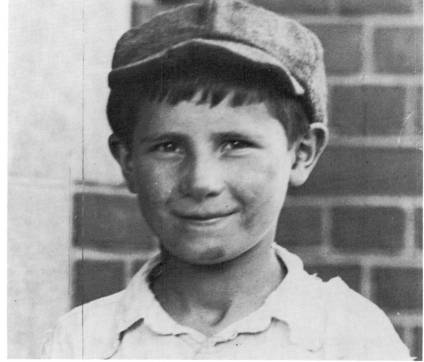

Minneapolis Public Library photographs

It wasn't only the foreigners who were on the outside looking in. Many blacks were migrating to Minneapolis from other parts of the country. A poignant observation in librarian Augusta Starr's 1921 report for the Thirty-sixth Street branch illustrates how isolated many blacks were as they came to the library looking for the same access to mainstream society that the immigrants were seeking. Starr wrote that a "fine-looking Negro man" brought *Roget's Thesaurus* to the check-out counter for the "umpteenth time." She observed that he used the book often. He replied, "I find it very useful in short-story writing," bowed courteously and walked away. "One wonders," wrote Starr, "what kind of stories he writes, where they are published, and ponders over the tragic life of these people who live beside us and yet are a world apart."[66] The Seven Corners branch, located in an area like that of the Thirty-sixth Street branch, where Scandinavian and other foreign residents were slowly leaving and blacks were moving in, reported in 1925 that not many blacks were using the library. The librarian said she didn't know if this was because of shyness (a characteristic whites often perceived in blacks who were subjugated by the whites' system) or because the blacks felt the library had nothing to offer them. She did say the Thirteenth Ward Improvement Club, a black organization, was using the library as a meeting place, and that some black professionals used library resources. She hoped these people would "spread the gospel of good books, of reading for education and for pleasure among their people."[67]

A few years later, Seven Corners did have more black patrons. Some were interested in learning about the art and literature of their own race, some were young kids interested in everything, and some were older people, like the one eighty-year-old woman just learning to read and write in night school who wanted a simple history of the United States.

Countryman and her staff regarded Americanization as crucial work. They saw it benefiting all the people of their communities, and they believed in its usefulness to the country as a whole. Countryman felt that much of their work had been successful when, in 1931, she was awarded a civic service honor medal by the Inter-Racial Service Council, a group of naturalized citizens, for her dedication in helping all classes of people.

Countryman received another honor when she was elected president of the American Library Association in 1933. In this two-year position, she and her library received much attention, with national publications lauding her work. The *ALA Bulletin* called the Minneapolis Public Library "the city's most human institution." The *New York Times* said, "In Minneapolis, the public libraries are as unacademic as Miss Gratia Countryman can make them." The *Christian Science Monitor*, in an editorial about Countryman, wrote, "Books she knows. Mankind she knows. To bring them together is her work."[68]

In 1936, after effecting profound change that would still be evident half a century later, Gratia Countryman ended her career as head librarian under a city law that mandated retirement at the age of seventy. "In lots of ways, I'll feel very lonesome to give up this job. I feel well and strong but on the whole I think the pension law is correct," she told an interviewer.[69] So she left the library that had been her life. She had never married, although in 1918 she had adopted a small boy named Wellington who had wandered frequently into the library. She had said in 1913 about library work, "It uses books, not simply as educational tools, but as a medium for bringing about better social and moral conditions. The work has all the satisfaction which comes from books together with that which comes from service."[70] That satisfaction, which embraced her instincts for literature, education, and social work, was hard to give up. After trying to farm her property near Mille Lacs, she returned to the library in 1938 to direct a Works Progress Administration (WPA) newspaper indexing project. She had been hesitant about taking the position, but was convinced when she heard the project would provide jobs for two hundred people. In 1941, an eye operation forced her to quit.

Countryman remained active, and in 1946, at age eighty, was quoted in the *Minneapolis Sunday Tribune* as saying, "Life is still an adventure and there's always tomorrow."[71] On July 26, 1953, Gratia Countryman died in Duluth, where she had been living with a niece. Her funeral was held in Westminster Presbyterian Church in downtown Minneapolis, and she was buried in Hastings. Countryman had been asked in 1934, for an alumni publication of the University of Minnesota, what her greatest accomplishment had been. She replied, "My greatest achievement—I think I haven't any. Just a busy life, full of interests and service."[72] A woman who loved what books could do, and who brought them to people throughout the state, was gone. But echoing behind her were fighting words, like these written during one of the many battles for funding during the twenties. "We are not discussing whether the library is a luxury or not. Americans do not usually consider intelligence and literacy as qualities of the rich. Reading is an essential part of any child's education, and an essential exercise for maintaining his development. Schools and libraries are not luxuries in a democracy."[73]

This outdoor reading room in the Gateway Information Center was part of the library's outreach program during the 1930s and 1940s. The Gateway area, where Hennepin and Nicollet avenues met, was once the proud entry to Minneapolis, where visitors from the east crossed the Mississippi into Bridge Square. But as the center of downtown shifted south down Nicollet Avenue, this part of town became known for its cheap hotels and bars. This reading room, shown in a 1940s photograph, was designed to give people down on their luck a way to improve it, and was an outgrowth of Gratia Countryman's social activism. The Gateway area continued to decline until the library helped spur redevelopment in the 1960s by locating its new central library just two blocks from where this reading room had been.

1936—1958

Windbreaks and Storms

The world in the late 1930s was tumbling toward war. The country's direction seemed often confused, with a dazzling variety of ideas, some of them spooky, bubbling out of the turmoil. At the Minneapolis Public Library, people's reference requests demonstrated an increasing interest in Europe. As the shadow grew and the war there became more widespread and tragic, Minneapolis readers went to the library to study the relative strengths of the air, land, and sea forces of the countries that were or would be involved. Those who knew that the fighting would touch even this peaceful prairie sought to prepare themselves with information about ordnance and small arms and infantry drill. But the library, like the country, was not yet ready for war. An embarrassed librarian wrote, "We are somewhat in a similar position as we were in 1916—at that time our military drill information bore the date of 1865."[1]

Chiang Kai Shek, the Chinese swashbuckler championed by Henry Luce and his *Time* magazine, was "the most popular personage of the day" at the reference department in 1937. At the library's hospital service department, it was reported that many employees at Minneapolis General had "joined the union and are deep in Marx and Communism."[2]

Two new directions that would change our lives more directly than Communism were visible in the library system in 1938. The technical department was trying to field ever-more-frequent calls about a magical substance called plastic, and the Sumner branch library found itself in the way of a four-lane highway. Sixth Avenue in front of Sumner was being widened into Floyd B. Olson Memorial Highway, and the library had to be moved one hundred feet north so commuters from the growing western suburbs wouldn't leave tire tracks on the books or the patrons. The cost was thirty-two thousand dollars.

Marjorie Kinnan Rawlings's *The Yearling*, Daphne DuMaurier's *Rebecca*, Margaret Mitchell's *Gone with the Wind*, and John Steinbeck's *The Grapes of Wrath* were all popular books as the thirties waned. Steinbeck's bittersweet story of domestic refugees in an America gone dry had a reserve list of seventy-one people at the end of 1939. But the public's reading taste still didn't suit some of the staff. "Some of us may look down our noses on ephemeral fiction and non-fiction, the escape or recreational type of literature, but there will always be these borrowers with us. Sometimes we can successfully suggest worthwhile books instead, but the reader is the ultimate judge of what he will take, as many of us have experienced if we tried in vain to imbue him with 'educational purpose' in his reading," wrote Louise Lamb of the circulation department in 1939.[3] Apparently, uplifting the public was a trying job.

In 1937, a new person took over the library that Gratia Countryman had made so dynamic. It was the beginning of a time of change for the library system. In many ways, the heyday was over, and the system would begin to contract—imperceptibly at first, and then more obviously. The notion of outreach and social mission had gone about as far as it would go. The focus started to change now, eventually bringing us to the leaner, more efficient, perhaps less ambitious system of today.

But the change was slow, and it was not away from quality. The new librarian, Carl Vitz, would, near the end of his tenure in Minneapolis, become president of the American Library Association, following in Countryman's path. Vitz was a perceptive man, well versed in his field, and a person who would stand his ground when he thought he was right.

Carl Vitz was born in St. Paul on June 3, 1883. He was educated at Western Reserve in Cleveland and at the New York State Library School, now part of Columbia University. He worked for the Cleveland Public Library while going to school, was an assistant at the New York State Library in Albany after graduating from library school, then returned to Cleveland's library in 1912, rising to vice-librarian by the time he left there in 1922. That year he became head librarian at the Toledo Public Library, the position he held when he was hired by Minneapolis. He arrived in Minneapolis on April 1, 1937, when the town was just coming out of winter hibernation, and discovered, as the weeks went by, a citizenry wild about parks and recreation. "I have never seen so much baseball played before in my life," he told an interviewer.

"And Minneapolitans play as though it were a matter of life and death." In a prescient view it would take the rest of the city decades to catch up with, Vitz criticized the commercialization of the Mississippi River banks, saying that if Minneapolis had done as well by its riverfront as it had by its lakes, there would be a bustling civic center by the great river downtown.[4]

Vitz was a construction expert. He had overseen the remodeling and expansion of the Toledo library system, and had served as a consultant for planning and construction at the Enoch Pratt Free Library in Baltimore. The Minneapolis library board hoped to make use of his expertise in planning for a new central library here. Vitz, almost immediately after his arrival in Minneapolis, joined the call for a new main library building to replace the "increasingly inconvenient, inadequate and obsolete" old one. "Is it too much to hope," Vitz asked, "that by 1939, the 50th year of existence, funds for a new building can be assured?"[5] In fact, it was too much to hope—far too much. Vitz would come and go, as would his successor, before that hope was fully realized. The new central building was a chimera that the library staff and board and city officials would chase for another two decades before it was finally caught, tamed, and put on display as one of the centerpieces of a new downtown.

Choosing a new librarian after Countryman's retirement was not an easy process. There was strong support on the library board to hire Glenn Lewis, who had worked for years in the system. Lewis had started part-time with the library in 1915, and had worked full-time for eleven years. He had the firm support of Farmer-Laborites on the library board and in the city, who felt the job should go to someone from Minneapolis and from within the library system. The politics of the choice became so involved that Gratia Countryman, in a private letter, said she was glad to be leaving the library if politics was going to play such a heavy role. Five conservative members of the board supported Vitz, while four Farmer-Laborites were for Lewis. When the Vitz faction prevailed and the Toledo librarian was offered the job, he hesitated, worrying about a divided board and its "uncertain future political complexion."[6] He also hesitated because Toledo had decided to match the six-thousand-dollar salary Minneapolis was offering. Finally, in late October 1936, Vitz accepted the job. To win him over, the library board had promised to pay his moving expenses and had allowed him to defer his arrival until the spring or summer of 1937 so he could help train a successor in Toledo and let his children complete the school year there. The library board issued a public statement saying the choice had caused some embarrassment, but that, in this crucial time for the library, experience had been chosen over promise. Glenn Lewis was made acting librarian until Vitz arrived, and Lewis's salary was increased to reflect his new, though temporary, status. Not everyone was satisfied.

Photograph from Bruce Sifford Studio, Inc.

Carl Vitz, Gratia Countryman's successor, the fourth director of the Minneapolis Public Library. The year Vitz started at the library, 1937, was also the year Dimitri Mitropoulos became the conductor of the Minneapolis Symphony Orchestra. The city was still experiencing disturbing echoes of the violent truckers' strike of 1934: in the fall of 1937 another Teamsters official, Patrick Corcoran, was shot and killed outside his Minneapolis home. And 1937 was the year Amelia Earhart was lost, the year of the Hindenburg disaster in New Jersey, and the year the Duke of Windsor married Wallis Warfield Simpson.

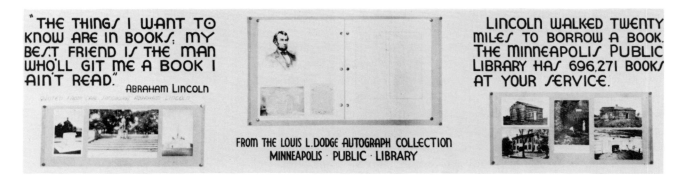

"THE THING/ I WANT TO KNOW ARE IN BOOK/; MY BE/T FRIEND I/ THE MAN WHO'LL GIT ME A BOOK I AIN'T READ." ABRAHAM LINCOLN

FROM THE LOUIS L. DODGE AUTOGRAPH COLLECTION
MINNEAPOLIS · PUBLIC · LIBRARY

LINCOLN WALKED TWENTY MILE/ TO BORROW A BOOK. THE MINNEAPOLI/ PUBLIC LIBRARY HA/ 696,271 BOOK/ AT YOUR /ERVICE.

A 1938 display highlighting an autograph collection in the Minneapolis Public Library. The display department placed material around the building and around the city, explaining what's available at the library. This tradition continues today, most noticeably in the display windows of the main library's lobby, where library material is often tied in with other events around town, from the opening of the baseball season to a celebration of Scandinavian heritage.

The Hennepin County Veterans Farmer-Labor Club passed a resolution condemning the library board for choosing an outsider instead of a Minneapolis citizen. But Glenn Lewis bided his time, graciously welcoming Vitz when he at last arrived to take over the library.

The new librarian said he approved of Gratia Countryman's policies of bringing books to the people, and stated he saw no reason to tear things apart just because there was a new man in town. So the library continued trying to serve people instead of just harboring books. One program that flowered under Vitz, although it started before he came, was a creative writing group. This was an offshoot of the reader's advisory service that Lewis had started in 1930, where people interested in a certain subject would be given guidance and a reading program. In the creative writing group, accomplished and aspiring writers worked on their writing and learned how to market their results under the direction of Mabel Oren of the library staff. Eight different classes met each week in 1938, with four hundred people participating. This was a time when far more magazine fiction was published than is the case today, and the group's record in 1938 was impressive: twenty-five short stories accepted for publication, twenty articles, eighty-five poems, three plays, three novels, one biography, one western, and two children's books. As usual, the social effects of the program were as interesting to the library as were the literary ones. Oren made notes on several of the library's aspiring writers, including "Miss Hazel Case—middle-aged spinster, also on relief and physically handicapped. Apparently had no special talent for writing except a willingness to work—and work hard. Had been despondent and ill; no prospects. Lived in one room in rather unpleasant surroundings. Selling her first short story only two months after she registered made her very happy and encouraged her as nothing else ever has. In less than a year she has sold 10 stories to children's magazines."[7]

The year 1939 brought the fiftieth anniversary of the central library. In 1889, the building had been a glorious step toward civilization; now it was a cramped old place that no one was very pleased with. But, as Gratia Countryman had said, "The library is the books in the hands of the readers,"[8] not the physical structure, and for this library there was much to be said. The newspapers lauded the library, calling it "education's second arm" and "a vital factor in whatever civilization that community can claim." *The Minneapolis Star* wrote, "Making books available to people who otherwise could not have them in their homes is, in itself, a civilizing influence of incalculable scope. Few of us can look back on the things that shaped our lives and find that some great book, or books, did not play a great part in our 'coming of age.' "[9] The *Minneapolis Journal* waxed sentimental and called the Minneapolis Public Library "Mother Library" (as in "Mother Church"). "If the walls could speak, after their long service," said the newspaper, "what tales they might tell of questing students and gentle readers and of worried, weary people being carried away on the printed page, as upon a magic carpet, into realms of romance, poetry and chivalry!"[10]

On the evening of December 16, 1939, there was a golden anniversary dinner at the Nicollet Hotel, sponsored by the Minneapolis Civic Council. Gratia Countryman was there, as librarian emeritus, speaking about that opening night fifty years ago for which she'd worked so hard to prepare. She recognized three others of Herbert Putnam's original staff who were there to celebrate the event: Jessie McMillan Marclay, Josephine Cloud, and Robert Kelsey. Countryman recalled that "the neighborhood then was one of elm-lined streets in a residence district; and the only sounds that disturbed the quiet were contributed by horsecars and carriages."[11] Also present at the dinner was Edward C. Gale, who had attended the library's opening with his father, Samuel C. Gale, one of the Athenaeum's founders. Edward C. Gale was now president of the library board, having succeeded T. B. Walker on his death in 1928.

The main speaker for the evening was author Christopher Morley, who could not resist addressing the gathering by starting, "Friends, Romans . . ."—and then giving a silent bow to the librarian emeritus. Morley, the vivacious humorist, then became serious as he paid tribute to the "great civic spirits" who founded and carried on the library's work, and who "saw the necessity for their fellowmen having a place which would satisfy the hunger for information, and the hunger for entertainment, and the hunger for intellectual stimulus and for intellectual shelter that a great library gives." Noting that the world was in parlous times, Morley used a metaphor to express his view of a library. "Coming up in the plane from Chicago this morning, I noticed in many places across that pale puppy-colored prairie, lonely farm-houses around every one of which was set a windbreak of evergreens, pines, or fir trees of some kind, planted usually on the northern and western sides, and I couldn't help thinking isn't that a good symbol of what a library is in a municipality? It is an evergreen plantation or a windbreak against the gales of economics, the gales of uncertainty, the distress and anx-

Photograph from the *Minneapolis Tribune,*
November 21, 1934

Author Christopher Morley, on
his way to Minneapolis to speak
at the fiftieth anniversary
celebration for the Minneapolis
Public Library, looked out his
airplane window at the farm
country below and saw a metaphor. A library, he said, is an
"intellectual windbreak" for a
city, providing shelter from the
tumult and a time for thought
and for hope for the future.

ieties and commotions of civilization, and behind that windbreak we
can to some extent shelter ourselves for thinking, and planning, and
believing, and hoping for the future. An intellectual windbreak is surely
as necessary to the mind and heart as the actual pine or evergreen plantation that the farmer puts out to shield his stock and his house and
his home from the northwest gales of winter.[12]

Morley and other speakers expressed the hope that the physical
quality of that windbreak could be improved soon by the construction
of a new library building. Guy Stanton Ford, president of the University of Minnesota and toastmaster for the evening, said, "The time is
long overdue for better accommodations for the library. Not primarily for the library's sake, but for yourself and your children."[13] Even
the newspaper called for a new library, *The Minneapolis Star* on
December 12 saying, "Maybe the celebration, among other beneficial
things, will put a little impetus behind the move, so far unsuccessful,
to get us a library building worthy of a modern city of half a million
population." The library's own fiftieth anniversary booklet pointed
out how almost every public concern in town had a new building—
except the Minneapolis Public Library. "This is now the oldest public
building in the city," the report wailed.[14]

The library had indeed outgrown itself, like a houseplant that from
a small, cramped pot spreads over the table and across the floor. There
were sixteen branches, libraries in eighty-two schools, and collections
in sixty-nine businesses and welfare centers and fifteen hospitals. The
total annual circulation was 3.75 million volumes, and the book collection numbered three-quarters-of-a-million. Phonograph records were
circulating, pictures were circulating, slides and projectors were being
loaned out, the Hennepin County libraries were administered from the
central library, and the whole operation had indeed become rootbound.
At the downtown library, more and more space that had once been
reserved for people reading books was being eaten up so that the library
system could continue to operate. Still, the call for more space would
echo for many more years before it would be answered.

In the Minneapolis Public Library's fifty-first year, a new service
started, one that would last for nearly another fifty years. It was
somehow symbolic of a society put on wheels, of a mobile life that would
spread people all over the map. The bookmobile arrived in Minneapolis
in 1938 and began service in 1939. In one sense it was part of the freeway
culture, chasing down the road after a population that was exploding
away from the central city faster than capital construction could keep
up. But in another sense it stood apart from hamburger drive-ins and
ice-cream trucks and convertibles along the lakeshore drives. For the
bookmobile offered, free, if not culture, than at least literate entertainment. For many in Minneapolis, including the author of this book,
it was one of the first places where little hands could paw over a treasure

trove of children's books. The delight was like breaking into the candy store when no one was around, even if you weren't always tall enough to reach the top shelves. The first bookmobile was twenty-six feet long, six-feet-six-inches high inside, and packed with twenty-five hundred books. You went through the narrow passageway like a frog through a snake, a little afraid of lingering too long, but awed by what you saw. The first bookmobile was painted green with gold letters outside, and it made most of its stops at grade schools around town. In the eleven months it operated during 1939, it circulated a very healthy total of fifty-two thousand books. That initial success ensured that more of the benevolent, bulgy, whalelike bookmobiles would follow this first one as it made its ponderous way through Minneapolis streets.

In 1939, the city council requested five-year programs from all city departments outlining major needs. Heading the library's request, to absolutely no one's surprise, was a new central building. The cost was estimated at between $1.5 and $2.5 million. But the library's report to the council added that new buildings were needed at the Camden and West Lake branches, and entirely new branches needed to be established in North, Northeast, Southeast, and South Minneapolis. South Minneapolis, in fact, was nominated for three new locations. This was whistling in the dark, but it sounded good, and was in tune with the old melodies. The library budget was shrinking again, after several years of relative prosperity, and book purchases were down.

To augment the buying power of the library's music department, a private group called the Minneapolis Record Society was organized in 1940, with members each chipping in two dollars to buy records that could be listened to on library equipment. After six months, non-members could use those same recordings in the library. The music department reported sympathetically that year on several German refugees who, when fleeing the Fatherland, had left their music behind. They came almost every night and listened with longing to German music on the library phonograph. And, as the war dragged on, and as Americans started dying in it, more Minneapolis librarians were sympathetic toward escape reading—light fiction that could transport one from the cares and woes of the day. In nonfiction, correspondent William Shirer's book *Berlin Diary* was at the top of the reserve list and remained popular for years as readers tried to figure out what rough beast had slouched out of Germany.

A battle was opening at home in 1940, between the library and the school board. What Gratia Countryman had sown, the library now reaped in a bitter struggle between the two cherished arms of education. Short of money and looking for ways to trim the budget, the library turned to the junior high school branches that Countryman had established some twenty years earlier to serve adults in the community as well as students. These branches had never been very successful

"It is the library in its representation of the immortality of the race and its task as curator of everything that is finest and most sensitive in ourselves—it is the library that preserves the wine of passion that was spilt in haste, and the rippling flow of youth that might go to waste if it had no place to pause and be fruitful. And that is the way of it, because no individual passion lasts long, and yet in the hands of the librarian the passion that lasted not does survive the voiceless tomb."

—Christopher Morley, at the December 16, 1939, dinner honoring the fiftieth anniversary of the library's opening

Windbreaks and Storms

Minneapolis Tribune photograph

Minneapolis Star and Tribune photograph

Books on wheels at the Minneapolis Public Library. The upper photograph shows the city's first bookmobile as the Minneapolis Public Library started the service in 1939. This bookmobile carried two thousand five hundred books and reached parts of the city not served by branches. The bookmobile got bigger in 1952, with the center photo showing the new truck that carried four thousand books. The lower photo shows the final, streamlined version, which provided bookmobile service until it was discontinued in 1982.

By the mid 1940s, overcrowding had become apparent inside the old
library building at Tenth and Hennepin. Storage room was so short that
fifty percent of the reading space inside the library had been given over
to stacks and cabinets holding the books and other materials. This
photograph shows the crowds at one end of the reference department.

in catching adults—a schoolyard full of little people was apparently
not the place big people wanted to go for books.

So the library board looked at its branches in nine junior highs—
Jordan, Lincoln, Bryant, Jefferson, Franklin, Nokomis, Sheridan,
Folwell, and Ramsey—and decided they were too costly. The library
board said the school board would have to pay more of the cost of the
libraries, or else those branches would have to be closed. But the board
of education said its situation was worse than that of the library board.
With city property valuation down, and taxes slipping, the library was
looking at a possible thirty-thousand-dollar deficit, while the school
board was facing a one-million-dollar deficit and the grim prospect of
closing elementary schools. It was not a good atmosphere for a fight,
and the fight became rough.

Each side disagreed on how much the schools were contributing

Minneapolis Public Library photograph

Junior high school libraries, like the one at Sheridan Junior High at Broadway and University avenues Northeast, became a battleground in 1940. Two institutions that should have been allies, the public library and the public school system, fought over who should support libraries in the junior highs. Both the library and school systems were short of money, each needed to cut expenses, and the controversy raged over what level of sharing resources was most fair. By 1941, with much bitter feeling left over, the public library got out of running the junior high libraries, turning over much of its collection on education and children's books to the schools. The Sheridan library, however, was reborn as a separate branch to serve the neighboring community. This photo was taken in 1954.

to the branch libraries in the junior highs. The library said the schools covered only ten percent of the cost; the board of education claimed the figure was greater than one-third. But the fight was really over philosophy and responsibility. Each side said the other was failing to live up to the original agreement that put the branches in the schools, and failing to live up to its commitment to the people of the city, who paid all the bills.

The school board caught the library on the point that if outreach made sense eighteen years ago, it still made sense now. A report prepared for the school board and referred to in public meetings and negotiations maintained that the library had opened the junior high branches not to help the schools, but to add readers to its empire. "The library has become a vast social enterprise," the report stated. "This desire on the part of the library to create a demand for books where it previously did not exist, just as a business concern might do to stimulate new business, has brought some acute financial problems to the public library." The report called the junior high branches "a specialized form of library service with distinct library purposes, just as the business branches are a specialized service with a specialized purpose."[15] The school board was saying to the library, you came in for your own purposes, not to magnanimously help us out, and even if your reach has exceeded your grasp, you can't now pull out and say it's all up to us.

The library fired back. In a report by Carl Vitz entitled "Junior High School Libraries: Whose Responsibility are They?" the library argued that school libraries were manifestly part of the educational curriculum, and thus the responsibility of the board of education. (This was not, of course, an argument that was heard in Gratia Countryman's time, when the library was expanding.) The school board already ran its own libraries in the three other junior high schools in the city, Vitz pointed out, which demonstrated that they accepted the responsibility.

For decades the question of who should run school libraries had been bouncing around Minneapolis. The partnership was a strange and often strained one, although Gratia Countryman thought of it as a joint venture in education that would avoid costly duplication. At various times it had been suggested that the library and school systems merge to coordinate educational efforts. This the library resisted, not wanting to lose its autonomy and identity. Other times it was suggested the library take over *all* school library duties in the interest of coordination and consistency. This the school board resisted, not wanting to lose all control. Vitz now said, again, that the library would be happy to take over all school libraries if the city would appropriate the money to cover the costs. He knew it couldn't happen.

Vitz charged that the board of education had not lived up to its end of a 1926 agreement with the library, an agreement that said space would be provided for library branches in all new junior highs on a corner of the ground floor, with separate entrances so that the libraries could be open to the community after school hours. Because of this breach of contract, Vitz argued, and because the library had many other responsibilities—such as adult education, Americanization, recreational reading, and now providing war information to an anxious public—

the library would have to give up the junior high libraries if the schools couldn't pay for them.[16]

The library won, if any side can be said to have won in this affair. The junior high school libraries were discontinued in June 1941, although many of the books for children and on the process of education were left behind for the schools. Vitz emphasized that the Minneapolis Public Library would continue to serve young readers through its community branches. But the image of the library had been tarnished in the struggle, as many people in town thought the library had run out on one of its purposes.

The public library still maintained libraries and classroom collections in grade schools across the city, so the issue wasn't fully settled. The fight over school libraries would reopen before the end of the next decade, this time with more vitriol and trauma. The public had been aroused on this issue in 1941, as a letter to Carl Vitz from the Sheridan School Parent-Teacher Association shows: "We really are a group indignant at the thought of losing something which rightfully should be ours."[17] The public would be heard from again in 1959.

Meanwhile, the war in Europe and the Pacific raged on. Readers were now being lost to the fighting. The Hosmer branch reported a drop in circulation as many of its patrons went into the service. "Dear boys of '41," the Hosmer librarian wrote. "How eagerly would they have been saluted by young Corporal James Hosmer who in '62 left his church in Deerfield to join the Massachusetts Volunteers. So, each generation meets its High Adventure."[18] There were also staff shortages due to the war, as men went into the armed forces and several men and women went off to run libraries at training camps or abroad. In 1942, both the bookmobile and county book truck schedules were curtailed due to gas and tire rationing, with stops being made less frequently and some distant locations being cut out altogether. Much of the book budget was diverted to purchases of defense training manuals and books on the technical and manufacturing skills needed to turn America into the arsenal of democracy. Information about the war itself was prominently displayed in the library, as were openings through the U.S. Employment Service for wartime production jobs. As one library bulletin said in 1942, the libraries must keep people aware of the cause, because "this war is not only a physical and mechanized one but it is also a war of ideas. It is not only a war of ideas but a war of words."[19]

Victory garden material became popular by 1943, especially through the Hennepin County system. Sumner library had its own victory garden, but through most of the summer, neighbors "who could not resist the lure of free food" stripped the tomato vines.[20] Books on do-it-yourself repairs of home appliances, bikes, and cars were popular as citizens found that their normal repair people were off providing a different kind of service.

Minneapolis Public Library photograph

The public library has always been a second home for a lot of children. Story hours, magicians, puppet shows, and summer reading programs have filled many hours for these small, sometimes slightly squirmy patrons. In this 1949 photograph, Mary Jane Dornack holds a story hour for children at Roosevelt branch in South Minneapolis.

Social diplacements due to the war were reflected in the library. "Of vast importance in wartime is the library work with children," wrote the librarian at the Roosevelt branch. "With the mother a defense worker out of the home, more and more children look to the library as a place of warmth and amusement."[21] The whole system was aware of the need to keep kids busy and keep their spirits up. Because circulation had dropped and most adults were busy with wartime occupations, the librarians had more time to give to the children who piled into the library after school, waiting for their mothers to come home. Juvenile delinquency was an increasing concern in Minneapolis, and the library pulled together information to try to help social workers deal with the problems. In 1942, sixteen elementary schools were closed and the students shifted to other schools, adding to feelings of fear and uncertainty already instigated by war and absent parents. The Social Service branch was busy dealing with the problems of working mothers and with finding information on setting up day nurseries for their children. The Business and Municipal branch reported requests about production control from the Twin Cities ordnance plant and questions about war bonds, rationing, and rent control.

The technological aspect of World War II would also transform postwar America, as Elizabeth Thorson of the library's technical department recognized when she quoted a publisher on the library's role in teaching technology: "For we have learned new techniques to open at least the fundamentals of technology, of science, to the vast generality of working men and women. And this is a lesson that, I assure you, we shall continue to study, for if man is to be at home in this brave new world that science plays so large a role in, then science must no longer remain so mysterious to him."[22]

At the Sumner library, the public schools' adult education department gave English classes so immigrant parents could write to their children abroad. One delighted parent brought in a letter from her soldier-son to show the librarian. "Dear Mom, I received your letter and believe me, Mom, I sure got the biggest thrill in my life when I read your letter. It was written very plain. I could read it plain as day. The first letter written by my Mom, I'm going to keep it forever. Thanks a million. I can't tell you what it means to me."[23]

By 1945 there was a "difficult and disturbing" aspect to the creative writing classes run by the library. Many parents of men killed in the war came to the library to get help in having their sons' letters collected and published in books. The parents believed such collections would give comfort to others. "It takes all one's reserve of control and understanding to meet the emotional crises that come up in these conferences," wrote librarian Mabel Oren. "To the parents, the letters are beautiful and inspirational. It would take a tough-minded person to tell them otherwise." Oren said that most of the burden of saying no was thrown onto the publishers, but "when a man in a wheel chair himself tells you that his only son went down on the Enterprise and he wants to write a record of the boy's life, it is only human to want to help."[24]

Some on the library staff were looking ahead to when the war would end, and they saw that returning soldiers would place a heavy demand on the library. The veterans would want to learn how to start over, they would want to escape awhile from some of their memories, and they would find the library useful in their readjustment. The library, several staff members said, should start preparing now to be ready when the deluge hit. That was a good idea, but resources were already tight, hours were reduced throughout 1944 and 1945, and the library was having trouble meeting current needs, to say nothing of planning ahead.

And the soldiers did start coming home—those who had made it. The circulation drop slowed in 1944, and by the end of the following year there was a slight turn upward. Material on starting businesses wouldn't sit still. Books on salesmanship, advertising, insurance, and real estate were called for constantly. Some men had sent for books on electrical repair or shoe repair even before they were discharged, so they could study and be ready to begin a new enterprise as soon as they returned. And it wasn't just the servicemen. People who had worked in defense plants that were now closed, or whose businesses had failed because they were nonessential during the war, were looking for ways to start over. People showed a great deal of interest in new businesses ripe for development, such as air conditioning, refrigeration, cold-storage locker plants, and home freezers. There were also many requests for information about small farms and living in the country, building log houses, and homesteading in Alaska. Life began to return to normal, with an extra jolt of energy left over from the war.

Many GIs headed back to school, which caused "a decided change in the type of books called for. The old standard books and classics have again come into their own and the reference work is more specialized and technical," Glenn Lewis wrote. Textbooks in the library collection had to be limited to a checkout period of seven days, because, when the University of Minnesota opened, "students descended like grasshoppers on a Dakota wheat field, stripping the shelves bare before the astounded staff could gather themselves together and make provision for some sort of fair practices act."[25]

But not all the ex-soldiers were so scholarly. The collection of westerns, which the librarians regarded rather like dead fish on their shelves, had moved very slowly during the war, with the readers gone to real shoot-outs. Now, after the war, the westerns began to disappear from the library, and the staff was probably happy to have them out of sight, even if they shuddered at the thought of someone actually reading them. The returned soldiers showed less interest in books about the war itself than did teenagers—no doubt the soldiers had seen enough while they were in it.

The library got a boost on June 11, 1945, when a public referendum to raise the maximum library levy from two mills to three was approved by sixty-five percent of the voters. Three months earlier, the library board had asked the city charter commission to put the question on the ballot. All spring library staffers had pushed the referendum, making phone calls, distributing leaflets, and talking to patrons over the checkout counter.

Then, at the end of the year, Carl Vitz resigned to become head librarian in Cincinnati. In 1941, he had been wooed by his old employer, the Cleveland Public Library, to become head librarian there, but he had turned down that offer because he wouldn't have had enough freedom to do his own hiring—and because he liked Minneapolis. But the Minneapolis Public Library's mandatory retirement rule finally chased him out, as it had Gratia Countryman. Vitz was sixty-two years old in 1945, only three years away from forced retirement; in Cincinnati, he could work until he was seventy-two.

Vitz had done well in Minneapolis, and was respected for his work. He was elected president of the American Library Association in 1944, a year that needed some brightening for Vitz and his wife, as they had just lost their son, Richard, in the fighting in France. No major changes came during his administration of the Minneapolis library, but he presided ably over a bustling system during troubled years. A new central building remained just talk as Vitz left, his construction knowledge unused here. But he did oversee the building of a new library in Cincinnati, which opened in 1955, the year of his retirement. In 1961, Vitz returned to Minneapolis to look over the new library that had finally materialized. He liked what he saw, especially the public's ready access to the books. "It's not much fun to go to a library if you can't handle the books," he commented.[26] Carl Vitz died January 8, 1981, in Fort Thomas, Kentucky; he was ninety-seven years old.

The reliable Glenn Lewis was appointed acting head librarian on December 18, 1945, to serve until a successor to Vitz was chosen. Lewis was a candidate for that job, of course, having come so close the last time. The board interviewed Lewis and a librarian from New Bedford, Massachusetts, and on February 25, 1946, unanimously chose Lewis. Lewis had the support of most of the staff, whose fondness for him was demonstrated by Charlotte Matson, head of circulation. When she heard the board's decision, she grabbed an old air-raid bell left over from the war and clanged it exuberantly to announce the choice.

Lewis was a gentleman—quiet, modest, courteous, and easy to talk with. He felt an affinity for the people who used the library, most of whom were working class folks. Believing many of them were a little lost among the library's offerings, he had started a reader's advisory service in 1930. It provided structured reading programs that guided readers through a variety of subjects, from the practical to the ethereal. His concern for the people he worked with, as well as for the library's patrons, gained him the support of labor. Born in Minneapolis on November 12, 1892, Lewis was a graduate of Central High. He earned a B.A. from the University of Minnesota in 1920 and an M.A. from Harvard in 1923. He taught English at the University of Minnesota, the University of Wisconsin, and at Lake Forest College in Illinois before becoming a full-time librarian in 1925 in Minneapolis. A veteran of

World War I, he was fifty-three years old at the time he became head librarian. He was married, had three sons, and his wife, Leah, was a professor of interior decorating at the university.

Lewis was a good choice for the six-thousand-dollar-a-year job. He had grown up with the Minneapolis Public Library, been with it during the booming years of expansion and the tougher years of tight money and controversy. As head of the central library since 1940, he

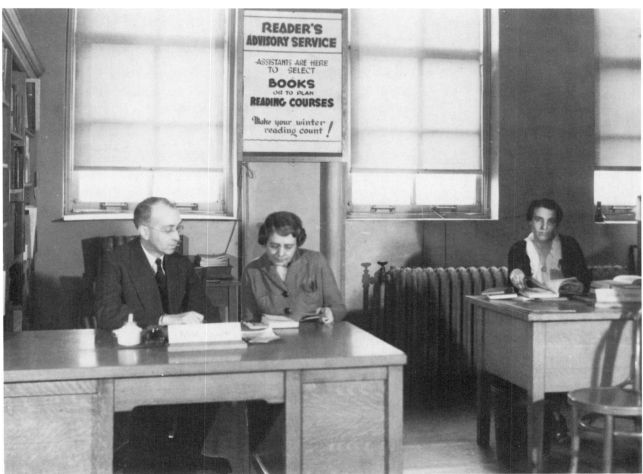

Waiting for patrons to uplift, Glenn Lewis sits at the reader's advisory service desk with librarian Lucretia Clapp in the 1940s. (To their left is librarian Katherine Yerxa.) Lewis, who became director of the library in 1946, started this advisory service in 1930 to help people he thought might be overwhelmed by what the library had to offer. Librarians hoped then, as they continue to hope, that people would use their library for the serious pursuit of knowledge rather than just for entertainment. Lewis's idea of a directed reading program was an early effort at what we would now call continuing or adult education.

Windbreaks and Storms

A *Daily Times* photograph, May 11, 1945

Librarian Glenn Lewis, right, works with Daniel Defenbacher, director of the Walker Art Center, to prepare one thousand art books for transfer from the art museum to the public library in 1945. The books were originally collected by T. B. Walker, founder of the Walker Art Center and first president of the Minneapolis library board. Gifts like this one are priceless and crucial to the library's service to Minneapolis over one hundred years.

knew the administration and operation of the library from the inside. Trained under Countryman, he shared her ideals and her view of the library's role, and hoped to keep it as vibrant a system as she had. He stated, in a refrain that was beginning to sound familiar, that his first priority was a new central library building.

The system didn't grow much under either Vitz or Lewis. Community branches reopened in two junior highs—Sheridan in 1941 and Jordan in 1947. Operated with the cooperation of the board of education, these branches kept their full hours and served communities that had high library activity but no regular branch.

In 1942, the Business and Municipal branch moved to rented quarters at 217 Sixth Street South. Ten years later, the building was purchased by board member Archie Walker, T. B. Walker's son, and given to the library. In 1954, the Camden branch was expanded after the library acquired the entire field house from the park board. The first floor was remodeled, the outside was painted, and the branch, renamed the Webber Park branch for the family that had donated the building in 1910, was formally opened on March 26. The population of this northern edge of the city, and of the suburbs beyond, had been growing, putting a great deal of pressure on the small space and collection of the original Camden library.

In 1946, the West Lake branch closed. It had started as a deposit station in 1899, and was made a branch in 1926. But its location at Lake and Pillsbury was near the Walker branch, and when West Lake lost its lease in 1946, it was simply phased out. In 1957, the Logan Park branch was moved to rented storefront quarters at 1224 Second Street Northeast, and was renamed for Pierre Bottineau, one of the guides to General Henry Sibley, the trader and Indian fighter who became Minnesota's first state governor. This kind of shuffling was the only capital activity under both Vitz and Lewis, who devoted most of their expansion efforts to trying for that new central building.

During the war, in 1941, a new system for selecting fiction had been set up. It involved a five-person committee made up of the chief and the first assistant of the circulation department, the head of the branches department, and two head librarians chosen from the community branches on a rotating basis. The head of the central library also served on the committee as an advisor. These people read the new fiction releases, or read reviews of them, and then came together to discuss what they were like and which ones the library should buy. The idea was to get a variety of views, so that not just one person's taste prevailed, and to try to achieve some coordination in buying. In 1945 this committee considered 663 books, purchasing 507 of them and rejecting 156. The number of books rejected varied from about fifteen to thirty percent through the years, with some books banished for being too lewd and others for just being lousy. Lewis again laid out the

Minneapolis Public Library photograph, 1949

Archie Walker, who succeeded his father, T.B., on the library board in 1928 and served as board president from 1944 to 1955. It was Archie who chose Paul Bunyan as the symbol for the Walkers' Red River Lumber Company. Recalling tales of the mythical hero he'd heard while working in the lumber camps, he had his cousin, W.B. Laughead, draw Bunyan and collect the stories, which the lumber company published in a series of booklets. By 1944, when the company was liquidated, a half million booklets had been given to customers and friends, giving Bunyan his earliest and widest public exposure.

Drawing by W.B. Laughead, courtesy of Louise Walker McCannel

148

justification that if a book appealed to the seamy side of life only to sensationalize and to sell books, it could be rejected. But he cautioned that books that might be objectionable to some could be instructive to others. He sounded like he was groping for the "redeeming social value" concept that the United States Supreme Court would try out later.

Margaret Mull, circulation department head in 1956, complained that there was too much sex in books, quoting a critic as saying, "The time has come for a change. The logical beginning would be to admit that man has a mind as well as entrails." She continued, "An outstanding example of such literature is the very much publicized *Peyton Place,* by Grace Metalious, which we did not buy and consequently have been severely criticized by several irate patrons who feel that we are trying

The Pierre Bottineau library, a storefront library at 1224 Second Street Northeast. This library bounced from Sheridan Junior High to the Logan Park field house, finally settling in 1957 in this rented building, where it remains today. This photo was taken in 1958.

to censor their reading. We certainly do not want to practice censorship in any way, but do feel that we must be selective not only from a literary but a monetary standpoint."[27] Several staff members were concerned about the effects of heavy advertising of books during and after the war. A strong ad campaign, a movie made from a book, or a review or mention of a book by columnist Walter Winchell would assure that dozens of people would ask for that book at the library, regardless of the book's quality. Some books that library staff thought were questionable were purchased but not placed on the open shelves, where young people might run across them at random. Some authors who today seem pretty tame were given this cold shoulder: Graham Greene's *The End of The Affair* and Feike Feikema's (Frederick Manfred's) *The Giant* were 1951 examples of books considered "sordid and depressing and of the type which would have to be handled with care." The circulation chief lamented, "There seems to be a cycle of realism in present-day writing which places an institution using public funds in a rather untenable position. The fiction selection committee is always faced with the problem of whether to purchase everything that is published, or to buy with caution and be accused of censorship."[28] Lewis advocated a middle-of-the-road position on the question of what to purchase and what to reject.

Something else was affecting reading habits after World War II. That was the new member of the family, the one that came in a box—the television. What would become English teachers' favorite excuse for their students' poor reading skills started taking a bad rap almost before it was warmed up. The central library's children's department reported that 1950 was a tough year for kids, with war jitters and television, which, "in its present state of development, hardly aids a child's mental balance or his emotional stability." Even though television was being blamed for a decrease in use of the Minneapolis Record Society collection in the music department, the children's room librarian reported with some jollity that, "despite dire threats to the contrary, the Children's room survived 1950 without losing its entire clientele to the monster Television."[29]

Although it would become obvious as the decade progressed that children were spending more and more time in front of a TV set, in 1951 the television and the library were peacefully coexisting. Circulation in the downtown children's room was up, as were reference requests. Story hour attendance at the Longfellow branch was way down on Saturday mornings, however, as children dug in at home to establish a tradition that continues today. But the head of the branch department, Alice Brunat, said that the group that was really losing reading time to television was adults. The library's hospital service, especially, where TVs were going into patients' rooms, was losing readers.

The library soon learned that television could be used, not just

Windbreaks and Storms

Photograph by Edward G. Edmundson, Minneapolis, October 1949

Television enters the library, perhaps as a Trojan Horse in the view of some librarians. Here football fans watch a 1949 game in the young people's room at the downtown library. While many authorities worried that TV would take over the lives of children, at the library it was the hospital service that felt the impact of the tube most, with adult patients putting aside their library books to watch TV in their rooms.

suffered. In 1952, a young critics club from the library did book reviews on Bee Baxter's KSTP variety show. They discussed, among many other topics, books on "the Negro" by Carl Rowan and Hodding Carter. By 1956 the library had a regular spot on Arle Haeberle's "Around the Town" show on WCCO. Betty Engebretson from the Athenaeum would explain the history behind some of the library's rare books, and public relations head Sarah Wallace would show other aspects of what was going on at the library.

The library staff even had to admit that television could stimulate reading in some youngsters. When Walt Disney put on shows based on biographies of Davy Crockett and Jules Verne's *20,000 Leagues Under the Sea,* calls for those books flooded the library. The same happened after TV productions of *A Night to Remember,* the story of the sinking of the Titanic, and of *War and Peace.* A 1955 special of *The Wind in the Willows* pried that book off the shelf where it had been languishing peacefully for years.

Adult reading trends flickered around several subjects during the 1950s, but strong and consistent interest was shown in books on religion and self-help, led by *A Man Called Peter,* the story of Peter Marshall, and *The Power of Positive Thinking* by Norman Vincent Peale. The quality of education was a topic much discussed and read about as baby-boom children flooded the schools. The subjects of desegregation, following the 1954 *Brown* v. *The Board of Education* Supreme Court ruling, and communism, following Joe McCarthy's tirades, were much read and talked about. As part of the library's outreach efforts in adult education, a "Great Books" program, designed by the University of Chicago, was started in 1947 and continued through the 1950s. Library staff organized the discussion groups, recruited leaders, and provided meeting space in the branches.

Despite services like the "Great Books" program and widespread support for the library, the public wasn't willing to hand over money endlessly to this institution. Another amendment on the city ballot in 1948 would have raised the library's mill levy limit from three mills to four. But it was defeated, "a smashing blow," as one branch librarian said. (This was also the year the government documents department at the library got a call from the mayor of Minneapolis, a brash man named Hubert Humphrey, asking about Republican Senator Joseph H. Ball's voting record and stands on the issues. A library staffer pored over copies of the *Congressional Quarterly* for several days to gather the information. Humphrey was pleased with the work, made good use of it, and launched his national career by sweeping Ball out of Washington.)

For some time, the library staff had thought the public didn't know enough about the good work the library was doing. Both Gratia Countryman and Carl Vitz had called several times for a group of "library friends" to be formed to help with library chores and to get the word out to the public about the library. Such a group, which many other libraries in the country already had, was especially needed when the library was campaigning for more money. In 1948, a Public Library Friends group was organized in Minneapolis by Evelyn Palmer. It grew out of an informal group that had worked for the 1945 mill-increase campaign, and its first two tasks were supporting the 1948 campaign and planning a sixtieth anniversary celebration for the library in 1949. The 1948 campaign was not successful, but the next year the Friends did help the library secure more money from the city.

Glenn Lewis, director of the Minneapolis Public Library from 1946 to 1957. Lewis was a man who cared for the average patron of the library, and wanted to help guide the public to make good use of the library. He also cared for his employees, and had a kind, common touch in dealing with people.

The group's first organizational meeting was in January 1949, at which Evelyn Palmer was elected president. A membership campaign was started for this "group organized to promote a better understanding of the Minneapolis Public Library, its resources, and its possibilities with adequate financial support."[30] The friends hosted a sixtieth anniversary open house at the library December 18, 1949, and about five thousand people attended. Off to a good start, the group continued with author luncheons and teas, fund-raising projects, book fairs, and the continuing struggle to get the library more money and a new building. The Friends, with occasional lapses in interest and involvement, remained close to the library and still provide valuable volunteer services, trying to bring the library, books, and authors into closer contact with the people of Minneapolis. In recent years they have brought in such writers as Alex Haley, Alistair Cooke, Frederick Manfred, Harrison Salisbury, Eric Sevareid, and Garrison Keillor for programs and annual meetings. They conduct tours of the library and raise money by selling used books culled from the library's collection and new books of a regional interest.

Glenn Lewis's twelve-year administration reflected what had become the traditional rollercoaster ride of the library's fortunes. Money was scarce and then adequate (somehow librarians never seem to say it is plentiful), the book budget expanded and contracted, hours were shortened and lengthened, including Saturday closings in the mid-1950s. The change from the old Minneapolis Public Library classification system designed by Herbert Putnam to the Dewey decimal system, which had been going on slowly for decades, was completed under Lewis. And always, always, there were hopes and dreams and work toward what would surely someday be a new central library building. Although Lewis helped to make that library a reality, he left his position before he saw it completed. He retired on his sixty-fifth birthday, November 12, 1957, a respected figure in the city. He would live until January 2, 1973, when he died at the age of eighty, in Hopkins.

In some ways Lewis was like an elderly minister who calms and soothes his congregation. He made his parishioners toe the line, to be sure, and do good works, but he kept the skies sunny and blue. The new minister who replaced Lewis was a young firebrand who would stir and awaken and challenge and aggravate and bring on the thunderstorms.

Raymond E. Williams seemed to be a man in a hurry. He was forty-one when he came to the Minneapolis Public Library, only four years older than Gratia Countryman had been when she began revolutionizing the place. Williams became head librarian when plans were beginning to be made for the move into a new building downtown. Some might have thought that the move would have been enough of an upset to a library system. But Ray Williams was going to change a great many more things to fit the library into the new age as well as into the new building. And he didn't dawdle around. He simply did it, now. His precipitate manner aggravated many people, and although he got the new library launched nicely, he found himself on his way back out of town shortly afterwards.

Williams was a native of Summit, New Jersey, although he attended grade school in Groveland, Minnesota, near Lake Minnetonka. His parents were graduates of the University of Minnesota, and his great-great-grandfather, a man with the delightful name of Tilestone Snow, had been a settler in Minneapolis in 1856. Williams got his bachelor's degree from Lehigh University in Bethlehem, Pennsylvania, and his master's from Syracuse University in New York. His library work in the New York cities of Syracuse, Elmira, and Rochester, and in Hartford, Connecticut, was interrupted by a stint as a submarine torpedo officer in World War II. When he applied for the Minneapolis post he was assistant director of the Enoch Pratt Free Library in Baltimore, one of the oldest public libraries in the country. One of his responsibilities there was overseeing a $6.5 million building program.

Two library board members went to Omaha to interview a librarian there after meeting with Williams. But Ray Williams emerged as the clear choice, and his appointment was announced on April 23, 1957. "The years immediately ahead will be challenging and exciting ones in the Minneapolis system," Williams told the *Minneapolis Tribune* two days later. He spoke the truth.

At the time Williams was hired, the new library was so close board members could almost taste it. Construction hadn't begun yet, but land acquisition and site clearing would start shortly. Floor plans were sent to Williams in Baltimore, and after studying them he came to Minneapolis to meet with the board. He immediately, although tactfully, began changing the plans to fit his vision of the new library. In Williams's mind, the library wouldn't only have a new outside shell, it would have a new organization as well.

Within a month of his arrival to take over as chief librarian (a title he changed to, simply, librarian), he presented his plan for reshuffling the library. Instead of the library being organized by administrative function, as with circulation, catalog, and reference departments, Williams organized the place by subject matter. He set up departments of history, literature, sociology, and, eventually, natural science. Existing departments, such as reference and the reader's advisory service, were absorbed into each new subject department. If a reader had a reference question about the First Minnesota Regiment at Gettysburg, for example, the question now went to the history, rather than the reference, department. A person who wanted to read more about the American Civil War would be referred to the history department, rather than the old, centralized reader's advisory service. A new department

Minneapolis Public Library photograph

Raymond E. Williams, the city's sixth librarian. Williams designed a new system for operating the main library, worked out its bugs in the old library at Tenth and Hennepin, then took his new, streamlined system into the new building in 1961.

Windbreaks and Storms

called the reference core dealt with simple reference questions—about the city and the library itself, for example—and also included an information desk, the card catalog, interlibrary loans, visual aids, and government documents. Ordering, cataloging, and binding operations were all merged into a new department called processing. The parent-teacher room, which had opened in 1926 to house information about the process of education, new developments in teaching, the education of teachers, and choosing colleges, was discontinued and its material

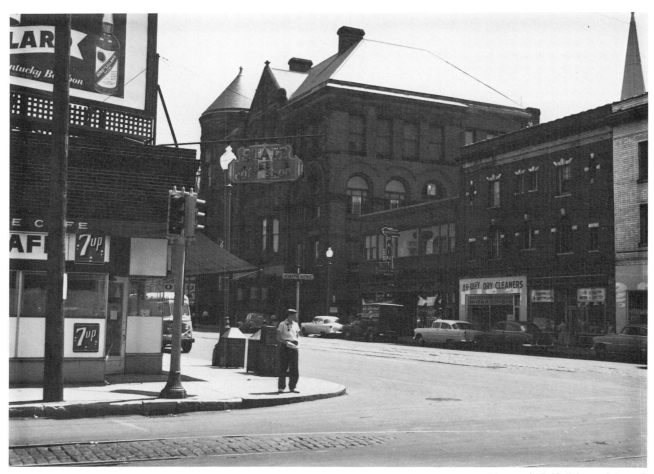

The old central library in 1955, seen from the corner of Eleventh Street and Hennepin Avenue. By this time the library was bursting at the seams, its neighborhood was declining, and the new library six blocks north was being planned.

absorbed into the sociology department. The Business and Municipal branch—the second-oldest special business collection in the country—was soon closed and its materials also brought into the central library under business and economics. All books and other material were now checked out at one central charging desk at the main library, instead of going through one of the nine charging stations spread out throughout the present building.

These changes stirred things up like a huge paddle swirled in a quiet pond. To Williams, the new system seemed more efficient, streamlined, and logical. It would keep administrative functions from overwhelming the library's main purpose: getting people face-to-face with books. To the staff, the new regime meant change, turmoil, and extra work. How could an already-busy desk librarian handle reference questions as well as requests for books and magazines? And who, in the middle of all this, would have the time to sit down thoughtfully with a patron as an advisor and map out a plan for studying the people, history, and language of France? There were sparks. Anticipating all this, Williams wanted to get the new system in place in the old library and take the whole business for a shakedown cruise before moving into the sparkling new quarters.

But reorganizing wasn't the only thing Williams had in mind. He was also going to lighten ship. He looked out over the extension system Gratia Countryman had put in place, and saw three areas that were duplicative, inefficient, or inconsistent: school branches, hospital service, and business house libraries. The business house libraries he did away with altogether in the winter of 1958. Many business firms, as they grew, were maintaining their own libraries, Williams said. Besides, he said, it wasn't fair or consistent to have public-supported collections in some companies and not in others, so he killed them all. The move would save money, and the central library would still handle business books and reference requests. The hospital service he cut in half, to save money and to get the service better in line with shortening hospital stays. The same number of hospitals would be visited, but only once rather than twice a week.

And then there were the schools, that murky area of uncertain responsibilities and volatile public opinion. The question of who should provide library service to the city's school children hadn't really been resolved since the fight over the junior high libraries. Several grade schools were gathering their own library collections, but there was no system-wide consistency. Williams didn't think the library belonged in the schools at all, and the library board basically agreed with him. On January 8, 1958, the library board voted to abolish classroom libraries in the grade schools. These were small collections, often a shelf or two, placed in more than two hundred individual classrooms around the city. The central libraries in the grade schools, twenty of them, would

Minneapolis Public Library photograph, 1954

The Business and Municipal Branch served the downtown business community for forty-four years. It opened in 1916 at 508 Second Avenue South and was moved to this building at 217 South Sixth Street in 1942. Ten years later the building was purchased by library board president Archie Walker and given to the library. At the end of 1960 it was closed, its collection moving to the central library under Ray Williams's new departmental plan.

remain for the time being, but the small collections in the classrooms would go.

The real trouble came when the central libraries in the grade schools were about to be pared off. The board of education operated libraries in thirty-eight grade schools in the city, while the Minneapolis Public Library ran libraries in twenty grade schools. The schools themselves had been slowly improving their library service, and Williams wanted to get out and leave all the school libraries to the schools. Money was again an issue. School teachers and school librarians had just had their salaries raised for 1959, widening the disparity between what an employee earned from the public schools and what that same person would earn from the public library. Some children's librarians were deserting the public library and going over to the schools for better hours, vacations, and money. Williams and the library board wanted to raise their librarians' salaries, but to do so some overhead had to be cut. The board voted on December 11, 1958, to close all grade school libraries by June 1959, with eight of those libraries going in January 1959.

Williams had encountered some choppy waters over his internal reorganization of the library and over complaints that he didn't communicate very well with his staff, but now he had sailed into a maelstrom. His announcement that eight school libraries would be closed by January 5 "brought forth a storm of controversy," according to a library report. "Denouncements from parents and school personnel descended like an avalanche. . . . Never in its history had the library been under more scathing criticism."[31] The board of education was very critical of Williams and of the closings, which the board members called "arbitrary." Board member Anders Thompson felt the announcement of the closing was a "disgraceful action," and said the library board and the librarian should be censured.[32]

Citizens wrote to the newspapers saying school libraries shouldn't be closed because the early grades are the times children learn to read and learn the value of books. One woman wrote, "To save money by destroying the usefulness and availability of books seems exactly contrary to the whole conception of a public library." The writer, Helen Grouse, said the library hours during the school day, the times when whole classes paddled down to the library room, were essential to the children's education. If the library branches were taken out of the school, the kids would never go to the libraries, she felt. "In appraising the library's financial problems, the board should not lose sight of the very purpose of a library. As a mother, if I were to choose between a new library building and a school library program, I would choose the latter. To me, the success of a public library lies not in the beauty and extent of the steel and stone structure that houses it, but rather in the number of books open and in the hands of people who profit by their use."[33]

The inadequate facilities of the old downtown library are evident in this photograph from the 1950s. Since there was no loading dock, bookmobiles were loaded at the Tenth Street curb, where staff members had to lug books amid pedestrian and motor traffic.

Letters like this had to hit soft spots in their target, for the writer here was quoting the gospel according to Countryman right back to the library board. And she was hitting another enormously sensitive area—the ground for the new library had been broken only a month earlier, and the cornerstone wouldn't be laid for another eight months. To challenge that new library building when it finally seemed about to materialize was heresy, and a most frightening heresy. Perhaps the thing could still be chased away and lost at this last minute if the library wasn't careful.

With some help from Dorothy Rood, the library board's president, Williams realized that his plan for the closings had been a little hasty. The library board thought it had warned the schools, at the time of closing the classroom libraries a year earlier, that the closing of the twenty central school libraries was also being contemplated. But the action had still come as a shock. President Rood felt the library should never have been in the schools in the first place, and the board agreed, saying in a letter to *The Minneapolis Star* on January 15, 1959, that "speaking realistically, from the beginning [the school libraries] should have been the responsibility of the school board." But now that the storm was upon them, a compromise would have to be made. Williams borrowed librarians from other parts of his system to cover the eight school branches one day a week. Library aides would cover the other four days, and, in this way, with reduced service, all the school libraries could be kept open for the remainder of the school year.

The Minneapolis Star was pleased with the compromise, agreed to through a series of joint meetings of the school board and library board. In an editorial on January 24, 1959, the paper said that, although the wrong choice had been made in closing some school libraries rather than reducing service but keeping them all open, Williams was still to be commended for admitting that a mistake had been made and that the proposed withdrawal had been too abrupt. The editorial said that school libraries should be a school board responsibility, and added that the school board hadn't met the responsibility very well in the past, a fact which had contributed to this crisis. But, the editorial continued, "the city librarian has shown his willingness to cooperate in trying to solve a difficult problem, and he has conceded with gracious candor the error of the earlier termination order. When public officials carry these attitudes into a job, even the thorniest issues have a way of getting smoothed out."

In a further compromise reached in March after another joint board meeting, the library agreed to keep seven school libraries open one day a week through the summer, and then to loan two part-time librarians to the school board to help train the school's librarians and staffs to run the libraries themselves. By September 1959, the Minneapolis Public Library was out of the schools entirely, with all twenty of its grade school branches turned over to the school board. Nearly seventy-nine thousand books from these branches were given by the public library to the school board, at an estimated value of three hundred and sixty-five thousand dollars.

The year-end report of the library's extension department tried to put a good face on the whole turmoil, saying that if the school libraries hadn't been so good, people wouldn't have been so agitated over losing them. "Although the protestations gave evidence of widespread misunderstanding of the library's true role in the educational and cultural life of the city, the raised voices gave high tribute to the excellence of the library's former school department services throughout the years."

Not everyone was placated. There were still neighborhood protests in the spring, and at least one school was picketed by parents carrying signs showing they didn't want to lose their school branch library. The controversy also sparked a lively debate during the autumn's election campaign for library board posts, with eight candidates running for three openings. In addition, a group called the Citizens Committee for School and Neighborhood Libraries successfully campaigned against a proposed one-mill levy increase for the library in the fall election. As the library planned for its move into a new central facility it seemed to some neighborhood residents that they were being abandoned by a library system that had once seemed to want to reach into every cupboard and corner of their homes. The library hadn't abandoned its outreach philosophy, but it was certainly trimming it. And like all changes, this one hadn't come easily or painlessly.

The public's confusion and resentment toward the library could be felt over the checkout counter during the controversy. Ingrid Pedersen, who worked in the library system from the Depression into the 1970s, said that when the school branches closed, "it was one of the few times that we felt the public was annoyed with us."[34]

Taking library service out of the schools was a reversal of the expansion that had started early in the century. It was an indication that fiscal realities would limit the vision seen by social missionaries like Gratia Countryman. Those limits would tighten further as the library approached its centennial year. But the late 1950s was not just a time of cutting back, for another vision, one that had danced tantalizingly before the eyes of city librarians for decades, was soon to be realized.

Photograph by the Citizens League

Library board president Dorothy Rood breaks ground for the new
library at Fourth Street and Nicollet Avenue on December 4, 1958. With
Rood, left to right, are H.P. Christenson, Sixth Ward alderman, Raymond D. Black of the Citizens League, and Mayor P. Kenneth Peterson.
Mayor Peterson estimated that the redevelopment of the area would en-
tail construction worth sixty-seven million dollars, nine million of
which would come from federal funds. The new development would
gain Minneapolis one million dollars annually in taxes, the mayor said.

1958—1964

Renewing Downtown

December 4, 1958, was a bitterly cold day. Snow blew across a vacant lot bounded by Hennepin and Nicollet avenues, Third and Fourth streets. Minneapolis Mayor P. Kenneth Peterson watched as library board president Dorothy Rood, clad in a bulky coat, stuck a shovel into the frozen earth. It was a moment many people had thought might never come. It was a moment that Gratia Countryman would have loved to have seen. Librarian Ray Williams must have heaved a sigh of relief. Ground was being broken for a new central library in downtown Minneapolis.

The location was significant, touching both the future and the past. One block farther down Hennepin, in 1866, the Minneapolis Athenaeum had constructed its first building, providing the roots for the present library. And all around the library site were hopes—hopes that the north end of downtown would experience a rebirth led by the new library building. If all went as the planners hoped, someday the Minneapolis Public Library would be surrounded by new hotels and public buildings and park space, instead of the dingy brick bars and flophouses that now crowded the area. It seemed an ambitious plan, that day in 1958.

Things had started moving toward the end of the war. Twice earlier, in 1939 and 1941, the city council had asked the library for long-range plans and had gotten the response that a new central library building was the greatest need. The song was old by this time, and nothing came of singing it again. In 1944, the library board set up a special committee to examine the question of a new library building, this time to document the need more carefully and to look seriously at alternatives. The committee said that remodeling the present building at Tenth and Hennepin was too expensive and would not provide enough space. Building an annex to the present building was considered impractical, not only because it would be hard to match the architecture and the floor and ceiling heights of the old building, but also because the old building would still need work. Building a new structure across Hennepin Avenue from the old building was an idea that was favored by many board and staff members. The new building, it was said, could be connected with the old by an underground tunnel, making use of the old building's heating system; the bindery, shops, museum, and meeting and storage rooms of the old building could also still be used. But the committee rejected this plan, saying that it would be expensive to operate two buildings of different vintages, and that the old building would still have to be extensively remodeled.

The library committee decided the best answer was a "complete new building. This is the most desirable solution and in the long run the most economical. With proper planning it should result in the best quality of service."[1] The cost of the new building was estimated at $2.5 million, and the library board came up with a new plan to help meet some of this cost: making the library a war memorial. How to satisfactorily recognize the service of Minneapolis's World War II fighting men and women was a question residents had been debating for some time. The World War I memorial, Victory Drive in North Minneapolis, with a parkway and plaques and trees planted for the dead, offered a guide. But the library board proposed that a living memorial to those who served be created by building a new library with memorial funds, "to the end that such library may serve such men and women and their families and descendants in helping to improve and defend the institutions they fought to save."[2] In the spring of 1945, Carl Vitz and the library board took the war memorial idea to the city council's postwar progress committee, explaining that books, alcoves, fireplaces, murals, rooms, flagpoles—almost anything—could be designated by a plaque as a memorial to a lost soldier. Carl Vitz, in a letter to the *Minneapolis Tribune,* said that a library could help prevent another war by educating the public to the country's national and international responsibilities. The new library could also help America remain as strong as she had proved herself to be in the war. The library serves all people, Vitz wrote, and "takes no notice of right or wrong side of the tracks. It is free but it is not charity. The user helps himself and his benefits depend upon his initiative. The library is the stronghold of the rugged individualist."[3]

Apparently, the rest of the city was less enthusiastic about making the library a war memorial than was the library board, and the idea, perhaps offered in desperation, died quietly. But 1945 saw help come from another quarter; a group of civic giants had looked at the tacky north edge of downtown and decided that a library there could help improve the tone.

The part of Minneapolis in question was the oldest except for old St. Anthony. When, in 1855, a suspension bridge to Nicollet Island completed the joining of St. Anthony and Minneapolis, the area at the end of the bridge in Minneapolis had become a focal point of the city. It was called the Gateway. Hennepin and Nicollet avenues converged near this point, and through the years there was a triangular-shaped building in the space between those avenues, and then a park with a building that served as an entrance to the city, a comfort station and a home for the city's chamber of commerce. Once the busy center of downtown, by the middle of the twentieth century the area had become run-down as the center of the city had moved south to Seventh Street and Nicollet Avenue. The Gateway area, with the Gateway Park as its center, was filled with old hotels, small shops, bars, and restaurants. And it was filled with men, some unemployed and vagrant, some working but poor. Many of these men lounged in Gateway Park, warmed by the sun and conversation and perhaps by hopes of better times, and, if that failed, by alcohol. To some, this "lower loop" area was a "vermin-infested rat-hole." To others, it was simply an old part of town that provided low-rent living to the kind of itinerant workers that are always needed in a city to cover odd jobs.

The end of World War II marked the beginning of a national effort to revitalize the great cities of America. Soldiers were coming home, production had to switch from wartime to peacetime output, and the high level of energy and economic activity that had pulled the nation out of the Depression had to be channeled into something that would keep prosperity at hand. Urban renewal was one of these new peacetime forces, and the federal government took the lead in many cases by constructing new federal buildings in many downtowns. Minneapolis would be the recipient of new federal court and public health buildings if it played its cards right, and a group of businessmen formed to make sure that would happen. In 1945, the Civic Center Development Association issued a report recommending the redevelopment of a section of the lower loop. Included in their plan were a public health building, a federal courts building, public safety and veterans' buildings, and a new public library, located between Third and Fourth streets and Nicollet and Hennepin avenues. The proposed developments were to be the centerpiece of a renovation of the entire lower loop area, one that would clear away the aged buildings, many more than fifty years old, which had degenerated to the point that they were "no longer capable of competition with modern structures."[4] As well as an eyesore to many and a center of moral decay, the area was a tax liability. New buildings in the lower loop would bring in more tax revenue. The Civic

Minneapolis Public Library photograph

Hubert Horatio Humphrey, who, as mayor of Minneapolis, helped locate the new downtown library at Fourth Street and Nicollet Avenue. Humphrey always had an eye for a good deal, and when federal funds were available to help renovate the lower loop if the city committed to locating one of its own buildings there, Humphrey advised the library board to "strike while the iron is hot." In 1945 Humphrey endorsed the recommendation of the Civic Center Development Association that the new library be built on the block between Third and Fourth streets and Hennepin and Nicollet avenues. In 1946, as ex officio member of the library board, Mayor Humphrey offered the motion that approved the site, thus helping assure the rebirth of the northern part of downtown.

Center Development Association carried a great deal of weight, for its board of directors included representatives from the General Mills, Pillsbury, and McKnight companies, and from major local banks, retailers, newspapers, and hotels. Their recommendation was endorsed by the city planning engineer, Herman Olson, who would soon start to work on a comprehensive redevelopment plan for the city, and by the mayor of Minneapolis, Hubert H. Humphrey.

So here again, as in the nineteenth century at the time of the founding of the Athenaeum and of the original Minneapolis Public Library, we see the enlightened self-interest of community leaders who hoped to use a collection of books for more than just reading. These civic leaders believed in the educational and recreational benefits of reading, to be sure, and liked the idea of a library providing a constructive alternative for people looking for something to do downtown. But they also wanted the library to be a catalyst, to take the point position as the new invaded the old. The physical fact of a new library could bring about other physical changes downtown—changes that could benefit all the firms represented on the Civic Center Development Association board. A healthy, vibrant downtown meant that the banks, stores, hotels, and companies there had a better chance of prospering.

These civic leaders were far sighted, as had been their predecessors in the previous century. Their own businesses benefited from the revitalizing of downtown Minneapolis, but so has each of us who lives in the Twin Cities metropolitan area. The development association's plan was solid, and although it never was fully implemented, the new library finally did rise, many years later, on the site the group chose. The officers of this group were William Brockman of Midland National Bank and Trust Company, Neil R. Messick of the Nicollet Hotel, Leo R. Pflaum of Maurice L. Rothschild and Company, Gordon Ballhorn of General Mills, and George C. Crosby of the S. T. McKnight Company. Also on the board of directors were men like Doddrick Olson of Powers Dry Goods Company, Donald Dayton of the Dayton Company, and Richard Pillsbury Gale, an attorney and former congressman whose father, Edward C. Gale, had been library board president from 1928 to 1943 and whose grandfather, Samuel C. Gale, was an original founder of the Athenaeum. These people recommended a library site that would more than fulfill Mayor Humphrey's words when he endorsed the plan: "Your program will rehabilitate an area which is becoming an economic liability. It is a sound and practical means for developing the industrial life of our community and for beautifying a section of our loop which has become increasingly blighted."[5]

But there would still be many years and a great many words between this recommendation and the actuality of a library functioning on that ground.

Building a new library, sooner or later, was an idea that had general support in Minneapolis. But the location was still far from a settled issue. The development association wanted the library to lead the way to a revitalized city, to make the location work not just for the library's purposes, but for the city's purposes as well. The library board was not so sure about this at the beginning. At the time of its 1944 survey of construction possibilities, the board stated that public opinion wanted the new library to be near the old library site—people were used to going there, transportation was available, and there was a good location across the street for expansion. There had been other sites suggested at the time—Nicollet Island, or near the Minneapolis Institute of Arts in South Minneapolis—but the board favored the old location. Carl Vitz, as he left in 1945, said he wasn't sold on the Civic Center site, and Gratia Countryman wrote from Duluth that she preferred a new building across from the old one, where the neighborhood was quiet, there was adequate parking and no building to tear down before construction could begin. In fact, the location across Hennepin from the old library was so attractive that, at the instigation of Archie Walker, who had taken his father's place on the board in 1928, the library board purchased a site there in 1942 for possible expansion. Walker, who became the library board's third president in 1944, opposed the Civic Center site when it was advanced, perhaps because the Walker family interests still lay at the south edge of downtown rather than the north.

But the Civic Center location had a certain logic to it for a library that had once professed to be a social-activist institution. On April 3, 1946, the *Minneapolis Daily Times* endorsed the site, which was formally proposed by the Civic Center Development Association to the library board the next month. A tentative decision on a site became necessary when federal planning money became available for urban renewal. To land the federal grant, a specific location had to be listed. The federal government had committed itself to building a new federal courts building downtown if it was convinced that Minneapolis was serious about redeveloping the Civic Center area. So there was pressure on the library board to throw in with the Civic Center location, not the least of which pressure came from Humphrey, ex officio board member and Civic Center advocate who said the board should "strike while the iron is hot." He said, "Public interest and private self-interest are both behind the Civic Center plan, a rare combination."[6] On April 10, 1947, on a motion offered by Humphrey, the library board approved the site at Fourth and Nicollet for a new building, and successful application was made to the federal government for planning funds. Several board members felt the decision was reversible, that the vote was nonbinding, and that the location could be changed later if they chose to do so. In fact, argument and vacillation over the site continued for the next ten years, but in the end the Civic Center

Renewing Downtown

Four views of the block of older buildings that gave way to the new Minneapolis Public Library in downtown Minneapolis (clockwise from the top left): The view of Fourth Street, showing the Hotel Russell and The Pit Bar B Q; Hennepin Avenue between Third and Fourth streets, with the Crystal Theater and Hamburger Heaven; a photo taken from the roof of the Nicollet Hotel, showing Third Street, with the B & B Hotel on the corner of Third and Hennepin; and Nicollet Avenue between Third and Fourth streets, with Nicollet Pants on the corner of Third and Nicollet, and Brown's Clothing. Many of the tenants of these buildings weren't eager to leave, but progress started leveling the block in 1958.

Development Association's proposal for the library was carried out in steel and concrete. Again, a civic-minded group of businessmen, working with government and with an eye to protecting and enhancing their own property, had changed the face of Minneapolis. The library they sited, with the library board's approval, became the wedge of renewal that cracked into the decaying facade of the lower loop, an area that now sparkles with soaring office buildings, condominiums, apartments, and hotels.

In 1948, architects were chosen to draw up plans for a new library. But by 1949, the library board was wavering on the choice of a location. So far, the whole idea of revitalizing downtown was like a dance with all partners wary of becoming too involved. The library didn't want to be the first to build in a depressed area and then find out no one else was going to come down to that part of town. The federal government wouldn't go in until it had evidence that the city was serious about rebuilding the Civic Center area, and private companies, such as Northwestern National Life Insurance, were waiting along the wall, ready to join the dance if others did. No one was talking about committing big money or breaking ground right away, but decisions still had to be made and planning begun. As Robert Cerny, executive secretary of the Civic Center Development Association, told the library board, "We cannot go on for generations saying we will not do any building unless someone else does it first. Someone has to start."[7]

To get more evidence that the Fourth and Nicollet site was the best, in 1949 the library board asked the city planning commission to conduct a survey of the advantages and disadvantages of the old library site, the Fourth and Nicollet site, and a site on Marquette just south of the Foshay Tower. The Fourth and Nicollet site was found to be the best in terms of access, the number of potential users, and the proximity to businesses, shopping, and other retail activities. As the planning commission had already endorsed the whole Civic Center Development Association's proposal, it came as no surprise that the Fourth and Nicollet location was favored. The library board, however, still heard opposition to that lower loop location. Hotel owners on the southern edge of downtown objected to moving the library. Some businesses near the proposed library site didn't want the library and the other urban renewal projects there because they would displace their operations. And for some members of the public, the lower loop was just a disagreeable place they didn't want any part of. At a public hearing on February 8, 1950, one Minneapolis resident was quoted as saying that the lower loop area was "not a fit place to send a boy or girl for a book. . . . Let's put the library where students can go in the family car without being accosted by a bunch of bums."[8]

But the next day, the library board officially confirmed the Fourth and Nicollet site. The Civic Center Development Association congratulated the board, and said the federal government would surely now agree to put the new courts building in the Civic Center location, at Fourth and Marquette. By November 1951, preliminary architectural plans for the library were approved. But things moved slowly, and while the drawings were there, the money wasn't. The city was engaged in long-range planning, and didn't want to start on a single project until the entire picture was clear. In the summer of 1954, journalist Barbara Flanagan wrote that, since the old library would reach retirement age, sixty-five, in December, it was time to get cracking on a new library. To add a little damaged civic pride to the pressure for a new building, she pointed out that new libraries had popped up recently in cities and college towns all around Minnesota—in Fargo, St. Cloud, Hibbing, Waseca, and St. Peter.[9] Still, it took another year for any perceptible movement on the issue, and the staff was becoming impatient. Elizabeth Bond, coordinator of the main library, wrote that trying to maintain 1950s services in the 1889 building was "a good deal like trying to ram a 200-pound dowager into the size 12 dress she wore at her debut."[10]

In the late summer of 1955, the Minneapolis Housing and Redevelopment Authority presented an eleven-million-dollar plan for redevelopment of the lower loop that superceded the Civic Center concept, but kept most of its proposals, including the new library at the Fourth and Nicollet site. The Downtown Council was formed at the same time, a private group of business people aimed at promoting and publicizing downtown development, and enthusiasm rose. A *Minneapolis Tribune* editorial said, "Blight runs through the lower loop like some virulent disease and unless it is checked by drastic measures it will ultimately despoil the whole area."[11] The paper said the library had patiently waited for the city to finish its planning process, and that now was the time to go ahead. The editorial supported a bond sale to acquire land at Fourth and Nicollet for the library. *The Minneapolis Star* also supported action on the library, saying not only was such a facility needed for the system's own patrons, but for "the part such a project could play in redevelopment of a section of the city which has become blighted over the years. The razing of old buildings in the block in question and the construction of an attractive library would greatly improve the appearance of the entire area."[12] The library was, at last, to lead the way to a new downtown. The new building, the *Tribune* said, would "serve to stabilize property values in this area and will encourage private investors to launch new businesses and industries in the lower loop."[13] That autumn, the city approved four hundred thousand dollars in bonds to acquire property for the library, after yet another round of suggestions to reexamine where the library should go. The city council accepted the Fourth and Nicollet site for a final time on October 28, 1955. The following

Renewing Downtown

The library was changed inside and out in the late 1950s and early 1960s. In this 1958 picture, librarian Ray Williams, at left, and administrative assistant Robert Rohlf look over a model of the new downtown library. To fit the new building and a new era, Williams had streamlined and reorganized the library, stopping some services and combining others. His changes brought turmoil to the library, although almost all the changes operated successfully once they were instituted. Two years after the new library opened, Williams resigned as director, in part because of the turmoil. Rohlf went on to become the director of the Hennepin County library system, for a time a competitor of the Minneapolis system. After a sometimes heated fight between the two systems, peace among libraries was finally restored in 1974.

summer, the city began buying up the property on which the new library would be built. One by one the old businesses in the area moved out, some by court order when they resisted. Brown Clothing, the B & B Hotel, Hamburger Heaven, the Russell Hotel, the Pit Bar B Q, the Baltimore Cafe, the Crystal Theater—all relocated or disappeared entirely.

Late in 1956, it became clear that the library board's preliminary plans for the new library were too ambitious. Each year of delay had meant an increase in costs, and now money was becoming tight again. By 1957, nearly $1 million was cut out of the construction budget, and the building plans were reduced from six floors to four. Those four remaining floors were enlarged, but administrative assistant Robert Rohlf, who was overseeing the construction plans, predicted that in thirty years the library would have storage problems because of the space cut out of the plans. On August 8, 1957, the library board approved final plans for the library, and an architect's sketch of the building as it appears today was run for the first time in the newspapers the following day. In January 1958, the board of estimate and taxation committed itself to bond sales of nearly $7 million over the next three years to finance the new building. On November 15, 1958, bids were taken for construction of the library, and they came in at $4.7 million, nearly $1 million below estimate. The next month, in the snow, the ground was broken for what would become "one of the cornerstones in a major face-lifting scheduled for the city's lower loop."[14]

The library so long awaited began taking material shape, and by June 1959, the curved steel of the planetarium dome could be seen rising above the corner of Fourth and Nicollet. By August, the framework for the sculpture in front of the building was going up. This was to be a thirteen-ton, twenty-seven-foot-high metal sculpture of a scroll, symbolizing communication from age to age. The sculptor was John Rood, husband of library board president Dorothy Rood. The sculpture had been approved by the board early in the year, with the understanding that it would be paid for by donations. In August, Dorothy Rood made a gift of the scroll to the library.

Dorothy Rood, the fourth board president and the first woman to hold that post, stood next to Mayor P. Kenneth Peterson on a festive autumn day when Peterson troweled the cement around the cornerstone of the new library. The date was September 27, 1959. Looking on were Librarian Ray Williams, city council president George Martens, Librarian Emeritus Glenn Lewis, and the chairman of the library board's building committee, Kenneth Backstrom. Sealed inside the cornerstone were microfilms of the Aquatennial Week editions of the *Minneapolis Tribune* and *The Minneapolis Star*, pictures of the old library building, floor plans of the new, and a tape recording of Christopher Morley's speech at the library's fiftieth anniversary

Renewing Downtown

The laying of the cornerstone for the new public library downtown, September 27, 1959. From left to right are retired library Director Glenn Lewis, library board president Dorothy Rood, city council president George Martens, Mayor P. Kenneth Peterson (holding the trowel), library Director Ray Williams, and Kenneth Backstrom, head of the library's building committee. The new public library in turn became the cornerstone for the redevelopment of downtown Minneapolis, a downtown that continues to grow and remains a model for urban development.

celebration. A new "intellectual windbreak," to use Morley's term, was taking shape on what would one day be the Nicollet Mall.

When the doors finally swung back at Fourth and Nicollet over a year later, on January 28, 1961, the occasion marked more than the opening of a new central library. The north end of downtown was reborn, beginning a slow process of growth where, by the 1980s, posh

Minneapolis Public Library photograph

By 1960, the new library finally began taking on a steel and concrete reality. Shown here are the beams of the science museum and the planetarium dome at the corner of Fourth and Nicollet. As an earlier generation of Minneapolis children had remembered the old library for its mummies, so the present generation would remember this new library for the star shows in the planetarium. Maxine Haarstick, the director of the planetarium when it opened, said it was an important tool to help children "open that door to learning and experiencing and exploring." In the early 1980s, Haarstick, then retired, joined with the Friends of the Library in a struggle to find funding to keep this educational tool open to another generation of Minneapolis citizens.

condominiums would replace the parking lots that had replaced the aged warehouses and bars. Downtown Minneapolis, working against the trend of many other major cities, would become a vital place for working, living, shopping, and playing, thanks in part to the public library, which first settled down in an unfashionable part of town.

The central library's opening also marked the beginning of a new era for the Minneapolis library system. It would not be an era of exuberant expansion, as the city had seen under Gratia Countryman. But it was to be a period where the library's place in Minneapolis was solidified—where, after some arguing and questioning, the people of Minneapolis decided to have a modern library system and to support it, if not lavishly, at least well. In the twenty years following 1961, eight new branch libraries would open, extending service or replacing old buildings. New ideas and services would be tried in an effort to keep up with the accelerating pace of change in the world. Some would succeed, and some would not. What the city would have, starting with that block-long building at Fourth and Nicollet, was a library system well built and well maintained enough to sail confidently to its hundred-year landmark and look forward to the years beyond.

In January 1961, the city, the country, and the world were poised on the edge of change. On January 20, John Fitzgerald Kennedy, the nation's youngest elected president, was inaugurated. Many saw signs for hope and renewed national vigor as Kennedy proclaimed, "Ask not what your country can do for you; ask what you can do for your country." Kennedy would talk tough with the Russians, but he would talk with them. From Havana, Fidel Castro said he hoped for a clean start with Kennedy and better relations with America, while in Nicaragua and the wilds of Florida the Central Intelligence Agency was training guerrillas to overthrow him. Late in January, the United States tested a new Minuteman missile equipped to carry nuclear warheads, and it came down on target in the Pacific four thousand miles from its launch site. The Soviet Union was said to have thirty-five nuclear-tipped rockets aimed at the heart of America, while we had only a dozen pointing back. On the last day of January, a chimpanzee named Ham rode a Redstone rocket from Cape Canaveral into the lower fringes of space and landed alive in the Atlantic. In Georgia, Governor Ernest Vandiver was threatening to close the state university rather than let two black students enter it. A federal court stopped him, the students went to class, riots followed, and it took several days for peace to return and for the students, black and white, to go back to class.

In South Minneapolis, a week before the library opened, a cross was burned in the yard of James Horris, a black social worker living in a mostly white neighborhood. The newspaper photo caption read, "It happened in Minneapolis." Marvin Kline was on trial for swindling money from the Sister Kenny Foundation, Mayor Peterson asked the city council for one hundred and fifty more police to combat a crime wave, Minnesota was in the throes of redistricting, and Elmer L. Andersen had just been sworn in as governor. Ground had been broken January 4 for the new West Bank Campus of the University of Minnesota, and a private group was forming to redevelop the nearby Riverside area. Interstate Highway 35W was creeping through South Minneapolis, and bridges to carry it over Minnehaha Creek near Page Elementary School had just been proposed. The Minnesota Gophers, under coach Murray Warmath, had started the new year by losing the Rose Bowl to the Washington Huskies, but January still provided hope for sports fans. A new National Football League franchise called the Minnesota Vikings drafted thirty-six players on January 26, and a week earlier Norm Van Brocklin, a South Dakota native who had just retired as quarterback of the Philadelphia Eagles, had been named to coach the new team. In the middle of the month, Harry "Cookie" Lavagetto, Harmon Killebrew, Bob Allison, Billy Gardner, and Earl Battey came to town for a baseball banquet. Local sportswriter Halsey Hall was toastmaster for the affair, which previewed the new Minnesota Twins. They would play their first game in Metropolitan Stadium as soon as the snow cleared.

Minneapolis was becoming a big city, a major-league city. The city proper had passed its population peak. In 1960 more than four hundred eighty-two thousand people lived in Minneapolis—eight hundred fifty thousand if its suburbs were counted. And the suburbs were where people were going. Highways that would carry them there and back were rolling into place—the first stretch of 35W had opened in 1959; a tenth revision of the route for the first part of Interstate 94 between Minneapolis and St. Paul was approved in January 1961; and Interstate 494 was on the drawing boards, with University of Minnesota geography professor John Borchert predicting heavy development where 494 crossed Highways 12 and 55 west of Minneapolis and where it intersected Highway 100 southwest of town. This move to the suburbs would strain central city resources, for many people still worked downtown but lived and paid taxes outside the city limits. That strain would, before long, trigger a fight between the city and the county over library funding and service. But Minneapolis was basically healthy, and, while it was no Chicago or San Francisco, the Mill City with its Foshay Tower, Rand Tower (now Dain Tower), Bell Telephone Building, and brand-new First National Bank Building was proud of itself.

On Saturday, January 28, 1961, while the Winter Carnival Parade crunched through the streets of St. Paul, a group of people carrying books walked through downtown Minneapolis. They were the city librarian, members of the library board, and city and state officials who were symbolically carrying a tiny part of the library's collection from the old building to the new. The new building on Nicollet had taken

Renewing Downtown

longer to open than anyone had thought, due to strikes and construction delays. The move had been put off through the fall and into January. But finally the books had been crated and moved, and the statue of Minerva, goddess of learning and wisdom, had been taken down from the front of the old library, cleaned, and placed on display outside the new building's main meeting room. Behind her, as another memory from the 1889 library, was one of the graceful mahogany fireplace mantels which had also been saved and moved. The Egyptian mum-

Minneapolis Star and Tribune photograph

Wisdom moves symbolically six blocks up Hennepin Avenue. The statue of Minerva, after looking down on Hennepin Avenue at Tenth Street for seventy years, is lowered and moved by flatbed truck to the new library at Fourth and Nicollet. The Woman's Club of Minneapolis paid for the moving and cleaning of the statue. In her new location, Minerva looks out over the arcade of the library.

177

mies from the museum had made the trip down Hennepin Avenue in a hearse in deference to their fragility and their dignity.

Now, with a cold wind making the day's twelve degrees seem colder, the marchers had reached the new library. The Patrick Henry High School band finished its music, and prayers of dedication were said by Rabbi Albert Minda of Temple Israel, Bishop Leonard Cowley of St. Olaf Catholic Church, and Dr. Howard Conn of Plymouth Congregational Church. The library's three flagpoles were inaugurated when Judge Luther Youngdahl raised the American flag, Governor Andersen raised the state flag, and Mayor Peterson raised the city flag. Frederick Wilson, the main contractor on the library job, presented a gold-plated key to library board president Dorothy Rood, who handed it over to city council president George Martens, who gave it back to Rood, who then presented it to librarian Ray Williams. Eleven-year-old Archie Dean Walker III, great-grandson of T. B. Walker, cut the ceremonial ribbon with scissors taller than himself, and the library was officially part of Minneapolis. The library, including the site, cost $7,838,920.26, about nineteen thousand dollars less than its allocated funding. Almost ninety-nine percent of that money had come from city bond sales.

Inside were 632,822 books, an impressive total compared with thirty thousand inside the first library when it opened more than seventy years earlier. The new building could hold 1.5 million books, and its system to circulate those books included pneumatic tubing for carrying orders from the various department desks to the stacks above and below the public floors, and a vertical conveyor for carrying the books from the stacks to the desks where people who wanted to read them were waiting. There were far more books, too, out in the open shelves and available for public browsing than there had been in the old library—one of the reasons a new facility had been requested.

The library was constructed in two parts, joined by an enclosed, marble-lined arcade that opened onto both Nicollet and Hennepin avenues. On the south side of the arcade were the planetarium, with its domed roof for projecting replicas of the heavens, and its improved-model projector being used for the first time. Also in this wing were a black-lighted hall of time and space, and a large auditorium. In the basement of this wing was the science museum, where the mummies resided. In the basement of the north side, the main building, were the library's shops—print and paint and carpenter's—and other supply and maintenance rooms. On the ground floor, when the patron came in the main library doors, she or he was faced by an information desk, and flanked by checkout and return areas. Behind the information desk was the card catalog, telling what the library had to offer. Lining the walls were open shelves of books from the departments of literature, language, and fiction; history, biography, and travel; science and technology; and business and economics. The first floor was basically

Minneapolis Public Library photograph

Making a connection across the generations, Archie Dean Walker III, T. B. Walker's great-grandson, holds the huge pair of scissors he used to cut the ribbon at the opening of the new downtown library on January 28, 1961. In 1889, T. B. Walker had greeted the crowd at the opening of the first downtown library at Tenth and Hennepin. As T. B. was largely responsible for the opening of the first library, so his great-grandson helped open the second.

one huge room designed to give a feeling of openness and light, with a few areas in the center closed off for work space and offices. On the side toward Hennepin Avenue was a drive-up window, modeled after the automobile-age innovations at banks. A person could call in an order for a book and, within half an hour, drive by and pick it up without leaving the car. There was also a twenty-four hour book drop, the only part of this drive-up service that still remains.

An escalator close to the information desk gave easy access to the second floor, also a public area. On that floor were the music, art, sociology, and children's departments. There was also a lounge area, which particularly tickled *Minneapolis Tribune* columnist John Sherman: "And mirabile dictu, there's a smoking lounge! The idea of books associated, in a public place, with one of life's finer minor pleasures, is something I never hoped to see. The only possible next step is a cocktail lounge in the courthouse."[15] The administrative offices were on the second floor, including a board room far more utilitarian than its predecessor in the old library. The third floor was largely book storage, although the county library offices were located here, as were six small study rooms, or carrels, which scholars could use for up to six months while working on a research or writing project. These study carrels were financed as memorials by the families of people important in the early cultural life of the city. Outside each room was placed the name, photo, and short biography of the person the carrel honored: Martin B. Koon, a district court judge and early library trustee; Thomas Lowry, the streetcar man; Anna Gale Lindley, a teacher and patron of the library, local theater, and the Minneapolis Symphony Orchestra; William S. King, a Minneapolis developer and Lowry's partner; Hugh G. Harrison, the second mayor of Minneapolis; and James Kendall Hosmer, the city's second librarian, in whose study carrel this book was written.

On the fourth floor of the new library was the Athenaeum, with its special book vault and display area for beautiful rare books. The Athenaeum's place at the top of the new library symbolized its importance in the library's history and the continuing role it plays in partnership with the main library, providing quality and depth to the collection. Also on the fourth floor were the bindery, the catalog and order departments, a staff lunchroom, lounge and locker areas, and more stacks for storage. In all, the stacks and open book areas in the new library contained enough shelving to reach from Minneapolis to Red Wing—if someone took it into her or his head to lay it all end to end.

The library opened to the public the Monday after the Saturday dedication—January 30. The place was jammed, as curious citizens turned out to see what their tax money had bought. Between 9:00 A.M. and 9:00 P.M. four thousand two hundred items were checked out of the library, twice the circulation recorded at the old library the previous Monday. During opening day, two hundred and fifty new library cards were issued, five times the normal haul. "It's been a record day all around," said Margaret Mull, chief of the central library. "We've had great lines at the three check-out machines all day. There hasn't been a moment's lull."[16] Some complaints about parking were heard, as there were still some moving trucks parked in the library lot, but the situation was expected to be eased when ramps were built in the area in the near future. The pneumatic delivery system carrying orders around the building broke down the first day, giving a touch of excitement to an already busy time. People seemed generally pleased just to wander around and check out the new place in town, browsing here and there and perhaps planning to return later when things calmed down. The new building's drawing power held throughout the year, as circulation at the new central library jumped forty-four percent over the last year in the old library.

The newspapers were far less ecstatic and effusive than they had been when the original library opened in 1889, but this was a more restrained era. There were no editorials in the Minneapolis papers lauding a new monument to civilization in our midst. The editorials at the time were preoccupied with the new Kennedy administration and with whether we could peacefully coexist with Khrushchev's Russia and Castro's Cuba. The news columns of the papers did give the library good coverage, however, including front-page treatment on opening day and picture spreads showing the building's facilities. And the following Sunday, in his column in the *Tribune*, John Sherman wrote, "If you can browse through this building and not feel an irresistible impulse to grab a book and read it, you're a clod. I've rarely seen, anywhere, a more alluring showcase for books and the values they represent, a more tempting invitation to enjoy the reading experience." He praised the ample light and bright colors, and then added playfully, "Set in the lower loop, the library by sheer proximity if nothing else threatens to make book readers out of nearby bankers and businessmen." The new library joined with the symphony, the university, local art museums, and the planned Guthrie Theater to round out the city's cultural image, Sherman concluded. "We're growing up fast, and we're beginning to look better, with a shine on our shoes and a new tie."[17]

So it was open at last, the new building that would take the Minneapolis Public Library system into its second century. It was not as stately as the original building, but it was functional and spacious. It had been worth the wait—even such a protracted wait. The new building sat bravely, tying together with its arcade rather faded but historic parts of Nicollet and Hennepin avenues. The neighborhood around the new building would bloom with new headquarters for Northwestern National Life and Northern States Power, with the new Sheraton Ritz Hotel (now the Minneapolis Plaza Hotel), and with new apartments and condominiums, while ironically, the area around the old library at Tenth and Hennepin was sliding into tackiness and would soon give way to dirty bookstores and dingy bars. The city that had started close by the banks of the Mississippi had been moving its downtown center slowly south, but now, thanks partly to the new library, the area near the river would come back into fashion.

But there was a shadow trailing the new library. The month before the opening, the library board had authorized an independent study of library operations. A three-member committee of the board would look into how things were working, in terms of administration and personnel matters, and would decide if an outside agency should study the library, and, if so, who that consulting agency should be.

Why? What was the problem?

Apparently there were many. Raymond Williams was a man who brought change to the library, and he had a personality that made that change very forceful and direct. Some of his changes the staff didn't like, and some of his changes the public didn't like, as in the closing of the school libraries. Some staff members felt Williams was abrupt and didn't communicate with them. Some on the library board had questions about some of the changes and about the way Williams was handling the library. The matter was brought to a sharp public focus when, on December 11, 1960, board member Yvonne Van der Boom resigned and submitted a statement to the Minneapolis newspapers criticizing Williams. "I have lost faith in the judgment and ability of the chief administrator," Van der Boom said. "In my opinion, there are administrative areas where the librarian has proven to be so ineffective that Board members have had to concern themselves with administrative details." She said money problems were mounting, service was deteriorating, the system was top-heavy with administrative staff, and staff morale was very low, with many employees and former employees saying they'd lost confidence in Williams. She didn't like the way Williams was handling the board; she felt he convened the board only to rubber stamp his own policies. Williams didn't communicate well with his staff, the board, or the public, Van der Boom concluded, and she called for an outside survey to be taken to see if her perceptions on the matter were correct.[18]

The charges were serious, and Williams was, understandably, stunned. He said he welcomed the idea of a survey, because he felt it would show that he and the staff had done an excellent job getting the library into a new building with only a short time to plan the move itself. Some board members, including president Rood, expressed support for Williams, while others thought that the outside survey was a good idea. So, at the board's last meeting of 1960, the survey was authorized.

Meanwhile, the library moved ahead, getting used to its new surroundings. In January 1961, the Athenaeum held its 101st annual

The John Rood sculpture and the fountains in front of the new library along Nicollet Avenue are shown in this 1962 photograph. Across Fourth Street from the library, where the Thrift Store is shown, Northern States Power would break ground in 1963 for its headquarters, which was completed in 1965, adding to the renovation of the Gateway area.

meeting in its new quarters, so close to where it had erected its first building. The new planetarium, under the guiding hand of Maxine Haarstick, gave its first star show on February 4 and became an immediate hit. In its first year of operation, the planetarium opened the heavens to one hundred forty-seven thousand people. The most-asked-for books in the library were Theodore H. White's *The Making of the President: 1960*, William Lederer's *A Nation of Sheep*, William Shirer's *The Rise and Fall of the Third Reich*, Harper Lee's *To Kill a Mockingbird*, Edwin O'Connor's *The Edge of Sadness*, and Irving Stone's *The Agony and The Ecstasy*. Books that were considered that year but found unsuitable for the collection were Henry Miller's *Tropic of Cancer*, Patrick Dennis's *Little Me*, and Harold Robbins's *The Carpetbaggers*.

Something else that was considered but didn't make it was another attempt at a levy limit increase. The public had said no to more money for the library in 1959, and it said no again in 1961, by a vote of fifty-four thousand to thirty-five thousand. An earlier request for more funding through the state legislature had died in committee, so the library again had to look to reduced hours and reduced staff. And the levy effort brought more dissension, as one board member, Mary Laddy, publicly said that the library needed a staff reorganization, not more money.

The legislature did pass an additional mill of funding for the separate Hennepin County library system, a recognition of the growing suburban population. But there would be no growth in the city system, despite the library board's approval of an ambitious twenty-year branch expansion program to reach into parts of the city not served at present. The plan included a Gratia Countryman branch to be built at Fifty-fourth Street and Penn Avenue South; but with no money, the Countryman branch and the entire plan went nowhere. In 1962, the city council didn't even put the library's expansion plan on its priority list because the prospects of funding were so grim. The library must have felt almost as bereft as the black children from the Deep South who began showing up at Sumner branch after moving in with their Minneapolis relatives to escape the racial tension and hatred at home.

In 1962 the consultants, those outside experts who had been studying the library system, spoke. The lengthy document issued by George Fry and Associates, a management consulting firm, was a middle-of-the-road report that placed no blame and said nothing terribly new. But it did clarify the problem at the library and make some good suggestions for solutions. The report said the "past several years of intense and continuous movement and change have had an unsettling influence" on both the library staff and the public.[19] Low staff morale was confirmed, partly because these changes had been unexpected. That element of surprise also affected the public, to whom the library board and administration had not done a good job of explaining the changes in advance. Williams was said to have been heavy on control in his early days as head librarian but some senior staff were also called "somewhat inflexible" by the report. "An effective working relationship" between Williams and the board had not been reached, the report confirmed, nor had Williams clearly delineated what administrative responsibilities his department and branch heads would have. Most significant, the report stated that much of the professional staff was overpaid in comparison to other libraries in the nation. While the Fry group acknowledged that the Minneapolis public schools still paid more for comparable work than the library did, it said the library offered more librarian jobs and better chance for advancement, so that salary equality wasn't as crucial. Since 1952, revenues for the library had risen thirty-five percent, while salaries were up fifty-six percent and comprised eighty-three percent of the budget. Only one major library in the nation allocated a higher portion of its budget to salaries, the report stated. While the Minneapolis Public Library was twenty-second in total circulation of all libraries in the country, it was sixteenth in total expenditures and sixth in per capita expenditures.[20]

The Fry report made two major suggestions. First, it recommended that the library write clear job descriptions and standards of performance for each of its jobs. Second, the report recommended that the library make more use of nonprofessional staff, meaning clerks, aides, pages, and other staff members who did not have library degrees. Since Gratia Countryman's time, the library's philosophy had been to have only professional librarians out in front dealing with the public. This had meant good library service, but the report suggested that nonprofessionals could work with the public without affecting service—and with a substantial savings in salary costs. This was a recommendation that has been acted upon; since the time of the Fry report, the percentage of professionals on the library staff has been slowly decreasing.

The Fry report, which came out in October 1962, hardly blamed Williams for all the library's troubles, but it didn't exonerate him either. Troubles continued. Williams had a verbal brush with board member Mary Laddy, and a conflict with the people who ran the library cafeteria, who told the board that Williams was uncooperative. The librarian had had enough. At the board's February 8, 1963, meeting, Williams submitted his resignation. In his statement to the board he said, "Apparently there is a never-ending supply of the desire for controversy, and I feel it unnecessary to spend the remainder of my professional career in such an atmosphere." Williams said he was proud of the work he had done with the new building and with the staff, and that he regretted "the lack of sufficient funds for staff and branches to complete the plans drawn to give full coverage of good public library service for the city, as well as a full integration of county and city library service."[21] Williams said he had been thinking of resigning for some time, but that he had no immediate plans for another position.

Board members were mixed in their reaction to the resignation, although, as an editorial in *The Minneapolis Star* noted, they accepted it "without much visible reluctance."[22] Board member Kenneth Backstrom said he regretted that Williams's administration was ending this way, and that not all the problems the librarian faced were self-created, as some charged. "I feel he has accomplished something here that took a great deal of courage and a great deal of determination, and in doing this he has offended a great many people," Backstrom said. "This is what happens perhaps when you exert too much effort to achieve the ideal goal."[23]

Williams's resignation was effective June 1, but by the end of May, Margaret Mull had inherited the library. As chief of the central library and the person most acquainted with the entire system, she was appointed acting librarian May 21, taking over Williams's job and his fourteen-thousand-five-hundred-dollar salary. Of the departed Williams, Mull later wrote, "Perhaps no greater compliment can be paid to him than to point out that the organization which he shaped in the

Margaret Mull was acting librarian between Ray Williams and Ervin Gaines. Mull took over the library at a rocky time in 1963, after the move into the new building downtown and after dissension within the library board and the staff over the operating style of Ray Williams. Mull helped calm things down for the new librarian, Ervin Gaines, and then went back to her job as head of the central library.

old building worked smoothly when transferred to the new and that it is now an established and accepted pattern."[24] On August 1, 1963, Williams began a new job as director of the public library system of Charlottesville, Virginia, near the home of one of the patron saints of America's libraries, Thomas Jefferson.

Margaret Mull calmed the waters. As a staff veteran, she was close to her coworkers, was frank and open with them, and was respected. She was in charge of the Minneapolis Public Library for fourteen months while the library board searched for a new permanent head librarian. In this tenuous position, she could not affect policy much or make plans for the future. But she could, and did, help stabilize the library in its public image and its internal relations, and for this the library board was extremely grateful. Her groundwork would make it easier for her successor to strengthen the library system.

There were still money troubles. Trying to get some Saturday service in the branches while still keeping to a Spartan five-day week, a scheme of being open on alternate Mondays and Saturdays had been tried in 1962 and 1963. Then some branches closed Wednesdays to be open on Saturdays. The whole thing confused the public, which never seemed to know when the libraries were open. By 1964, the central library was closed three nights a week. That same year, the hospital outreach program was ended to save money, and the Seven Corners branch was closed, a victim of highway construction and declining circulation. The Jordan branch was also on the chopping block, but community pressure kept it open. Circulation declined to 2.5 million in 1964, down nearly a million from a peak six years before.

A general library problem got some national publicity in 1963 when it was found that low-income city dwellers made the least use of public libraries of any group in the population. Many argued that this was precisely the group that most needed to make use of libraries, that should be increasing their literacy skills and studying new developments so they could be trained for new jobs in a society that was finding less and less need for unskilled workers. This lack of use by the urban "underprivileged" would become an increasing frustration for librarians and social activists in these idealistic years of the New Frontier and the Great Society. At the Franklin branch, located in a poor part of South Minneapolis where immigrants, blacks, and Native Americans had historically been on the low end of society's scale, several attempts were made to get in closer touch with the community and to attract readers. Visits were made to high schools, art exhibits were placed in junior highs, programs were mounted in the branch. (One gets the feeling here of well-meaning people floundering, having recognized the problems but not knowing what to do about them.) In 1963, the Franklin and Sumner branches started a program to get neighborhood people with problems in contact with social workers and others who could offer help. The idea was that with the library sponsoring this kind of referral service, people using it would avoid the negative feeling of going into a welfare center. Information and contacts on health, alcohol abuse, camping, nursery school, and civil rights were offered at the library. The program was renewed in 1975 as part of a pilot program to distribute information about two thousand public and private social service agencies offering assistance on everything from food stamps to landlord problems. "People come here because there's no stigma in any way in coming into the library for information. We are trying to reach the people who might not go to other agencies—people who aren't aware of the services or are timid or shy," said Janice Raivo, an information specialist at the Franklin branch in 1975.[25] These outreach attempts were mildly successful, but, of course, the problems remain.

Into this library that was looking for calm after turmoil now came a man who managed to spark controversy from half a continent away. In fact, controversy seemed atmospheric to this man, and he headed into it with the dash of a plucky sailboat heading into a gale. He was Ervin J. Gaines, the Minneapolis Public Library's seventh librarian.

Photograph by Earl Chambers, June 8, 1962

The growth of the Gateway area downtown after the library moved in is shown in this 1962 photograph taken from the Nicollet Hotel just north of the new library. Under construction is the Sheraton Ritz Hotel and parking ramp, which was completed in 1963 and renamed the Minneapolis Plaza Hotel in 1984. Behind the hotel is the Times Building, white with arched windows, the last vestige of "newspaper row" as it stood in the early 1900s. The Times Building and its annex were renovated in 1978 and 1979. Less fortunate was the Metropolitan Building, at left under the municipal clock tower, which was just beginning to fall victim to the wrecking ball. The parking lot in the foreground would become the Federal Reserve Bank in 1973. In 1964, Minneapolis won its second All-American City award in a dozen years, on the strength of twelve new high-rise apartments for low-income elderly people, expansion of the Minneapolis Auditorium, the beginning of the skyway system, the previous year's opening of the Tyrone Guthrie Theater, and the Gateway redevelopment.

1964—1985

Challenge and Change

Ervin Gaines was an Easterner who came to the Midwest and made sure, by his presence and his actions, that life would not be dull out here on the prairie. He was described as quiet, but he was earnest, and could fight hard—some said too hard—for his beliefs. He wasn't afraid of adversity, as he demonstrated when he took a job heading a library that had financial and political troubles. Nor was he afraid of the future, for he had seen some of its push-button technology and was sure it could be made to work for libraries. He understood that libraries had to fit in with changes in the world, suggesting, for example, that the wide availability of television and of paperback books meant that libraries could concentrate less on escape reading and more on non-fiction.

But most of all, Ervin Gaines was a man who was not afraid to express himself. Although his speech was measured, genteel, and articulate, when he was finished, you knew he had spoken.

During his ten years as librarian in Minneapolis, Gaines managed to arrive in the midst of a controversy over his qualifications, and then to participate heartily in controversies over pornography, racial attitudes, dirty words, revolutionary talk, and the city's relationship with the county. When he left, he sailed into another storm within his new library, attracted to turmoil like a kid to a fire.

Like two of his most illustrious predecessors—Hosmer and Countryman—Gaines was not educated as a librarian. His background

Minneapolis Public Library photograph

Ervin Gaines became the director of the Minneapolis Public Library in 1964. He saw the library as an information center where citizens and businesses could keep up with the bewildering proliferation of new knowledge and ideas. "The public library," Gaines wrote, "has become in our time the major, if not the sole, information resource for the average citizen."

was a blend of scholarship and practical management experience. He had three degrees in English literature from Columbia University, and taught there from 1946 to 1953. Finding teaching too restrictive, he went to Europe, working with a radio service in Germany until he came back to start a personnel training job with a Connecticut electronics firm. From there he became a management consultant in New York City, and found himself doing a personnel study for the Boston Public Library. After the study was completed, Boston offered him a job as personnel director. He jumped at it, seeing it as an opportunity to combine his interests in books and in dealing with people. Gaines stayed in Boston for six years, developing a rather tough reputation for dealing with unproductive staff members. While working with the library, he was elected to the school board in the suburb of Boston where he and his family lived.

When this New York City native came to Minneapolis in 1964, he was forty-seven years old. The board considered his experience ideal, but almost didn't hire him because of his lack of academic library training. A question arose at the time of his hiring as to whether the Minneapolis library could qualify for federal funding if the head librarian did not have a library degree. With money tight at home, the Minneapolis library was looking for funding from any source that seemed even slightly promising. A small bit of federal money was becoming available to libraries, but the state agency that disbursed the money said that, to qualify, a library must have a director with academic library training. Some members of the library board thought the board should ask the state to change its rules, although the Friends of the Public Library didn't like that, nor did the state's professional library schools and organizations. The issue might not have mattered much, since one state official said the money available to Minneapolis wasn't much to begin with, and that the library might not be awarded it anyway because the library was already well supported. Still, Minneapolis Mayor Arthur Naftalin said that, although he had no objection to Gaines, he wanted to be assured the city library would not lose federal funding with Gaines as director. There were some suggestions that Gaines be hired as a consultant while he earned his library degree, with Margaret Mull serving as director in the meantime.

Gaines, worried by the split on the board and by the lack of warmth he felt from Minnesota's professional library community, announced in early June he was reversing his decision to accept the Minneapolis post. The city's newspaper mourned the loss of Gaines, saying the state should be more flexible, and that in a library the size of Minneapolis's, where many administrators already had library degrees, the director should not be required to have one as well. The library board's finance chairman, Bruce D. Smith, the man who would soon replace Kenneth Backstrom as board president, flew to Boston to talk things over with

Gaines. After he assured Gaines that the board would take full responsibility for any loss of funding, Gaines once again agreed to take the job, starting in August 1964.

Gaines came to a town where, the *Minneapolis Tribune* said, the library was in bad straits, with costs rising, service dropping, and the tax base falling, making money scarce. In addition, library board members were bickering among themselves, and the public was generally apathetic about the whole system, the paper said.[1]

This was a challenge, indeed. By the time Gaines left, however, things would be different.

But along the way there were bumps. Gaines was said to be a man who didn't talk passionately but felt deeply. Yet he was hardly timid or retiring. In a 1966 letter to the city's Capital Long-Range Improvements Committee asking for funding for branch expansion, Gaines said, "The neglect of public library facilities in this city falls just short of scandalous."[2] Some city officials, feeling they were being browbeaten, took umbrage at this observation. *The Minneapolis Star*, however, backed Gaines up, saying that while the paper didn't admire his tact, he was, in fact, correct. The last new branch built had been Linden Hills in 1931. The *Star's* editorial said the library should be given more money so it could begin to catch up.[3]

In 1967, Gaines jumped into an argument over another hot topic: sex. At an American Library Association convention in San Francisco, Gaines proposed that major libraries build collections of current pornography so future scholars could understand its meaning and role in our culture. "So persistent an art form as pornography deserves to have its better forms represented for historical purposes," Gaines told the group. "Pornography must be important or it would not be so prevalent. It has some meaning in our lives that we do not understand. Some libraries had better begin to collect it so that it can be preserved for future scholars."[4]

While this was not a major proposal (and in fact a sociologically and historically sound one), it was bound to cause some friction. A *Minneapolis Star* editorial, thinking about the trouble the courts had been having defining pornography, said rather jocularly, "At last we may find out what pornography is. Pornography will be whatever is placed in the pornography collection of a public library."[5] One reader didn't find the issue so funny, saying in a letter to the editor, "Such amoral thinking has no place in Minneapolis library policy. Gaines needs to be relieved before he can do more damage to our youth and community."[6]

The most serious flap came in the fall of 1970. Tensions in the country were high, dissent over the Vietnam War was fragmenting and polarizing society, people were clashing over approaches to government and private lives, and Spiro Agnew had been loosed upon the world. In September, library material that Minneapolis's conservative mayor, Charles Stenvig, considered objectionable was brought to his attention. An acquaintance of the mayor had discovered that underground newspapers were available to readers in the Linden Hills branch, and that poetry containing four-letter words was on the shelves of a junior high school library that the Minneapolis library used to operate, but that was now run by the school itself. Before a meeting of the board of estimate and taxation that was considering library funding, Stenvig questioned the library's selection policy and threatened that no money would be coming from the city until he was assured of a tighter selection process. "I don't care if a person can go buy this garbage, but I don't want my tax money spent to have this on the library shelves," Stenvig said, holding up an underground paper. These "underground papers" were counter-culture publications with a very open attitude toward sex and a very critical, sometimes violent, attitude toward the government and "establishment" society. They often contained advertising for sexual material and services and photographs of sexual acts, and vituperative criticism of government policy and officials, sometimes advocating violent overthrow. "I don't want my kids subjected to this—it's filth," Stenvig said.[7]

Gaines defended the library material, saying, "I will not remove a book because it has some dirty words." As for the revolutionary material, Gaines said the library had always carried such fare, and many of these words could be found now in the central library. "I refer to Thomas Paine," Gaines said.[8] At a special library board meeting held October 8, at which supporters of both sides of the controversy were heard from, Gaines further defended carrying the underground papers. "A library worth its name must be a repository of information about the major controversies of society. . . . The great strength of the underground press is that it reports events and opinions not easily obtained in other places. The library would be poorer without them."[9] Martina Brown, head of the history department, where most of the underground papers were kept, agreed. "Not to include these papers would be a great disservice to future historians," she said, for they gave a unique view of young people and their opinions.[10] Dan Teisberg, head of the literature department, added, "If people pick up a book and find it objectionable, they can do what I do. They can close it and bring it back to the library."[11]

The controversy raised the question of book selection policy, and Gaines explained that department heads made recommendations on what books and material in their area should be purchased. The staff tried to read reviews and descriptions of the material before it was obtained, but very few books were read in their entirety before being placed on the shelves. The library's small staff could not possibly examine the large number of new books and other material added to the library each year, Gaines said. This explanation of the selection process did not satisfy the mayor, but a policy announced in the newspaper on October 25 helped to blunt his criticism. Gaines said the library had formalized its practice of handling underground papers: they would be removed from the open shelves; a patron would have to ask for them, and only adults would be allowed to read them. The policy didn't specify at what age a person was considered an adult, and Gaines left that up to the discretion of the staff member, which would allow for some flexibility in the policy. Twenty-four underground papers were kept on this basis, including *The Village Voice, The East Village Other, Rolling Stone,* the *Berkeley Barb, Muhammed Speaks, Black Panther,* and a local magazine called *Hundred Flowers.*

The conflict spurred interesting discussion and pointed out what current library director Joseph Kimbrough calls the liberal attitude of Minneapolis people, who wouldn't stand for censorship. It also brought again to public light Ervin Gaines's libertarian view of free expression. Gaines was an outspoken supporter of free speech, and participated in public debates in Minneapolis in opposition to an antipornography bill that had been introduced in the state legislation. He was a member of the Minnesota Civil Liberties Union and chairman of its Freedom of Expression Committee, as well as chairman of the Intellectual Freedom Committee of the American Library Association. His view of intellectual freedom got him into yet another controversy in 1973. In a book review, he discussed the subject of black people's alleged genetic inferiority. Two recent books had gathered information about learning ability, and had advanced the theory that not all learning differences between blacks and whites could be explained by cultural and physical environment. The books stated that genetic differences also had to be considered. Gaines said these books should be taken seriously and their research examined, for if this genetic difference was correct, we should know about it and work with it, rather than try other social approaches that might end in just more frustration. Gaines didn't accept the genetic-difference theory, but said the theory should be given intellectual consideration. Some local residents objected, saying Gaines was racist. The biggest problem came the following year, when Gaines was being considered to head the Cleveland Public Library. Cleveland's black community wanted his views examined very carefully; his appointment there was postponed while the issue simmered.

In at least one other area, Gaines was a straight speaker. For as long as there had been a public library, an argument had burned over people who used the library less for reading than for simply getting in out of the weather. The poor, the dispossessed, the dispirited often came to the library just to have some place to go. Some people called them bums and winos and said they should be chased out. Others were frightened by these drifters, either for themselves or for their children.

Gratia Countryman had wanted to reach out to some of these people who had more time than money on their hands. She saw in them potential readers who might be uplifted by the library's treasures. She made sure they washed their hands before they used the books, but she felt that those who behaved had a place in the library. But there had been, as there continue to be, some problems—"improper use of the restroom," sexual advances and harassment, and drinking. Some mornings the janitors picked up dozens of empty liquor and wine bottles in and around the library.

In 1974, Gaines was asked about these unemployed people who came into the library mostly to sit and get out of the rain. "Why shouldn't they?" he replied directly. [12] When he had been hired ten years earlier, a reporter asked him about the problem of the "seedy old men" hanging out in the library. He replied that it didn't seem to him a problem, as long as the men behaved and followed the rules of the library. He said more problems in libraries were caused by children than by older people, yet no one suggested that children be excluded.

The situation has remained the same for one hundred years. Some library patrons are still bothered by the ragged people who find refuge in the library. The library's tradition includes them, and the library's location downtown almost invites them. Some come to read, passing the time, escaping, perhaps improving themselves. Some come to sleep in a dry and warm setting. Some come to lift purses and wallets that aren't carefully watched, and some come to leer at women. Since 1970, a full-time police officer has been on hand at the central library to control things, and those who are caught violating the rules against drinking and drunkenness or disorderly conduct and abuse are expelled. But Joseph Kimbrough, the current library director, feels as Gaines did that anyone who behaves, regardless of the conditions of her or his life or clothing, may come to the library.

Gaines saw the public library as more than a repository of books, more than a warm and dry place. He saw it as an information center. This wasn't a new perception in library thinking, certainly. What *was* new was the pace of change in the world surrounding the library. Things were changing fast in the 1960s, as they had been since the industrial revolution more than one hundred years before. But the speed of change and development was itself increasing, so that innovations and discoveries, new techniques and problems, piled in upon one another so quickly it was hard to keep track of them. Things were jumping enough in the sixties at the dawn of the space age; through the seventies and eighties the mirrors and magic hats would whirl at ever-more-dazzling rates. Gaines felt the library should help people keep up. It should be a repository for the mountains of information being generated, and a guide to help people get answers from that information.

By 1968, Gaines saw people using the library differently than they had in the past. There was more interest in magazines and current reports, with frequent requests for material on topical issues such as race relations. People wanted current information, to be on top of what was happening now. Keeping alert to contemporary issues would help change the library's traditional image as a conservative institution, Gaines said. Reference questions were up, with nine hundred thousand requests logged, ranging from the light ("How do you address an Italian countess in conversation?") to the practical ("Can one take a pet cat into Canada?") to the seriously academic and technical. People were using the electronic media more than ever, with film and record circulation way up. In 1968, 1.2 million people saw library films—twice the 1966 number—either by checking them out or by attending showings at the libraries. Two years later, reference questions topped one million, and Gaines wrote, "The public library has become in our time the major, if not the sole, informational resource of the average citizen."[13]

But it was not just the average citizen asking questions. More than ten percent of the reference questions in 1968 had gone to the business and economics department, and many were highly technical and time-consuming to answer. The service was obviously valuable to businesses in town, and Gaines wanted to explore the feasibility of increasing that service. By 1970 the groundwork was done, and beginning April 1, a fee-based research service for business was begun, called "Search and Deliver." For an hourly rate, library staff would search the available literature for information on any topic required by the client. The city's chamber of commerce helped sponsor and publicize the service, which started slowly but grew steadily. The service was used primarily by the many Twin Cities businesses in the food industry, most often on questions about current market information. By 1972, the service logged five hundred hours of personalized, confidential research annually. Renamed INFORM in 1972, this service continues to prosper, and now includes on-line computer research capabilities.

The year 1972 also saw the opening of another specialized information service dealing with a current issue of immense importance. The Environmental Conservation Library, going under the acronym ECOL, was opened in April with speeches by naturalist Sigurd Olson and Minnesota Department of Natural Resources Commissioner Robert Herbst. ECOL had first been proposed in 1967, when Gaines suggested to the Athenaeum board that it might want to work on a special collection dealing with the variety of environmental crises coming to public attention and with the science of ecology then becoming popular. The Athenaeum agreed, and worked on a proposal for a collection that would "focus on the natural resources of Minnesota and the surrounding area, with emphasis on the impact of man's actions upon these resources."[14] The Athenaeum's board members raised private money from local businesses and leaders, and succeeded in landing an annual

Challenge and Change

The Minneapolis Public Library responded to the environmental crises coming to public attention in the late 1960s and early 1970s by opening a special collection in 1972 called the Environmental Conservation Library, or ECOL. At the suggestion of librarian Ervin Gaines, the Athenaeum took on the project, raising private and government money to fund the collection. The Athenaeum's sponsorship of ECOL would have pleased Dr. Kirby Spencer, the dentist and scientist who was the Athenaeum's prime benefactor 102 years earlier, and who wanted the Athenaeum's collection to deal with serious and consequential subjects. Shown cutting the ribbon at the ECOL opening April 16, 1972, is Mrs. Clara C. Lyman, president of the Athenaeum board, with Minneapolis Public Library Director Ervin Gaines looking on.

state appropriation for the project as well. Located at the central library, ECOL had three thousand books by the end of 1972, along with articles, reports, government documents, and newsletters of environmental agencies and groups. Material on current topics was gathered into subject packets for quick reference. When government reports on environmental questions were issued, ECOL often collected and kept the documentation, as with a study of copper-nickel mining in Minnesota. ECOL also published special catalogs, such as a directory of state environmental organizations in 1978. Over the years, the collection has served as a statewide reference resource, enhancing Gaines's view of the Minneapolis Public Library as a reference backup for all Minnesota libraries.

"America moves on information, and key units in the information system are the public libraries," Gaines said.[15] He foresaw that access to information and the ability to assimilate, connect, and act upon it would be the key to running a successful democratic society. As the world became more specialized and complex, it would be crucial that the people have easy access to reliable information so they could retain their knowledge of that world and their power to direct it. What was needed, Gaines said, was "solid information and responsible, respected librarian specialists to dig it out and put it in the hands of patrons."[16] Gaines didn't fully trust the mass media to bring information to people. He felt mass media, such as newspapers and television, simplified issues so much that the information was shallow and narrowly selected. He wanted people to be able to go to the original sources of information, through their libraries. Because information was crucial to self-government, and because collecting that knowledge and making it available to the public was more expensive than many libraries could afford, Gaines, like many in the library field, pushed for state and federal aid to libraries. He said society put a disproportionate amount of money into schools, where a small percentage of its population was educated, and not enough into libraries and other resources for adult and continuing education, which serviced the bulk of the population. To share informational as well as monetary resources, he proposed a three-level system of libraries, with local libraries being backed up by larger regional libraries, and with the whole system being backed up by a single, well-equipped state library. That main facility, of course, would have been the Minneapolis Public Library. He began talking in language that has since become common, saying central data bases needed to be collected for quick reference on a variety of subjects. "Press buttons and get actions," he said in 1968. "Computers are heady stuff, but we have to realize that books are not intrinsically precious."[17] The library of the future would be at least partly electronic.

The library in other ways made information more accessible to people during Gaines's time as librarian. A Municipal Information

Library was reinstituted in 1972, housed in city hall and assisted by city funds. The library's entire collection was slowly switched from the Dewey decimal classification system to the Library of Congress system. A machine-assisted research service, which allowed patrons computer time for information searches, was begun. The *Minneapolis Tribune* and *The Minneapolis Star* were indexed for the first time, beginning in 1970. And cassette tapes were brought into use during the 1970s. Gaines was so convinced that the business of brokering information was going to be a more and more important part of the library's role that he repeatedly asked the board to change the library's name to the Minneapolis Public Library and Information Center. Some called this a cosmetic and trivial change, but to Gaines it represented an attitude about the world. The change was finally approved in 1974, the year Gaines left the library.

The library would have to be two things if it was going to get all this information to people: solvent and accessible. This would require new funding, and new life in the branch system.

The funding came first. The years 1964 and 1965 were bleak, with cutbacks in book purchases, services, and hours. Then, in 1966, another levy referendum was put before the public, and this time it went over. A citizens' group called Citizens Organized for the Preservation and Expansion of Library Services helped push the millage campaign. Signs were placed on buses and buildings, there were radio and TV ads, brochures and flyers. *The Minneapolis Star* ran a week-long series of editorials supporting the increase and printed pictures showing all kinds of people—old and young, businesspeople and church groups—using the library. On September 13, two thirds of the voters said yes to raising the levy limit for the library from four to six mills. That year, with the prospect of more funds on the way, fifteen thousand books were added to the collection, compared with only two thousand the year before. The library's future looked better. Apparently, its reputation with the voting public had improved after two previously unsuccessful efforts to raise the library's funding limit.

One way of saving money on book acquisitions was to make use of paperback books. In 1963, the year the Tyrone Guthrie Theater opened, the library anticipated a demand for the plays the Guthrie was staging and purchased several dozen paperback copies of *Hamlet, The Miser, Death of a Salesman,* and *Three Sisters.* In 1964, duplicates of the year's most popular books were provided in inexpensive paperback editions: the Warren Commission's Report on John Kennedy's assassination, Barry Goldwater's *Where I Stand,* Minneapolitan Charles W. Bailey's and Fletcher Knebel's chiller *Seven Days in May,* and John Updike's *The Centaur,* which won the National Book Award. The Guthrie's second season of plays was also available in paperback: *Saint Joan, Volpone, Henry V,* and *The Glass Menagerie.* By 1965, paperback editions of children's books were showing up in the branches and in the bookmobile. This allowed the library to buy several copies of books of passing, rather than timeless, interest without seriously denting the book budget. Generally, by the time the books were worn out, so was their popularity.

With the library on more solid footing, thoughts of strengthening the branches became more realistic. Gaines was interested in fewer, but better-stocked, branches, and the idea of regional branches was developed. When Hennepin County decided to build a large branch

Photograph by Rapson A.I.A. Architects, Inc.

The Southeast Community Library at 1222 Fourth Street Southeast, near Dinkytown in the university area. This building was converted from a credit union office and opened as a branch library in 1967. In the early 1980s, this branch was a candidate for closing if the library's budget had to be deeply cut.

The sculpture by Donald Celender inside the Nokomis library captures in metal and water the feeling of nearby Minnehaha Falls.

for the southern suburbs, Minneapolis decided to look north for a large branch to serve as a regional center. The idea for a Gratia Countryman branch in the south part of the city was put on the back burner, then dropped. City officials approved a new branch at Thirty-fourth Avenue and Fifty-first Street South to replace the Longfellow branch, but the first new branch to open would be neither north nor south, but near the university. The State Capital Credit Union Building at 1222 Fourth Street Southeast came up for sale, and planning officials found it ideal to house a library. So on December 29, 1966, the building was purchased for four hundred and thirty thousand dollars and remodeling began. The four-year-old building was a one-story affair, with a basement, a block from the heart of Dinkytown. It opened as the new Southeast library on December 26, 1967, replacing the old Pillsbury branch, which was then closed and eventually sold. Southeast was a pleasant, small facility, with a good collection catering to the student interests of the area. A collection of protest books was displayed there in 1969, for example. A sunny corner was devoted to a wide collection of periodicals, which were well read. In 1970, a consortium of private environmental interest groups leased space in the library's basement and set up an Environmental Resources and Information Center in an agreement that proved helpful to both parties.

The year 1967 was a good one for branch development. Construction began on a new Nokomis branch, and the city approved construction of a North Regional branch and a branch in South Minneapolis at Lyndale and Minnehaha Parkway. The Nokomis branch would serve the old Longfellow area, a solid part of town whose residents had good income and education. The new branch opened in September 1968, and immediately doubled Longfellow's circulation. Nokomis was the first library branch to be constructed by the library system in thirty-seven years, since Linden Hills in 1931. The long drought was over. The one-story building was small, with a low tepee design to follow the Longfellow theme of Hiawatha. The tepee area in the center provided a loft that became popular for children's story hours. The branch was decorated with a "wind and water chime" that caught, in bronze, brass, and water, the image of nearby Minnehaha Falls. The artist was Donald Celender.

The next new branch opened in a book-hungry part of town. The area of South Minneapolis near Minnehaha Creek and Lake Harriet, while not as fashionable as Kenwood or the Lake Minnetonka settlements, was a well-to-do section. Students at Washburn High School were derisively called "cake eaters" by rival students at other city schools. Income and education here were high, and in the past some of the busiest bookmobile stops had been in this area. When the new Washburn branch opened, it broke records. The building had 14,451 square feet of space and a collection of eighteen thousand books—but that wasn't enough.

Minneapolis Tribune photograph, 1968

The Nokomis Community Library, at 5100 Thirty-fourth Avenue South. When this branch opened in 1968, it was the first new building constructed by the library system since 1931.

Soon after Washburn opened in September 1970, calls went out to other branches for more books. Phonograph records and children's books had been cleaned out almost immediately. In its first full year of operation—1971—Washburn circulated two hundred and seventy-three thousand books, the highest total ever for a branch. The building, including land, books, and furnishings, cost seven hundred and thirty thousand dollars, of which one hundred and nine thousand dollars came from federal funding. The one-story branch features an original millstone from an early Minneapolis mill, donated by General Mills, the corporate descendant of the Washburn-Crosby Milling Company. The opening of Washburn corrected the situation of not having a library branch from Thirty-eighth Street to the southern city limits between Lakes Harriet and Nokomis.

The next branch had been a long time coming. First proposed in 1964, North Regional didn't open until 1971. Site selection and fund-

Challenge and Change

The Washburn Community Library, 5244 Lyndale Avenue South, opened in 1970, and immediately began breaking circulation records. In the early 1980s it still led all branches in the amount of material its patrons checked out.

ing were debated and delayed for several years for what was to be the largest branch and the second most important library in the city. Both Gaines and the library board felt it was important to place this major resource in the northern part of Minneapolis, which housed some of the city's poorest residents and which had been hit by racial disturbances during the turbulent sixties. Gaines pointed out in 1968 what most people in Minneapolis already knew: the majority of cultural amenities in Minneapolis had always gone to the southern half of the city, making the north in some ways only a dormitory for workers. This "cultural vacuum" in the north, Gaines said, "fostered the ghetto in the first place and will continue to suck into itself corrosive and destructive forces."[18] A new library facility would be a step in the right direction, he said.

The building was finally sited on Lowry Avenue North between Fremont and Girard avenues, and opened October 24, 1971. To attract residents' attention to the opening and the new facility, twenty-five thousand brochures were mailed to the library's neighbors on the North

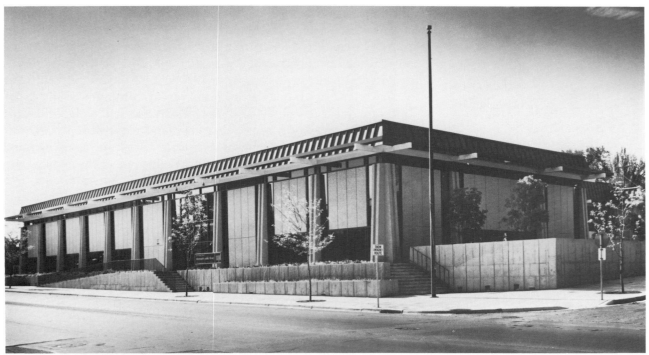

The North Regional Library, the largest library in the system outside of the main library downtown. Located at 1315 Lowry Avenue North, the library was placed in North Minneapolis in a conscious effort to help redress the imbalance of cultural amenities between North and South Minneapolis. The building opened in 1971.

Side, a technique that had been used on a smaller scale for the opening of the Washburn branch. North Regional had thirty thousand books, and space for fifty thousand. A two-story building with a dramatic white front on Lowry, it immediately attracted patrons, building a strong circulation that in its first year doubled the previous year's total of all North Side libraries. The bookmobiles and their collection were soon centered at North Regional instead of downtown, adding to the activity of the branch. Films, records, and cassettes did a brisk business here. The branch also became a magnet for neighborhood kids. Some came to devour the children's collection and some came, unfortunately, to vandalize the building. Washburn, too, experienced vandalism, a problem that has always stretched across societal lines.

The North Regional branch has one feature that makes it unique. A lifelong Minneapolis resident and first-class bookman, J. Harold Kittleson, had, in 1969, donated to the library five hundred rare books by and about New England authors. Included in the collection are many

In this 1975 photograph, a member of the Minnesota Weaver's Guild demonstrates a spinning wheel at the second annual Northside Art Fair, held at North Regional Library.

first editions of Emerson, Thoreau, Dickinson, Whittier, Longfellow, and Lowell. It is a treasure that reaffirms in Minneapolis the New England spirit of learning and letters that so many of the original members of the Athenaeum had brought West with them. Kittleson, a book buyer for Powers department store from 1930 to 1945 who served with the Library Friends and later on the library board, continued to add to the collection over the years. The library board decided to place this collection in the new North Regional Library, and designed a special room on the second floor that replicates the study of a nineteenth century scholar. Called the Emerson room, it remains one of the gems of the library system, and is open by appointment to scholars, students, and historians. The room now houses nearly five thousand volumes and related material in its Nineteenth Century American Studies Collection.

The last branch to open during Gaines's administration was Northeast, at 2200 Central Avenue Northeast, replacing the old Central Avenue branch, a Carnegie library built in 1915. Another one-story building, designed to fit the craftsmanlike tone of "Nordeast," the library

The Ralph Waldo Emerson room at North Regional Library. This replica of a nineteenth century study contains the library's Nineteenth Century American Studies Collection, including books and memorabilia from many of New England's giants.

Photograph by Dale Peterson, Minneapolis, 1971

The interior of the North Regional Library, with a spacious two-story room housing books, magazines, and areas for reading and study. At the far end of the building is the children's collection, with a circular set of risers for story hours. On the second floor is a community room and the Emerson room.

opened January 21, 1973, with a speech by Congressman Don Fraser. The branch has 15,275 square feet of space, room for thirty thousand books, and a fireplace to link it with the branch buildings of the past.

A similar branch—East Lake—opened on the South Side in May 1976 under the new administration of director Joseph Kimbrough. A replacement for an older branch of the same name, the single-story building at 2727 East Lake Street has fifteen thousand square feet of space and thirty-seven thousand books. East Lake joined the nearby Minnehaha Mall, along with Target and Super Valu stores, in bringing new growth to an aging area.

The next replacement branch was at Webber Park, where the building, formerly shared with the park board, was becoming an antique. A new branch was built near the old one, at 4310 Webber

Challenge and Change

Photograph by Les Turnau

The Northeast Community Library, 2200 Central Avenue Northeast. The branch opened in 1973, the last branch to open under chief librarian Ervin Gaines.

Photograph by John Croft, 1976

The East Lake Community Library opened in 1976. Located at 2727 East Lake Street, it joined several other new buildings in the area in an effort to revitalize an aging business community.

Parkway, and opened October 12, 1980. Because a Hennepin County regional library was planned for the nearby northern suburbs, an area that used to send many patrons to Webber, the new branch is a very small building—four thousand square feet with a collection of eleven thousand volumes. It cost three hundred thousand dollars and opened before all its permanent furniture was in place to a very eager and loyal clientele.

The most recent addition to the Minneapolis system, the new Walker library, differs radically from its neoclassical, 1911 predecessor. The replacement building, at 2880 Hennepin Avenue, is just across the street from the original building, but you might not know it at first glance. The new Walker is underground. Building below ground level was a decision made to maximize the use of the space at the site, but it also provides energy efficiency through the earth's natural insulation and temperature-moderation properties, and it makes the reading rooms more soundproof. Opened for service on February 23, 1981, the building's two below-ground levels provide eighteen thousand five hundred square feet of space and house a collection of forty-six thousand volumes. The building and land cost $2.3 million. The only parts of the library on ground level are a bus shelter and the entrances. The "minus one" level houses community meeting rooms, while the "minus

The new Webber Park Library, at 4310 Webber Parkway, opened in 1980. This building replaced the old field house, which the library had shared with the park board.

Challenge and Change

Opened in 1981, the new Walker Community Library was the first
earth-sheltered building constructed by the city of Minneapolis and one
of the few public libraries in the country to use underground
construction. A sunken courtyard (at left in photo) provides an outdoor
reading area that is relatively quiet in this busy Uptown area at
Hennepin and Lake in South Minneapolis. At grade level, a landscaped
plaza and parking lot remain as open spaces over the roof of the
building. The new library is directly across Hennepin from the original
Walker library, which was built on land donated by T. B. Walker and
which served the community for seventy years.

two" level is the library proper. A sunken, outdoor courtyard, entered
from the lower-level reading room, provides abundant natural light.
An angled mirror also brings light from the surface into the bottom
level. The building attracted national attention for its design, by Minneapolis architect David Bennett of Myers and Bennett Architects.

Some library-goers no doubt miss the older buildings—the stately Pillsbury branch and the solid Walker. But the system had to grow,
consolidate, and change. Nor has the city lost all the old library buildings
to demolition crews. The original North branch stayed open for six
years after the coming of North Regional—until architects told the
library that it could cost one million dollars to bring the old building
up to code. North branch was closed in 1977; but it and the old East
Lake, Walker, and Pillsbury branches still stand and are now preserved
either in the hands of private businesses or public agencies.

By the Minneapolis Public Library's centennial year, the system consists of fifteen facilities: the central library, North Regional Library, and thirteen community libraries (East Lake, Franklin, Hosmer, Linden Hills, Nokomis, Northeast, Pierre Bottineau, Roosevelt, Southeast, Sumner, Walker, Washburn, and Webber Park). The system is a mix of old and new, although even the old were remodeled during the 1970s to provide handicapped access. Each building has its own distinct physical character, suiting the flavor of the neighborhood it serves.

Not all activity was centered in the branches during Ervin Gaines's time; changes occurred at the main library downtown, as well. In 1966, the Athenaeum enlarged its space on the fourth floor, making more secure storage area for the rare books and providing a comfortable reading room and display area. The strength and depth of the Athenaeum's contribution to the library was illustrated in the late sixties and early seventies, when Native Americans became more aware of the need to understand their people's history and heritage, and when society at large became more interested in the nation's nearly forgotten people. The Athenaeum's collection of books and material on American Indians, built over more than a century, began seeing more use. Also in 1970, in the aftermath of the National Guard shootings of protesting students at Kent State University, James Bowdoin's 1770 account of the Boston Massacre (in which five colonial protestors were killed by British soldiers) was used frequently by the public in the Athenaeum.

In 1967, less scholarly books than this were collected in what was known as the Popular Library. This collection, which replaced a reading and smoking lounge on the second floor just east of the escalator, represented, in a way, the library giving in to public taste while still hoping to do a touch of uplifting of reading habits. The Popular Library took the best sellers of the day, along with categories of books that always enjoyed high circulations, and put them in one place, easily accessible to the public. Here were five thousand volumes for recreational reading—current books, perennial favorites, science fiction, mysteries, adventures, romances, historical novels. These books, so well loved by the people whose taxes built the library, had always made some librarians grimace. But the staff wasn't giving up entirely. The Popular Library would be salted, almost subversively, with quality. One librarian wrote, "Care has been taken to give it some depth by providing classics in attractive editions, Pulitzer and Nobel Prize winning books, landmarks in social, political or ethical thought, and both background and current material on contemporary problems, trends and events."[19] It worked. The good stuff held its own with lighter fare, and the Popular Library remains a very interesting and well-used collection. In 1983 it was moved to a more central location, smack in the middle of the first floor.

In 1971, a new gadget appeared at the central library. Detection equipment was installed at the first floor checkout positions to cut down on book theft. Gradually, books were fitted with a magnetic tape that would set off a beeper in the electronic detector if the book hadn't gone through the checkout process. The library staff was worried that patrons might resent this system, but most seemed to accept it with no problem, and many who did speak up said it was a good way to protect the public's investment in the library.

Late in the sixties, books and other material on the explosive issues of the day were, of course, well used. Race relations, the draft, the war, urban riots, drugs, hippies, politics, Martin Luther King, and Robert Kennedy were all frequent topics of information requests. In the children's departments, more interest was noticed in black history, integration and its problems, and in biographies of black leaders. In 1969, an Afro-American room was opened at the Hosmer branch, a Native American Collection was centered at Franklin, and the Sumner branch continued its long-term practice of gathering material on minorities. These collections had some success in attracting readers, but not as much as the librarians had hoped. They were still having trouble making library patrons out of inner-city residents. Gaines said in 1973 that the library's lack of success in reaching the so-called culturally deprived of the urban centers was a reflection of nationwide experience. "Watching the social efforts from Minneapolis we have come reluctantly to the conclusion that reading and use of libraries is a personal choice which is not easily induced by techniques available to libraries," he said. "Libraries do not direct social and cultural change; they respond to it."[20] This must have been a rather hard admission for someone sitting in Gratia Countryman's chair to make. Librarians have to believe in the educational power of their libraries; if they don't, they might as well run amusement arcades. But in this situation, libraries seemed unable to help the nation ease a disturbing social dilemma. Some said it was the entire culture that needed changing, not just those people at the bottom of the scale, and that therefore it was a job beyond a library's capabilities. Still the admission of failure must have been hard for Minneapolis librarians. The social intervention that Gratia Countryman had proclaimed in her first year as librarian was over. The library still wanted to be involved in people's lives, but the idea of taking the lead in changing those lives was receding, accompanied by many of the idealistic, but perhaps unrealistic, notions of the sixties.

But service was still there. In 1973, the Friends of the Minneapolis Public Library began an outreach reading program, spreading gifts of books among poor families. With the help of the Friends, the library also started a program called Service to the Homebound. In this program, volunteers brought books to people who couldn't leave home. The volunteers got to know their patrons' reading tastes and delivered a selection of books, including special requests, once or twice a month. The person confined to home due to health or age had the world of books brought to her or his chairside table, and the volunteer received the satisfaction of doing something useful for another. By 1978, in these and other programs, the Friends and the volunteers they supervised logged seven thousand hours in service to the library. The next year, with government money tightening as the city and state felt the pinch of recession, the Friends took over the library's volunteer services entirely, directing the homebound program and recruitment for library volunteers. This freed a full-time library staff person to return to other duties.

As Gaines had forseen, the library was serving adults more and more. While general circulation slowly increased, juvenile circulation and bookmobile patronage declined. This was due partly to the school system strengthening its own libraries, and partly to a general increased emphasis on adult education.

There was one more good fight, one more raging controversy that nearly consumed the Minneapolis Public Library before Ervin Gaines left for Cleveland. This fight had a long history and an implacable demographic force behind it, and Gaines was only one of many combatants to become embroiled in it. This was the struggle between the Minneapolis Public Library and the Hennepin County Library.

The Hennepin County Library had been formed in 1922 as part of the Minneapolis system. It was one phase of the octopus outreach favored by Gratia Countryman. She served as librarian for both the city and the county, and for decades the city library board doubled as the county library board. The relationship was easy. The county library used the city library collection and had its office in the downtown building. The county's operation was much smaller than the city library, and although its logistical problems were made rather tough by the sheer mileage from Dayton to Bloomington, from the Crow River to the Minnesota, the system was easily run.

Then came the 1950s, and America's urban landscape shifted. The cities were being surrounded—by new governments, new ways of life, new powers, a new state of mind. The suburbs were in ascendancy. Once only satellites, parasites even, the suburbs were discovering a life of their own. The population rode tail-finned cars from the central cities to the broader back yards, newer houses, and more homogeneous social mix of the suburbs. There was rivalry, there was jealousy, there was competition for resources.

In Minneapolis, the city library began experiencing hard times while the county library system was booming. Circulation wavered and dropped in the city, while it grew in the county as surely as a maple. Money became scarce in the city, except for construction of the new central library building, while the legislature kept authorizing more

Minneapolis Public Library photograph, 1982

A Friends volunteer visits a Homebound client with a welcome supply of reading material.

and more taxing power for the county library system. The trend continued irresistibly, as more prime Hennepin County farmland turned into subdivisions and fewer people lived and paid taxes in the city. By the end of the 1960s, Hennepin County had surpassed Minneapolis in population and property valuation. The Hennepin County Library was straining under the old system that had given it birth. The child educated in the family business was threatening to take over the store.

And threat is the right word, for that was exactly how some city library people perceived it. The struggle between the two libraries had been heated for about twenty years, and positively ferocious for the last few. Several proposals had been advanced to merge the two systems, something the city library looked forward to the way Harvard would look forward to a merger with Yale.

Ervin Gaines stated the city's side of the problem simply. The struggle was symptomatic, he said, of the urban-suburban conflict happening nationwide. The central city had a diminishing tax base, but suburban residents still placed a heavy demand on city services and amenities, for most suburbanites still worked and played in the city. Unless it drew a financial contribution from the people of the suburbs for these services and amenities, the city could not make it. If the city folded, then the focus of the metropolitan area would be gone. To redress this imbalance, Gaines concluded, county residents would have to pay for the city library service they used.

The county's argument seemed equally clear, and it had a fine historic ring to it: "No taxation without representation." Through most of the struggle, the county had no representatives on the city library board, which, after all, decided county library policy. The county also argued that its own growing system reached more county residents than the Minneapolis Public Library, which admittedly had better resources. If the county's system was to continue to grow, county residents would have to put up the money—leaving them little to spare for the city's system.

The problem, so simply stated, should have had a simple solution. It didn't, partly because of territoriality, jealousy, politics, and the natural desire to look out for one's own. A partial solution would finally come in 1974, when both sides gave up a little and bowed to a less parochial authority.

Back in the early fifties, Hennepin County paid the city library thirty thousand dollars annually to cover the cost of service to county residents. In 1956, the Minneapolis library board hired a consultant, University of Minnesota professor Frederick Wezeman, to study the relationship of the two libraries. Wezeman said there should be closer cooperation between the two entities, and that the city should get more money from the county for library service. With city and county citizen input, a new committee was formed, chaired by Wayzata Mayor

H. O. Kallestad, to lobby in the legislature to allow the county more tax money for libraries, with some of that going to the city. In 1957, the committee succeeded. The county levy limit was raised to 2.5 mills for 1958 and 1959, with the proceeds from half-a-mill going to the city as reimbursement for its library services to county residents. In exchange for this support, the city library dropped its two-dollar library card fee for nonresidents. But problems remained. County librarian Helen Young warned Hennepin County to be careful. The county should not, she said, help the city finance capital expansion "unless a reciprocal capital construction program is planned for the county." She also believed that county representatives on the city library board were essential, "as the present situation of 'taxation without representation' cannot long continue."[21]

By 1958, county library circulation broke the one-million mark for the first time, and the system kept growing. In 1961, while city efforts to raise the levy limits for the Minneapolis Public Library failed, the legislature raised the county library levy to 3.5 mills, with the proceeds from 1 mill going to the city. An additional mill was added for a county building program in 1965, the same year a separate Hennepin County library board was finally created. The board included six members of Minneapolis's board and six members representing the county. Two years later, the board was reduced to nine members, with only three from Minneapolis—and the county levy was raised to 6.5 mills. Several studies that looked at library service in the metropolitan area were done during these years. One study suggested that the Hennepin County Library build three regional libraries to complement the smaller community libraries already in the system or planned for the future. Another set up a formula that would pay the Minneapolis library for service to county residents according to use. This formula resulted in the county paying the city three hundred eighty-seven thousand five hundred dollars in 1967 and four hundred ninety-eight thousand dollars in 1968. By 1970, when the county's bill for city library service for the following year was set at eight hundred and three thousand five hundred dollars, things started getting sticky.

In 1967, both library boards had agreed in principle that a merger of the two systems was a good idea. Gaines reiterated this idea in 1969; but by 1970, when prospects of a merger seemed imminent, the Minneapolis library began to retreat. Hennepin County had named Robert H. Rohlf director of its library system. A very capable librarian, Rohlf had worked for the Minneapolis library and was largely responsible for planning the new central building. Some Minneapolis board members now feared that a merged library, under the control of Hennepin County, would give the job of overall director to Rohlf, displacing Gaines. It was also feared that a merged library would not consider and serve the best interests of Minneapolis. So in 1971, the Minneapolis

Public Library opposed a move in the legislature, initiated by Hennepin County representatives, to merge the two systems, and the merger bill died in committee. Hennepin County's support of the merger bill caused suspicions and fear on the part of the Minneapolis people, and relationships began to deteriorate further, polarizing the two systems. The struggle continued over how much the county should pay the city, over whether county headquarters should stay in the downtown library, and over whether suburban residents should again pay for city library cards. The *Minneapolis Tribune* commented in an editorial, "As a result of the disagreement, residents of Hennepin County, including Minneapolis, are being treated to the spectacle of a feud between two library systems that ought to be serving city and suburbs jointly instead of trying to devise ways to penalize each other."[22]

Protracted negotiations continued throughout 1972 in what Gaines called the "Minneapolis-Hennepin County collision." It took a long time for the two sides to agree on the county's annual reimbursement to the city. The often-abrasive negotiations strained friendships in the Twin Cities librarian community and tarnished the public's view of the library system. Finally, in 1973, the sides separated physically; the Hennepin County Library moved its headquarters from the downtown Minneapolis library to the county's new regional library in Edina. Located near the Southdale shopping mall at Seventieth Street and Xerxes Avenue, the Southdale-Hennepin Area Library was the first of the county's three regional libraries. It opened in May, with fifty-nine thousand square feet of space, a futuristic inverted-pyramid architecture, one hundred and forty thousand books, and a great deal of audiovisual material. The move did not improve relations with the city, however. The 1974 negotiations over contract payments were just as tough as before. The county still wanted a merger, and the city wanted more money.

Finally, in the summer of 1974, the library war ended—"through what amounts to an admission of mutual defeat," according to *The Minneapolis Star.* The two sides agreed on a total payment of three hundred and fifty thousand dollars for 1974, from the county to the city for library service, and then agreed there would be no more such payments. In return for the city giving up the annual contract for reimbursement, the county agreed to give up its drive to merge the two systems. Both sides agreed to work together to find more sources of state and federal funding, to be shared through a metropolitan area library organization. Both the *Star* and *Tribune* editorial headlines used language from the Vietnam War to mark the agreement ("Library peace, 'with honor' " and "Libraries: Peace is at hand"), showing, in a gruesome way, how bitter the struggle had been. Hennepin County commissioner Thomas Ticen said, "It's a great day. For the first time we've eliminated the confrontation over a merger and we're not standing on either side of a line shooting at each other. The fight is over."[23]

The umbrella organization that would help assure library cooperation was MELSA, the Metropolitan Library Service Agency. It was established in 1969 to join nine library systems in the Twin Cities area in a service agreement. Under the agreement, the libraries provide reciprocal borrowing privileges and interlibrary loans, and share reference services. MELSA also helps disburse federal and state funds to metropolitan libraries. MELSA minimizes squabbling among libraries, and it provides tremendous service and convenience to library patrons. A person can check out a book from a St. Paul library and return it to a Shakopee library more than thirty miles and several governmental units away. A small library in a surburban community can draw on the resources of the Hennepin County, Minneapolis, and St. Paul library systems. Cooperation through MELSA is one of the things that ties a metropolitan area of such numerous and diverse political entities into one large collection of cultural resources.

By 1974, with the city-county battle over, Ervin Gaines was looking for a new challenge. He found it at the Cleveland Public Library, which was experiencing some of the same troubles Gaines had first encountered in Minneapolis. He was eager to do in Cleveland what he had done in Minneapolis. As he left town, the Minneapolis papers praised him for his work here, crediting him with eliminating library deficits, expanding service and collections, and improving facilities. There was an admiring tone in the papers toward this man, as he rode off to another trouble spot. He had been sometimes stubborn, but always thoughtful and dedicated to improving Minneapolis's library service.

After Gaines resigned on November 15, 1974, Mary L. Dyar, the associate librarian, was named interim director while a search for a new director was conducted. Dyar chose not to be a candidate for the job, and would retire in 1976.

One of the things the library board was looking for in a successor to Gaines was someone experienced in interlibrary cooperation. The battles with Hennepin County had, everyone hoped, come to an end, and MELSA was being looked on as an increasingly important part of the library's future. After some turbulent periods, during which the Minneapolis Public Library had belied the traditional staid, quiet image of a library, the person who now took over should be a bit of a politician, and should be able to cooperate rather than confront. That person was found at the Denver Public Library, where he had been the assistant librarian and director of public services since 1970.

He was Joseph Kimbrough, forty-five years old at the time he took over the Minneapolis Public Library and Information Center on May 15, 1975. A genial man with an easy laugh, he bears a striking resemblance, except for the beard he wears, to former President Jimmy Carter. A native of Kentucky, Kimbrough retains a hint of the

Minneapolis Public Library photograph

Mary Dyar, who served as interim director between Gaines and Kimbrough and as associate director under both.

stretched, Southern slowness in his voice. Kimbrough had a bachelor's degree in library science from Western Kentucky University in Bowling Green and a master's from Indiana University in Bloomington. He also studied library administration and management at the University of Maryland and Washington University in St. Louis. He began his library career as a shelver—the person who puts books back on the shelves after they're returned—and worked in seven academic and public libraries before coming to Minneapolis. Library board president Marie Goss said the library had heard of Kimbrough's reputation and invited him to apply. Before going to Denver, he had been librarian in Lansing, Michigan, for four years, and had worked in other Michigan libraries as well, so even though Minnesota put on one of its best January blizzards for him when he came to interview, he wasn't scared away.

Kimbrough said Gaines would be a tough act to follow, calling him "a giant in our profession." Kimbrough sees himself as a much less publicly visible person than Gaines, and less inclined to enter into discussions of issues and ideas. Although not a shy man, he doesn't feel at home in controversy, saying "I think more things get done in social settings than . . . around negotiating tables."[24] He says he gathered from his hiring that "a low-profile, ameliorating kind of a person was going to be appreciated around here" after the tumults of the past. Kimbrough does not label himself as an intellectual; pehaps because of that, he seems open and easily approachable.

Kimbrough's management style is to delegate authority and trust his staff to carry out library service. Recognizing that the library staff included a great many people with years—indeed, whole careers—of service to the Minneapolis library, Kimbrough wanted to involve them in decision making. One of his first moves was to have library administrators and department heads draw up goals and objectives for library service, so progress could be measured at the end of the year and service coordinated with overall aims.

"I'm an experimenter; I like trying out new ideas," Kimbrough says, adding that he's not frightened of failure. If one idea doesn't work, it should be dropped and something else given a chance. One of the ideas he brought with him from Denver was for a program of library-assisted independent study. With emphasis on adult education increasing, and with many people looking for new skills—from crafts to new careers— Kimbrough wanted to have the library help self-learners define their goals and direct their search for information. He didn't want librarians to be teachers, but facilitators. "Why pay someone to fix your TV when your librarian can help you find out how to do it yourself?" he asked in a newspaper interview.[25] By 1977, Learning Unlimited guided study programs were going in all community libraries, with people working on projects from high school equivalencies to Federal Communication Commission licenses. But the program never achieved the hoped-for participation of the public, and by 1980 it was abandoned, although the same sort of individual assistance is still available on a less formalized basis. Kimbrough recognized that Minneapolis has many other options available for informal education, so this program wasn't pushed beyond its need.

Some of the inner-city branches were having trouble getting adult programs going. The Hosmer branch reported in 1979 that a free showing of the television series "Roots," which the Friends had purchased and donated to the library, drew no one and was cancelled. A book discussion group met once, with participants active and expressing satisfaction, but no one returned for a second meeting. The old problem of trying to court an inner-city audience was felt again. Kimbrough, like Gaines, recognized that people can't be forced to use the library. "It's not a frustration, it's a fact of life," Kimbrough says. "The library is a middle-class institution."[26] The great bulk of library patrons are from the middle ranges of the socioeconomic scale, he says, with neither the very high nor the very low ends of the scale well represented. This doesn't mean that the library abandons the needs of any group, he says, again pointing out that the library can indirectly benefit the entire community. But, concludes Kimbrough, you can't kill yourself trying to reach everybody directly.

One 1979 program did reach a great many Twin Cities residents. "Minneapolis: Portrait of a Life Style" was a series of talks, tours, seminars, town meetings, workshops, plays, movies, exhibits, and discussions that tried to capture and examine what it is that makes Minneapolis an interesting and enjoyable place. The program was conceived when money from the National Endowment for the Humanities became available for local projects. Kimbrough put out a call for any staff members interested to help brainstorm ideas for a local program that would focus on what is unique about Minneapolis. The idea that came out of the group was, as Kimbrough explained, that "Minneapolis is consistently in all the lists of the top-ten places to live in this country. Maybe we ought to capitalize on that. Find out why and if it really is."[27] So four staff members were assigned to spend half their work time for seven weeks coming up with a proposal for funding. "They came up with a gorgeous, gorgeous proposal, and it flew right away," Kimbrough said. The project landed three hundred sixty-two thousand eight hundred dollars from the National Endowment, and an advisory council, chaired by Wenda Moore of the University of Minnesota board of regents, worked with project director Amy Raedeke to organize the multidimensional portrait of Minneapolis.

The theme was expressed in a brochure this way: "Minneapolis, Minnesota. Cruelly cold in the winter, oppressively hot in the summer. And, as hundreds of thousands of people will attest, one of the best places in the country to call home. Why?" The library's project

Minneapolis Public Library photograph

Joseph Kimbrough, the library's eighth director. Perhaps more than any other chief librarian, Kimbrough has involved his staff in planning and goal setting for the library. At brainstorming retreats with staff members, Kimbrough has tried to foresee the future and determine how to meet the community's upcoming information needs. "A library is nothing more than a mirror of its times," Kimbrough says.

Quote from interview with the author, September 1981

Minneapolis Public Library photograph, April 7, 1979

When the library was awarded a $362,800 grant from the National Endowment for the Humanities in 1979, Vice President Walter Mondale brought special notification of the grant on a visit to the Twin Cities. He is shown here congratulating library board president Frances Naftalin. The grant was the largest ever made to a library in Minnesota and the second largest made by the NEH to any public library in the country.

attempted to answer that question over a three-year period, from the fall of 1979 to the early spring of 1982, making use of some of the leading minds and resources in the city and the country. Several areas were examined: people, health, social justice, politics and government, arts, work, environment and resources, and information and learning. National observers Fred Graham and David Halberstam appeared on library platforms, as did Minnesota Governor Al Quie, Minneapolis Mayor Don Fraser, Urban League Director Gleason Glover, Minnesota Supreme Court Justice Rosalie Wahl, Minneapolis police chief Anthony Bouza, Hennepin County Commissioner Nancy Olkon, attorney Ron Meshbesher, and writer and humorist Garrison Keillor. Kimbrough called the project a great success in helping Minneapolis-area people engage in introspection and analysis, and in bringing the library and its resources to the public's attention.

In the late 1970s and early 1980s, the library engaged in another kind of effort to reach out to people. Southeast Asian refugees, fleeing from the decades-long shattering of their homelands in Vietnam, Laos, and Cambodia, were moving to the Twin Cities area in large numbers, making this one of the leading areas in the nation for Southeast Asian resettlement. Library staff searched for children's books and classics in the immigrants' native languages to give them some connection with the home from which they were so far removed. Additional material for teaching the newcomers English was included in the libraries, particularly in the children's collections. Kimbrough sees this as a continuation of the effort that started early in the library's history. "I think this tradition is being carried on, and I'm real pleased that we're doing that," he said.[28]

The special book collections got a boost in the seventies with the acquisition in 1974 of an extensive collection of antislavery material. More than eight hundred books, pamphlets, letters, and broadsides by and about abolition leaders were purchased from Chicago attorney Robert Huttner. Frederick Douglass, W.E.B. DuBois, William Lloyd Garrison, Harriet Beecher Stowe, and others are represented in this collection. And in 1977, Robert E. Hoag of St. Paul donated two hundred and fifty books and pamphlets by Mark Twain. The collection included first editions, some by Twain's own publishing company, of books such as *A Connecticut Yankee in King Arthur's Court, A Curious Dream and Other Sketches*, and *Following the Equator*.

Another special collection that continues to grow is one dealing with World War II, begun by J. Harold Kittleson. Early in the war, Kittleson discussed with librarian Carl Vitz the need to document the conflict, and the library accepted from Kittleson some two hundred and fifty items to start the collection. Since that time, additional gifts and purchases have increased the collection to more than ten thousand books, posters, photographs, and other documents, including books autographed by Presidents Truman and Eisenhower, and papers signed by Adolf Hitler, Rudolf Hess, Heinrich Himmler, Martin Bormann, and others. This special collection, like the others in the library, provides tremendous resources for those studying history. The strength of the library's special collections was demonstrated in 1978 when Dan Cohen's biography of Hubert Humphrey, *The Undefeated*, was published. Cohen acknowledged that ninety percent of the book's research was done in one room: the Minneapolis History Collection of the Minneapolis Public Library, where librarian Dorothy Burke helped him work through a wealth of specialized information on the city, the state, and Minnesota's people and leaders. This collection was organized in 1940 by librarian Ruth Thompson, who, quoting Woodrow Wilson, often said, "The world's memory must be kept alive." Thompson herself wrote, "Each generation must accumulate its own historical material for the benefit of its successors."[29] Following Thompson's lead, the Minneapolis History Collection today not only includes material from the city's earliest days, but still accumulates the historical evidence of the present—from letters written to *Minneapolis Star and Tribune* colum-

Photograph by Dale Schwie

J. Harold Kittleson, benefactor to the library's special collections, in the Emerson room at North Regional Library.

nist Barbara Flanagan to memorabilia from the famous Minneapolis restaurant Charlie's Cafe Exceptionale, which closed in 1982.

Reference resources were deepened again in 1981, when the Minneapolis Public Library became a depository for the United States Patent Office. A Bush Foundation grant allowed the library to purchase microfilm copies of patents from as far back as 1790. The library now has a complete set of U.S. patents, an invaluable resource for businesses and individuals.

In 1980 the Science Museum of Minnesota took a five-year lease to run the library's science museum and planetarium. It added a retail store, with books, experiments, scientific equipment, and toys, where the time and space gallery had once been.

By 1982, however, the Science Museum had to close the store and give up the lease, for the national recession and slow business had forced cutbacks in the organization. It also looked as if the planetarium would have to close. But in 1983, after many people in the community voiced support for keeping this educational tool in operation, the Friends of the Minneapolis Public Library came to the rescue. The organization's volunteers got to work, as they had so many times before, and searched for funding to keep the star shows going. Contributions to subsidize the operation began coming in, and attendance at planetarium shows has remained steady. In August 1983, the Friends opened a bookstore in the space that previously housed the Science Museum's store. The bookstore sells used books from the library collection and from donations, and new books of regional interest, and has been very successful.

The library is busy as it marks its centennial year. Economic recession and unusually high unemployment in Minnesota did what they've always done in the past—sent more people to the library for inexpensive entertainment and self-directed learning. Circulation goes up, funding goes down, and the library struggles to provide service to the community when it is needed most. Doris Northenscold, then chief of the central library, made a study in 1980 that showed a direct correlation between higher unemployment in Minneapolis and increased use of the central library. Some history remains current.

There was one fatality in 1982—the bookmobile. The recession meant the library's overall budget had to be cut, and the bookmobile, with circulation dropping and expenses rising, was a good candidate for elimination. In its last full year, 1981, the bookmobile circulated slightly fewer books, about fifty-two thousand, than it had in its first year, 1939.

A brighter prospect was delivered in 1983 when city funding was approved for the Minneapolis Automated Circulation Control System, nicknamed MAX. Capital funds, plus additional money from MELSA, were allocated for this new electronic system, which will improve the speed and accuracy of checking out library materials. And in 1984, the

Minneapolis Tribune photograph

Minneapolis Public Library photograph

In 1982 a tradition passed from the Minneapolis scene. The bookmobile, after more than forty years of service, made its last run. Although the mobile library had introduced several generations of Minneapolis children to the world of books, when bookmobile service was canceled the library heard very little public complaint. A well-balanced branch system and the increased mobility of Minneapolis residents helped contribute to the bookmobile's extinction. These photos show the bookmobile's heyday. Fifth and sixth graders from Gresham School, Thirty-sixth Avenue and Fifth Street Northeast, check out the rolling stock in 1939; kids ducking in and out of the truck in 1954.

library's budget appropriation allowed restoration of Saturday service during the summer. For the first time since 1949, the downtown library and five community libraries were open Saturdays year-round, instead of closing on Saturdays from Memorial Day weekend through Labor Day. Also in 1984, the library launched a public awareness campaign called "Read . . . By All Means" to promote the importance and pleasure of reading.

And the immediate future? What will the library be like? In discussing the future, Director Joseph Kimbrough makes a statement that hasn't often been heard at the library. "We have plenty of space to last us for another twenty years." The central library's excellent design and new ways of storing information on computer disks and microfiche indicate that space shouldn't be a problem for perhaps two decades. But Kimbrough is more interested in the service of the library than he is in the physical plant, and he thinks the future will see a change in service. He agrees with Ervin Gaines that the library will play a crucial role as an information center in the years immediately ahead. Although he himself cherishes books (the fine craft of bookbinding is one of his hobbies), Kimbrough sees electronics solidly in the library's future. He intends to spend time listening to the community, especially the business community, about their information needs, and will then try to find a role for the library in meeting those needs. Without change, the library may be passed by. "The library is an institution that's only been around a hundred years. The world got along quite well without it before that, and it could again," Kimbrough warns, "unless the library understands and serves the ever-changing needs of the community that supports it."[30]

"Books are the windows through which the soul looks out," Henry Ward Beecher wrote. Through the library's history, millions of Minneapolis citizens have caught the glimmer of that soul by making use of the library's collection. This late-1960s photograph shows a young patron at the card catalog. Although that catalog has since been replaced by microfiche readers, which will someday be replaced by on-line computer terminals, the library's role as teacher, historian, and resource for the future remains the same.

Learning for the Future

Chester Sikorski lives with his wife, LaVerne, a half-dozen blocks from the North Regional Library in Minneapolis. He's a retired railroad man and a regular at North Regional. He is why the library exists. T.B. Walker would have liked him. Tom Lowry would have talked rails with him. Gratia Countryman would have smiled to see him walk in the door, again and again.

Chester Sikorski is what the mill rate is all about, what the ordering and the budget fights and the shelving are all about. He uses the library constantly.

Sikorski was born in Northeast Minneapolis, went to a parochial school there, and used the library of a nearby public school. He remembers a nun, Sister Gertrude, who taught him the value and the joy of reading. "This nun took time out in class every day. We would stop and take out a book, and we'd read so many paragraphs, and then the next one would read, and then the next one," Sikorski recalls. "And she always said, 'If you can read, you can do anything.'"

The Sikorskis moved to the North Side during the 1940s. Thirty years later, they watched as the new North Regional Library was built. "I think it improved the neighborhood," Sikorski says, referring to an area where freshly remodeled houses can now be found next to others with boards over the windows. The new library "improved my reading habits and everything else because it's so handy," he says. Twice each week, Sikorski covers his thinning silver hair with one

"Love of reading enables a man to exchange the weary hours which come to everyone, for hours of delight."

—*Montesquieu*

of the two hundred hats and caps he collects and walks to North Regional, smiling and waving to friends as he goes. His relationship to books is like that of a barn cat to mice: His eyes light up at the sight of them, he plays with them and fondles them, and then he wolfs them down. He keeps a log of the books he reads and the dates he finishes them.

"I'm always getting books," Sikorski says. "It moves me. It expands my knowledge—of people and territories and everything." Reading transports him. "When I read a book, I live it. I pick me a character and I'm right there with it."

Thomas Hale Williams or Kirby Spencer or Margaret Mull might want to "upgrade" the kind of reading Sikorski does; the books he chooses are mostly mysteries, adventures, and historical novels. But Sikorski understands the magic in books; he knows why the library is there. At home in his favorite chair, he grabs a borrowed library book and takes off.

For forty years, Sikorski worked for the Northern Pacific and the Burlington Northern, the lines that built America's Northwest. He put together a life for himself and his wife, and for their children and grandchildren. He still hikes his grandchildren down to North Regional when they visit, to rub them up against the magic of books—a third generation of readers fed by the public library. Sikorski was never educated beyond vocational and high school, except in the library amid all those books. He's an interesting man, a good conversationalist, well spoken, bubbly, and straightforward.

North Regional Library is Sikorski's second home, and he's glad his tax money has helped put it there. He walks into the building, nods to friends, and looks around the way a farmer looks over a lush soybean field. "This is a real nice place," he says. "People sit here and relax and read the newspapers and books." Sometimes the kids get a little too rowdy, and he quiets them down. "There's still some of 'em think I'm a flatfoot," he notes with a smile. The library staff, he says, are helpful and friendly, giving him information and, just as important, companionship. "It's kind of like family."

Sikorski says he couldn't afford to buy all the books he reads, especially in hardcover. And he's one of those people who prefers the heft of a solid hardback to the wisp of a paperback. The library is part of his everyday life. He reads there, he chats there, and there he finds dreams.

Steve Baxter and his family have haunted the Washburn branch and the downtown central library the way Sikorski haunts North Regional. Baxter is a past president of the Friends of the Library, that group of dedicated volunteers who work so hard to provide the extras that the library just can't afford. Baxter, who still hustles the group's newsletter back and forth from the printers, believes in the library.

"Our kids used it," he says. "They were always up at the library a couple of times a week." Baxter believes libraries are especially important for children. "Kids can get acquainted with the idea of books, get started at an early age, and keep on with that until they drop," he says. One of his sons, now in his twenties, still "keeps on" at the downtown library, picking out Roman dramatists and historians in the original Latin for "light" reading.

A neighborhood library can provide children with the same kind of cultural stimulation as a home full of art, books, and music, says

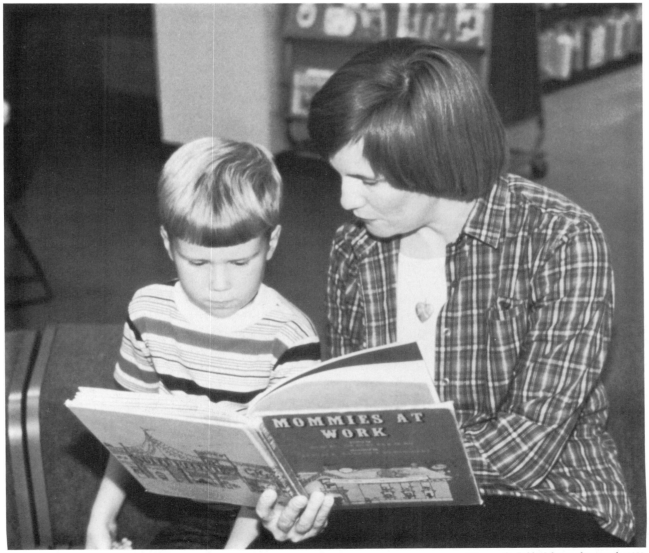

Minneapolis Public Library photograph, 1982

A mother and son take time for sharing at North Regional Library.

Minneapolis Public Library photograph, 1979

Two patrons at a special program at Washburn Community Library.

Baxter. But a library's usefulness goes beyond children, of course. "It is the basic reference source for everybody—industry, individuals, culture, science, anything at all," Baxter adds. From finding phone numbers to digging up points of history to uncovering what companies produce what and who their executives are, just "call the library," continues Baxter, "and they know instantly what the answer is." A library, in the long run, is part of education, and part of democracy. "We want a society with both curiosity and the means to satisfy it."

A public library provides that means to the whole public. "The magic of it is, it serves just about everybody. It's a very democratic institution," Baxter says. Going into the branches or the downtown library, he sees the full spectrum of the city's people, from bankers to students, from fur-clad readers to ragged itinerants who have no place to sleep at night. "The library is more likely to be used by the generality of the population," Baxter says, than almost any other service the city provides. It's part of what people expect of a city. "You might make the case that it's rather similar to the fire department—you don't use it all the time, but when you need it, it's there." Police protection, fire protection, water and sewer service are of primary importance to a community, Baxter adds, "but right after survival comes the importance of the general state of culture of the society."

According to Baxter, access is what a public library is all about. Large companies and wealthy individuals can afford to find answers to questions on their own, although they, too, use the library and recognize its value by contributing to its support. But for many individuals, small companies, and citizen groups, the library is the key to the world's knowledge.

Access to information has always been the motivating force behind assembling a library. Improved access was the reason the members of the original Athenaeum pooled their books into a private library. Wider access was what T.B. Walker fought for in making the library public. Nearly universal access was what Gratia Countryman strove for as she filled settlement houses, hospitals, firehalls, and factories with books. Access through technology was what Ervin Gaines was after when he said the library was an information center and a data base. And continued access is the issue confronting Joseph Kimbrough and his associates.

While many challenges face the Minneapolis Public Library as it begins its second century, two of the most important involve access. One is an old problem—funding. The future financial resources of the library will affect what's in the library and how people use it. The other revolves around the ongoing computer revolution, and how information is collected and made available to the public.

The problem of money has been a constant in the library's hundred-year history, although Minneapolis, because of its commitment to education and literacy, has generally done well by its library system. But the future may be more difficult. Recent government policy has had an effect on state funding, taking the responsibility away from the federal government and putting it back in the hands of localities. Minneapolis taxpayers, as state and local taxes rise to support local services, may become less eager to fund libraries as liberally as they have in the past. The library's administrative staff foresees the need for innovative sources of funding, including the possibility of charging for more library services to keep the library operating at the level of quality it and its patrons have become used to.

Basic services should never carry a fee, according to the library administration. And the idea of putting a price on any library service is generally repugnant to most librarians. But service charges have existed throughout the library's history, and they exist today, from fines for overdue books to fees for extensive reference work or computer searches. Zella Shannon, the library's associate director, sees charging for unusual and extensive service as a way of rationing that service and of assuring that traditional service remains free.

"Rationing" makes sure that a single patron doesn't tie up a service for a long time, Shannon says. For example, in reference service, a company or individual that wants a small amount of information can have it at no charge. But when extensive research is needed, work that would monopolize a reference person for many hours and keep that person from serving the basic reference needs of average patrons, the company or individual is charged a reasonable hourly fee if they choose to have the work done. As a result, the library's fee-based research service, INFORM, has become nearly self-supporting, and other reference personnel are available on the floor or on the phones serving the basic needs of the average patron. The same rationing idea applies to a computer search of available literature on a given subject. Through the library's Machine Assisted Reference Service (MARS), eight minutes of computer search time, enough to satisfy most requests, are free to anyone who needs the service. A patron who needs more time is charged. This technique may have to be applied to more library services in the future.

Fees for services should only cover extra work, Shannon says. "There should never be a charge for checking out a book from the library," she stresses. Library Director Kimbrough also says fee services should be a limited proposition. Many library patrons are "ill-clothed and ill-fed," he notes. If library service becomes a matter of money, then the library may soon serve only an elite, destroying the ideal that gave birth to the library a century ago. Curtailing a citizen's access to information would limit that citizen's knowledge and power, Shannon adds, and that hurts society as well as the individual. "People need to have access to that information, with no questions asked," she says.

"I have very fond memories of the time I spent in my hometown library, researching facts, finding interesting literature to read and just poring over the shelves and shelves of interesting books filled with people and far-away places to discover.

"Libraries have always been a big part of my life, whether it was in my hometown library in Collegeville, or during my school years at St. John's, or while I was going to law school at the University of Minnesota (the library was so much a part of my everyday life while I was in law school, it should have been my mailing address!). Later, as an attorney in the Twin Cities and as a father of four sons I spent many hours at the Minneapolis public libraries with my children and was happy that they found the same fascination and zest for learning among the shelves as I do."

—*U.S. Senator David Durenberger in a letter*

Minneapolis Public Library photograph

The library has been using Computer Output Microform (COM) catalogs like the microfiche catalog shown above since 1979. The COM catalogs currently include titles added to the library collections since 1968; by 1989, they will be complete for all titles added 1890 to date. Because COM catalogs are easily duplicated, they provide all service desks with information about titles located throughout the library system. COM catalogs are the forerunners of on-line catalogs, which undoubtedly are in the library's future.

The library may also save money in the future by limiting the amount of time library personnel spend with patrons. Gratia Countryman probably would have objected to this idea at first, although she was involved in one of the earliest projects that moved in this direction: a finding list, a forerunner of the card catalog, that let a patron find a book without the assistance of a librarian. Librarians say patrons will be seeing more of this "self-service" in the future. As in so many other places, technology will lend a hand. Advances like the computerized catalog and the microfiche reader help patrons see what's available and locate it on their own. In the future, on-line computer terminals linked directly to the library computer will take this process another step further. When patrons can help themselves with the simpler tasks, the librarians' time is saved to help patrons with more difficult questions.

Inherent in these changes is a fear of technology and a worry that people will be replaced by machines. Early signs indicate, however, that patrons will become more and more at ease with future technological advances at the library, especially children who are being trained now to use computers routinely in school. The library staff, noting that there has been very little resistance to advances like the microfiche catalog, is confident that patrons will have little trouble handling the next steps. For the librarians themselves, this technology may actually be liberating. By having some of the drudgery and the mundane tasks taken from them, librarians should be able to act more as educators, helping patrons make sense of the information they've found for themselves, helping them explore new connections and relationships within that information. That's a role Gratia Countryman would have approved. Technology may take jobs away, but the jobs that remain should be more rewarding.

The central library itself may look different in the future, if an idea to sell some of the library property materializes. With downtown continuing the boom the library helped initiate, the library's location increases in value. The library board is considering selling air space above the library site to a private developer, which could result in the construction of a high-rise building connecting to the city's extensive skyway system. Such an arrangement, while preserving the integrity of the library building, would give the library a supplemental source of income beyond local property taxes that could, among other things, fund renovation projects.

Whatever the techniques used to raise money, save money, and save time, Zella Shannon is convinced the library's operation will have to become more streamlined. "I think we're coming into very, very stringent times," she says. Management will have to be creative and resourceful, but that may not be enough. If funding falls short, as it so often seems to, some very tough decisions will have to be made. If the budget needs to be trimmed, should a community library be closed, or should all departments be cut back little by little? If the cutting of fat gives way to cutting of bone, should all services suffer, or should one be sacrificed?

Shannon says that careful scrutiny of government budgets is a good thing, and that the library, like all agencies, has a responsibility to stretch the public dollar. She says it will be up to the library to show the public what the library does and demonstrate that its service, like that of the street and fire departments, is essential and well managed.

While there is concern over money and the cutback of services at the library, the very technology that might help with these problems raises another concern. Already, a great deal of information useful to the library and its patrons is collected in computer data banks. Material ranging from professional journals and other standard reference works to sports scores and daily newspapers is stored in electronic computer memory, waiting to be tapped by a user. In the future, more and more information will be preserved this way. Some librarians are worried about the quality of this information. As the computer business booms and terminals become common sights in homes and offices, more and more private services go into the business of offering access to information for a fee. Librarians, the traditional custodians of the country's memory, fear that private businesses will not take the responsibility of preserving information as seriously as librarians have. Too many new companies are jumping into the electronic information business, librarians say, and not all of them will be good. Inaccuracies could slip in during shoddy processing of material; if not caught, these mistakes would be on the record forever. So access may improve, but the accuracy of information may not.

This concern about computer information runs parallel to another concern librarians and others have had for years—the fear that as corporate conglomerates take over the publishing industry, merging and absorbing what used to be smaller family companies that dealt only with publishing, the quality of what is published will diminish. A huge corporation may simply want good financial statements from a publishing house. It may view publishing as a profit center rather than an institution contributing to the nation's education and culture. This shifts the focus away from quality books of limited appeal to mediocre books of mass appeal with blockbuster sales. Again, this is a concern about the stability and quality of the information that librarians have to collect and preserve. The best access in the world won't matter if there isn't much useful or enlightening information to look at.

However the new information systems develop, the library's use of these systems will be consistent with history. Computerized data bases will be expensive to get access to, and not all citizens will be able to afford the subscription rates or user fees. Those who can't afford to tune into the data bases from their homes or businesses may be able

"[Libraries] are almost as important as the public school system in spreading education in a democratic fashion. It is hard to imagine this country without them."

—From a letter from Eric Sevareid

Learning for the Future

to use them in the library—just as people who can't afford a magazine subscription or the purchase price of a new hardcover book use the copies at the library now. Citizens pool their tax money, the library subscribes to an electronic information system and then uses that system to help the citizens get the information they need. It's a question of access, whether it's opening a leather-bound book in the Athenaeum in 1860 or punching a key on a computer console in 1985.

Minneapolis Public Library photograph, 1981

Preservation of library materials is a key issue in the library's future. Public libraries around the country are recognizing the need to retard, halt, or prevent deterioration of library materials and to restore deteriorated materials to their original condition. Along with this recognition comes the need to develop policies on surveying collections and identifying items that deserve preservation treatment, assuring adequate measures for disaster prevention and preparedness, microfilming of collections, and educating staff and public on proper handling of materials to prevent abuse. The library has a philosophical commitment to preserve its collection, but funds are needed to back it up. During its centennial year, the Minneapolis Public Library plans to seek funding for an endowment to finance book preservation. Shown above is a shelf of books in tenuous condition in the library's stacks: volumes of *Hansard's Parliamentary History* dating back to the 1600s.

The library's role in providing access will become even more crucial in the future. As the amount and complexity of information continues to grow at an explosive rate, the individual's need for the knowledge and power that information can give also grows. Libraries and other educators must be there to help the citizen wade through and make sense of an overwhelming mass of confusing information. That service is essential to a self-governing society.

The need is there, the job may be difficult, and the resources may be scarce in the future. In addition, more and more people will be making use of the library. Leisure time is increasing; the "how-to" movement continues, with people trying to cut costs by learning to do things like home repairs themselves; and career changes are becoming more frequent, so people want more information about new fields and new jobs. All these things mean more people at library desks and microfiche readers, more people on the phone, and more people in the building. Added to these factors, according to Zella Shannon, is the fact that the growing elderly population is increasingly better educated. In the past, people routinely went to a job instead of college after high school; when they retired, they still had little formal education. During the past few decades, however, a greater number of Americans have been going to college, so people are, for the most part, better educated and more likely to be library users when they retire. This trend will continue for decades. Shannon hopes that as the elderly gain political power by the strength of their numbers and their energy, they'll be on the library's side in the battles for funding.

Whatever the problems and challenges of the next one hundred years, the staff of the Minneapolis Public Library believes things will work out. Ruth Johnson, chief of community libraries, says, "the staff's philosophy is for quality," and other administrators agree that this applies to everyone, from delivery people to librarians. They have a tradition to maintain, a one-hundred-year-old tradition of feeding knowledge and entertainment to Minneapolis. A tradition of quality that has produced four presidents of the American Library Association and one Librarian of Congress. A tradition that reflects well on the library, but also reflects well on the town that supports the library. Kimbrough says the people of Minneapolis know they have an excellent library system, one of the best in the country, and are willing to support it. From the beginning, he says, the value of a library was recognized when the original legislation creating the Minneapolis Public Library set up an independent, elected library board to set policy and hire directors. This independent board, Kimbrough says, is the best guarantee that the library will be as useful to the people of Minneapolis in the future as it has been in the past.

Ingrid Pedersen is a retired librarian whose career started during the Depression. She worked in the children's department, the junior

"There is no limit to the ways in which the world of books through the effort of librarians may fit itself to human needs in this growing world. Intelligence, capacity for thinking and for making seasoned judgements is democracy's crying need.

—Gratia Countryman (from "Building for the Future," an undated talk, copy in Gratia A. Countryman papers, Minnesota Historical Society.)

"For the existence of a library, the fact of its existence, is, in itself and of itself, an assertion—a proposition nailed like Luther's to the door of time. By standing where it does at the center of the university —which is to say at the center of our intellectual lives—with its books in a certain order on its shelves and its cards in a certain structure in their cases, the true library asserts that there is indeed a "mystery of things." Or, more precisely, it asserts that the reason why the "things" compose a mystery is that they seem to mean: that they fall, when gathered together, into a kind of relationship, a kind of wholeness, as though all these different and dissimilar reports, these bits and pieces of experience, manuscripts in bottles, messages from long before, from deep within, from miles away, **belonged** *together and might, if understood together, spell out the meaning which the mystery implies."*

—Archibald MacLeish

From **Riders on the Earth**,
by Archibald MacLeish, Houghton Mifflin Company (Boston, 1978)

high libraries, and in the extension and acquisitions departments. Her view of what the library has meant to Minneapolis is simple and clear. "I think what the library has done is what a library ought to do," she says. "It's just been here, and quietly, most of the time, provided just exactly what the people wanted. They want books to read, they want records to play, they want answers to questions, they want whatever, all those millions of things. And it's just been here and done it and done it well. That's what it's done. It's served its purpose."

Mary Dyar was acting director before Kimbrough came on, and she looks at the library's usefulness on an individual level. "I think there are individual persons whose total entertainment was found in the library," she says. "And some people," she continues, received "their total education" here.

It isn't just the patrons of the library who have benefited these past one hundred years. Retired central library chief Bob Simonds recalls working with "a tremendous faith that what we were actually doing was something worthwhile." Dyar, too, felt that the work was of value to those who did it, that it gave them as much as it gave the patrons. "I think there was kind of the missionary spirit, too," she says. "It was very strong in our predecessors, but I think it still is a little bit in all of us—the desire to share the excitement that you can find in books."

The excitement. The magic. The worlds that lie waiting. "You know, I don't know if anybody can explain to somebody who doesn't read a book, just what a book means," Ingrid Pedersen says. "Any old book, just a book, is something special. Isn't it really, you know? I don't mean that it's sacred, or anything like that. It's just—fascinating."

Books. Fascinating, magical. Since the first homes were banged together from rough lumber at the falls of St. Anthony, books have provided a link not just to the past of literature but to the past of home. By setting up a room full of books in this crude new town, the first settlers felt not so far distanced from the halls of New England or Pennsylvania or Ohio where they'd grown. For some, books meant the glitter of civilization, a beacon to the rest of the world that here were people of learning and distinction. For others, books and the places they were gathered meant a piece of eternity, a pushing forward of their names beyond the reach of their own time. For merchants and developers, the magic of books would attract other ventures—mills, banks, companies, tall buildings, and people willing to shop and work and spend money amidst it all.

For still others, the magic in books could work toward social justice, toward true equality of possibilities. Books could lift people out of their poverty and despond and carry them to solid jobs and well-kept homes and help assure the nation's strength. For thousands of immigrants, books did in fact hold the key, the language and knowledge that would allow them citizenship and a chance to join all the others making their

Minneapolis Public Library photograph, 1981

The pleasure of books—even when they are "read" aloud by a machine—spans generations. Here a boy and his grandfather share a story presented on a filmstrip viewer in the downtown library Children's Room.

"Books are the treasured wealth of the world and the fit inheritance of generations and nations."

—Henry David Thoreau

way in what was still a brave new land. For some people in power, the words in books would keep the American machine well oiled, with each cog in its place and working smoothly, without complaint. For a great many who kept the books, their magic would enlighten the readers and raise the level of human intercourse. And perhaps for most readers, the magic in books would simply transport them, carry them away from the losses of war or the pressures of bills or the simple burdens of living.

All these roles the public library, this collection of knowledge and dreams, has played in the story of Minneapolis.

The books. The magic. It's been here for a hundred years, is here today, will be here tomorrow. Behind that John Rood scroll, the magic is stored, wafting between the covers of books, spinning on the surface of records, glowing in the synapses of a computer. The magic is ours. It is part of America.

Librarians of the Minneapolis Public Library

Herbert Putnam 1888-1891
James K. Hosmer 1892-1904
Gratia ̇A. Countryman 1904-1936
Carl Vitz 1937-1946
Glenn M. Lewis 1946-1957
Raymond E. Williams 1957-1963
Margaret M. Mull, Acting Librarian 1963-1964
Ervin J. Gaines, Director 1964-1974
Mary L. Dyar, Interim Director 1974-1975
Joseph Kimbrough, Director 1975-

Presidents of the Minneapolis Public Library Board

Walker, Thomas B. 1885-1928
Gale, Edward C. 1928-1943
Walker, Archie D. .1944-1955
Rood, Dorothy Bridgman Atkinson 1955-1962
Backstrom, Kenneth A. W. 1962-1964
Smith, Bruce D. 1964-1972
Kremen, Virginia F. 1972-1973
Goss, Marie C. 1974-1977
Naftalin, Frances H. 1978-

Elected and Appointed Members of the Library Board

Atwater, John B. 1885-1892
Johnson, E. M. 1885-1890; 1893-1898;
                                    1899-1900; 1907-1909
Koon, M. B. 1885-1890
Lowry, Thomas 1885-1892
Oftedal, Sven 1885-1894
Walker, Thomas B. 1885-1928
Moore, J. G. 1890-1896
Goodrich, A. M. 1890-1896
Cameron, C. R. 1893-1899
Truesdale, Verdine 1895-1896
Gale, Samuel C. 1897-1908
Crocker, A. L. 1897-1902
Wells, Charles L. 1898-1899
Kitchel, Stanley R. 1899
Fish, Daniel 1899-1905
Carleton, Frank H. 1900-1916
Crafts, Lettie M. 1901-1912
Stone, Jacob 1903-1911
Wells, Frederick 1905-1906
Deutsch, Henry 1909-1912
Gale, Edward C. 1909-1943
Dayton, D. Draper 1911-1923
Northrop, Cyrus 1913-1916; 1918-1922
Pence, Harry E. 1913-1933

Cross, Norton M. 1916-1924; 1926-1928
Lum, Bert 1916-1917
Decker, W. F. 1919-1929
Smith, Charles V. .1923-1931
McLain, John 1925-1926
Walker, Archie D. .1928-1955
Junell, John 1929-1935
Osgood, Dr. Phillips E. 1929-1932
Palmer, Ben W. 1931-1943; 1944-1949
Bull, Daniel F. 1933-1935
Erickson, Anna 1933-1939
Harding, Leila W. .1935-1941
Harris, Myrtle R. 1935-1941; 1943-1947
Larson, Margaret 1939-1945
Blanchard, Clifford 1941-1945
Strong, Harlan 1941-1945; 1947-1954
Norbeck, Abel 1944-1947
Stone, Nellie 1945-1951
Bessesen, Paul S. 1947-1951
Kachelmacher, Thomas O. 1947-1949
Ericsson, Bernard E. 1949-1960
Rood, Dorothy Bridgman Atkinson 1949-1962
Haglin, Mildred Daunt 1951-1963
St. Denis, Charles .1951-1953
Wichman, Florence Earle 1953-1959
Goldie, John A. 1954-1955
Paul, Angelus 1955
Backstrom, Kenneth A. W. 1955-1967
MacDonald, Helen 1955-1958
Van der Boom, Yvonne 1958-1960
Laddy, Mary 1959-1965
Kohout, Frank M. .1960-1961
Beeman, St. Clair 1960-1961
Kunze, William F. .1961
Willard, Grant R. 1961-1963
Ennen, Grace Mulcahy 1961-
Smith, Bruce D. 1962-1975
White, Robert J. 1963-1967
Barron, Caroline K. 1963-1967
Forester, Ralph 1965-1971
Kent, Frank C. 1965-1968
Sorauf, Francis J. 1966-1969
Kremen, Virginia F. 1967-1973
Denny, Robert J. 1967-1971
Ueland, Arnulf 1967-1971
Byrd, Johnaton H. .1969-1971
Anderson, Lloyd C. 1969-1970
LeRoy, Richard W. 1970-1972
Doty, David S. 1971-1979
Goss, Marie C. 1971-1983
Naftalin, Frances H. 1971-

Jackson, James O. .1971-1975
Van Krevelen, Robert J. 1972-1973
Solberg, Neil A. 1973
Wadley, Denis 1974-1976
Kittleson, J. Harold 1974-1982
Higgins, Ann 1975-
Thorbeck, Jo Anne 1975-1983
Ziemba, Helen 1976-1977
Rice, Sean 1978-1980
Sudduth, Gary Neil 1980-
Burress, Lee A. 1980-
Sussman, Ross A. .1982-1984
Doty, Mary 1984-
Rapson, Richard 1984-
Hofstede, Diane 1984-

Ex Officio Members of the Library Board

The Mayor of the City

Pillsbury, G. A. 1885-1886
Ames, A. A. 1887-1888; 1901-1902
Babb, E. C. 1889-1890
Winston, P. B. 1891-1892
Eustis, W. H. 1893-1894
Pratt, Robert 1895-1898
Gray, James 1899-1900
Haynes, James C. 1903-1904; 1907-1912
Jones, D. P. 1905-1906
Nye, Wallace G. 1913-1916
Van Lear, Thomas 1917-1918
Meyers, J. E. 1919-1920
Leach, George E. 1921-1929; 1937-1941
Kunze, William F. .1929-1931
Anderson, William A. 1931-1933
Bainbridge, A. G. .1933-1935
Latimer, Thomas E. 1935-1937
Kline, Marvin L. 1941-1945
Humphrey, Hubert H. 1945-1948
Hoyer, Eric G. 1949-1957
Peterson, P. Kenneth 1957-1961
Naftalin, Arthur 1961-1965

Legislation passed in 1965 permitted the mayor to appoint a representative to the library board.

The President of the University of Minnesota

Northrop, Cyrus 1885-1911
Vincent, George E. 1911-1917

Burton, Marion 1917-1920
Coffman, Lotus D. .1921-1938
Ford, Guy Stanton 1938-1941
Coffey, W. C. 1941-1945
Morrill, James L. 1945-1960
Wilson, O. Meredith 1960-1965

Legislation passed in 1965 deleted this officer from the library board.

The President of the Board of Education

Johnson, J. W. 1885-1886
Oftedal, Sven 1887-1888
Austin, A. C. 1889-1890
Ankeny, A. T. 1891-1894
Gjertsen, M. Falk .1895-1896
Crays, Jennie C. 1897-1898
Quinby, Thomas F. 1899-1902
Schlener, John A. .1903-1904
Pratt, Robert 1905-1906
Bintliff, C. J. 1907-1908
Elwell, George H. .1909-1915
Leighton, H. N. 1915-1921
Ortquist, A. P. 1921-1926
Jepson, L. E. 1926-1927; 1930-1932
Meyers, J. E. 1927-1928
Gould, J. F. 1928-1929
Kilgore, Helen 1929-1930
Johnson, Walter E. 1932-1933
Bauman, Helen L. 1933-1934; 1937-1938;
. . . . .1940-1941; 1942-1943
Thompson, Lynn M. 1934-1935; 1938-1939;
. 1941-1942
Drake, Dr. Charles R. 1935-1936; 1939-1940;
. 1943-1944
Bessesen, Henry J. 1936-1937
Cunningham, Owen 1944-1946
Robinson, The Rev. Morris 1946-1949
Rustad, Constance W. 1949-1951
Jensen, George M. 1951-1956
Adams, Frank E. 1956-1957
Lehmann, Florence 1957-1958
Pettersen, Einar T. 1958-1960
Leslie, Arnett W. 1960-1961
Gale, Stella 1961-1963
Mikkelson, Gordon A. 1963-1965

Legislation passed in 1965 deleted this officer from the library board.

INTRODUCTION *Granaries of Knowledge*

1. Quoted in Ditzion, *Arsenals of a Democratic Culture*, 18. This preamble was omitted from the final form of the law as passed in 1851.
2. Ditzion, *Arsenals of a Democratic Culture*, 10.
3. Quoted in Ditzion, *Arsenals of a Democratic Culture*, 103.
4. DuMont, *Reform and Reaction*, 137.
5. Quoted in Garrison, *Apostles of Culture*, 36-37; J.P. Quincy, "Free Libraries," U.S. Bureau of Education, "Public Libraries in the United States of America: Their History, Condition and Management," Special report, part I, 1876.
6. U.S. Commission on Education report, quoted in Ditzion, *Arsenals of a Democratic Culture*, 74.
7. Ditzion, *Arsenals of a Democratic Culture*, 135.
8. Garrison, *Apostles of Culture*, xiii.
9. Harris, "The Role of the Public Library in American Life," 14.
10. Quoted in Harris, "The Role of the Public Library in American Life," 15.
11. DuMont, *Reform and Reaction*, 39, from the 1910 American Library Association pamphlet, "Why Do We Need a Public Library?"
12. Ditzion, *Arsenals of a Democratic Culture*, 108, from an 1893 publication by T.L. Kelso, "Some Economic Features of Public Libraries."
13. Harris, "The Intellectual History of American Public Librarianship," in *Milestones to the Present*, ed. Goldstein, 234.
14. Kittleson to the editor, *Minneapolis Tribune*, 10 April 1955.
15. *Minneapolis Tribune*, 17 Nov. 1974.
16. Quoted in Barbara Flanagan column, *The Minneapolis Star*, 21 Jan. 1966.

CHAPTER 1 *Frontier Readers*

1. *Minneapolis Journal*, 16 Dec. 1889, quoted in Freestone, "Spatial Evolution," 138.
2. O'Brien, *Minnesota Pioneer Sketches*, 193-194.
3. Stevens, *Personal Recollections*, 86.
4. Stevens, *Personal Recollections*, 213.
5. Quoted in Thompson, "Minnesota Memories" column, *Minneapolis Tribune*, 12 March 1945.
6. Williams, "Sketch of St. Anthony," 29.
7. Kane, *The Waterfall That Built a City*, 28-29.
8. *Old Rail Fence Corners*, 34.
9. Quoted in Thompson, "Minnesota Memories" column, *Minneapolis Tribune*, 12 March 1945.
10. Hudson, *A Half Century of Minneapolis*, 12.
11. *St. Anthony Express*, 30 Aug. 1851.
12. *St. Anthony Express*, 4 June 1852.
13. Quoted in Flanagan, "Bayard Taylor's Minnesota Visits,"401.
14. Jackson, *Gold Dust*, 330.
15. "History of the Minneapolis Athenaeum," Minnesota Writers' Project, 2.

16. Hosmer to Williams, 22 Dec. 1900, Thomas Hale Williams Papers, Minnesota Historical Society.
17. Williams letter home, 8 Nov. 1837, Minneapolis History Collection, Minneapolis Public Library.
18. Williams letter home, undated, Thomas Hale Williams Papers, Minnesota Historical Society.
19. Williams to Samuel Hill, 29 Sept. 1900, Thomas Hale Williams Papers, Minnesota Historical Society.
20. Williams letter home, 16 Nov. 1854, Thomas Hale Williams Papers, Minnesota Historical Society.
21. Williams, "Sketch of St. Anthony," 7.
22. *The State Atlas*, 27 March 1864.
23. Quoted in Engebretson, "Books for Pioneers," 225.
24. Minneapolis Athenaeum Annual Report, 1869, Minneapolis Public Library.
25. Minneapolis Athenaeum Annual Report, 1872, Minneapolis Public Library.
26. Minneapolis Athenaeum Annual Report, 1875, Minneapolis Public Library.
27. Minneapolis Athenaeum Annual Report, 1877, Minneapolis Public Library.
28. Louise Walker McCannel, interview with author, 25 April 1983.
29. Walker, "Memories of the Early Life and Development of Minnesota," Minnesota Historical Society.
30. Walker, "Memories of the Early Life and Development of Minnesota," Minnesota Historical Society.
31. Nelson, unpublished biography of T.B. Walker, 218.
32. Nelson, unpublished biography of T.B. Walker, 272.
33. Atwater, *History of Minneapolis*, 287.
34. *St. Paul Pioneer Press*, 2 March 1880.
35. *Minneapolis Tribune*, 25 Oct. 1903.
36. "Testimonial Dinner in Honor of Thomas B. Walker," Minneapolis History Collection, Minneapolis Public Library.
37. "Testimonial Dinner in Honor of Thomas B. Walker," Minneapolis History Collection, Minneapolis Public Library.
38. Louise Walker McCannel, interview with author, 25 April 1983.
39. Undated interview in "American Magazine," Walker Papers, Minneapolis History Collection, Minneapolis Public Library.
40. Walker, "Contribution of Capital," Minneapolis History Collection, Minneapolis Public Library.
41. Walker, "Character as Related to Citizenship," Minneapolis History Collection, Minneapolis Public Library.
42. Nelson, unpublished biography of T.B. Walker, 446.
43. Quoted in Nelson, unpublished biography of T.B. Walker, 435.
44. Nelson, unpublished biography of T.B. Walker, 436.
45. Nelson, unpublished biography of T.B. Walker, 441.

46. Stevens, *Personal Recollections,* 384.
47. Atwater, *History of Minneapolis,* 294.

CHAPTER 2   *The People's University*

1. Lowry, *Street Car Man,* 102.
2. Freestone, "Spatial Evolution," 127.
3. Lowry, *Street Car Man,* 116.
4. Minneapolis Athenaeum Annual Report, 1885, Minneapolis Public Library.
5. Mearns, "D.C. Libraries," 4.
6. Minneapolis Public Library Annual Report, 1890, Minneapolis Public Library.
7. Quoted in *North Minneapolis Post,* 3 Oct. 1957.
8. Quoted in *North Minneapolis Post,* 24 Feb. 1965.
9. Mearns, "D.C. Libraries," 6.
10. Minneapolis Public Library Annual Report, 1890, Minneapolis Public Library.
11. Hosmer to Sven Oftedal, 3 Jan. 1892, Minneapolis History Collection, Minneapolis Public Library.
12. Hosmer, *The Last Leaf,* 231.
13. Testimonial, Hosmer Papers, Minneapolis History Collection, Minneapolis Public Library.
14. Hosmer, *The Color Guard,* 241.
15. Hosmer to Sven Oftedal, 18 Jan. 1892, Minneapolis History Collection, Minneapolis Public Library.
16. Minneapolis Public Library Annual Report, 1903, Minneapolis Public Library.
17. Hosmer, *Anglo-Saxon Freedom,* 11.
18. Hosmer, *Anglo-Saxon Freedom,* 199.
19. Minneapolis Public Library Annual Report, 1893, Minneapolis Public Library.
20. Minneapolis Athenaeum Annual Report, 1895, Minneapolis Public Library.
21. Minneapolis Athenaeum Annual Report, 1898, Minneapolis Public Library.
22. Minneapolis Public Library Annual Report, 1893, Minneapolis Public Library.
23. "Community Bookshelf," March 1926, Minneapolis Public Library.
24. Hosmer, *The Last Leaf,* iv.
25. "Community Bookshelf," June 1927, Minneapolis Public Library.

CHAPTER 3   *Countryman's Vision*

1. Rohde, "Evangel of Education," 3, Minneapolis History Collection, Minneapolis Public Library.
2. Countryman, speech at Hamline University, 31 March 1917, Gratia Countryman Papers, Minnesota Historical Society.
3. Rohde, "Evangel of Education," 11, Minneapolis History Collection, Minneapolis Public Library.
4. Putnam to Library Board, 25 April 1903, Gratia Countryman Papers, Minnesota Historical Society.
5. Interview with author, 7 Sept. 1982.
6. Interview with author, 7 Sept. 1982.

7. Countryman, "Safeguards of the Suffrage," 1889, Gratia Countryman Papers, Minnesota Historical Society.
8. *Minneapolis Journal,* 7 April 1911.
9. Dyste, "G.A. Countryman, Librarian," 72, Thesis, Minneapolis History Collection, Minneapolis Public Library.
10. *Minneapolis Tribune,* 1 Oct. 1911.
11. Dyste, "G.A. Countryman, Librarian," 110, Thesis, Minneapolis History Collection, Minneapolis Public Library.
12. Countryman, "Publicity in 1932," *American Library Association Bulletin XXVI,* 1932. Quoted in Dyste, 111.
13. "A Quarterly Magazine," Minneapolis Civic & Commerce Association, 1928, Minneapolis History Collection, Minneapolis Public Library.
14. "Community Bookshelf," Sept. 1926, Minneapolis Public Library.
15. Minneapolis Public Library Annual Report, 1920, Minneapolis Public Library.
16. Ditzion, *Arsenals of a Democratic Culture,* 56.
17. Ditzion, *Arsenals of a Democratic Culture,* 70.
18. DuMont, *Reform and Reaction,* 52.
19. DuMont, *Reform and Reaction,* 62.
20. Minneapolis Public Library Annual Report, 1928, Minneapolis Public Library.
21. Countryman, "School Life," April 1929, Minneapolis History Collection, Minneapolis Public Library.
22. Countryman, magazine article draft, 1932, Gratia Countryman Papers, Minnesota Historical Society.
23. "Community Bookshelf," March 1924, Minneapolis Public Library.
24. Richardson, "Woman's Home Companion," April 1935.
25. Minneapolis Public Library Annual Report, 1908, Minneapolis Public Library.
26. Minneapolis Public Library Annual Report, 1907, Minneapolis Public Library.
27. Minneapolis Public Library Annual Report, 1928, Minneapolis Public Library.
28. "Community Bookshelf," May 1923, Minneapolis Public Library.
29. "Community Bookshelf," May 1923, Minneapolis Public Library.
30. *Minneapolis Daily Herald,* 1 June 1962.
31. "Community Bookshelf," Nov. 1923, Minneapolis Public Library.
32. Minneapolis Public Library Annual Report, 1930, Minneapolis Public Library.
33. Minneapolis Public Library Annual Report, 1932, Minneapolis Public Library.
34. Minneapolis Public Library Annual Report, 1936, Minneapolis Public Library.
35. *Minneapolis Daily Herald,* 1 June 1962.
36. Minneapolis Public Library Annual Report, 1927, Minneapolis Public Library.

37. Minneapolis Public Library Annual Report, 1915, Minneapolis Public Library.
38. "Community Bookshelf," March 1927, Minneapolis Public Library.
39. Minneapolis Public Library Annual Report, 1904, Minneapolis Public Library.
40. Minneapolis Public Library Annual Report, 1910, Minneapolis Public Library.
41. Minneapolis Public Library Annual Report, 1917-1918, Minneapolis Public Library.
42. Countryman to Mrs. A.E. Zonne, 15 Jan. 1919, Minneapolis History Collection, Minneapolis Public Library.
43. Minneapolis Public Library Annual Report, 1917-1918, Minneapolis Public Library.
44. Freestone, "Spatial Evolution," 145, quoting *Minneapolis Journal*, 10 Dec. 1921.
45. Freestone, "Spatial Evolution," 147.
46. "Community Bookshelf," Feb. 1926, Minneapolis Public Library.
47. Minneapolis Public Library Annual Report, 1906, Minneapolis Public Library.
48. "Community Bookshelf," Feb. 1931, Minneapolis Public Library.
49. Freestone, "Spatial Evolution," 35.
50. Minneapolis Public Library Annual Report, 1933, Minneapolis Public Library.
51. Minneapolis Public Library Annual Report, 1933, Minneapolis Public Library.
52. Minneapolis Public Library Annual Report, 1917-1918, Minneapolis Public Library.
53. Minneapolis Public Library Annual Report, 1922, Minneapolis Public Library.
54. Countryman, "Parent-Teacher Broadcaster," Feb. 1931.
55. Wilson, "Journal of the American Association of University Women," June 1934.
56. Minneapolis Public Library Annual Report, 1931, Minneapolis Public Library.
57. Minneapolis Public Library Annual Report, 1931, Minneapolis Public Library.
58. Minneapolis Public Library Annual Report, 1932, Minneapolis Public Library.
59. Minneapolis Public Library Annual Report, 1932, Minneapolis Public Library.
60. *They Chose Minnesota*, ed. Holmquist, 11.
61. Minneapolis Public Library Annual Report, 1917-1918, Minneapolis Public Library.
62. Harris, "The Role of the Public Library," 13.
63. Minneapolis Public Library Annual Report, 1919, Minneapolis Public Library.
64. Minneapolis Public Library Annual Report, 1921, Minneapolis Public Library.
65. "Community Bookshelf," Dec. 1923, Minneapolis Public Library.
66. Minneapolis Public Library Annual Report, 1921, Minneapolis Public Library.
67. "Community Bookshelf," Dec. 1925, Minneapolis Public Library.
68. *American Library Association Bulletin*, quoted in Dyste, "G.A. Countryman, Librarian," 89. *New York Times*, 28 June 1934. *Christian Science Monitor*, 27 June 1934.
69. *The Minneapolis Star*, 27 Nov. 1936.
70. *Minneapolis Tribune*, 1 April 1913.
71. *Minneapolis Sunday Tribune*, 24 Nov. 1946.
72. Countryman to University of Minnesota "Alumni Weekly," 7 Sept. 1934. Gratia Countryman Papers, Minnesota Historical Society.
73. "Community Bookshelf," Nov. 1923, Minneapolis Public Library.

CHAPTER 4 *Windbreaks and Storms*

1. Minneapolis Public Library Annual Report, 1939, Minneapolis Public Library.
2. Minneapolis Public Library Annual Report, 1937, Minneapolis Public Library.
3. Minneapolis Public Library Annual Report, 1939, Minneapolis Public Library.
4. *Minneapolis Athletic Club Gopher*, July 1937.
5. Minneapolis Public Library Annual Report, 1937, Minneapolis Public Library.
6. Vitz telegram to E.C. Gale, 26 Oct. 1936, Minneapolis History Collection, Minneapolis Public Library.
7. Minneapolis Public Library Annual Report, 1938, Minneapolis Public Library.
8. *Northwest Architect*, Jan.-Feb. 1954.
9. *The Minneapolis Star*, 16 Dec. 1939.
10. *Minneapolis Journal*, 1 Jan. 1939.
11. *Minneapolis Tribune*, 17 Dec. 1939.
12. Morley, "Friends, Romans..." The Ampersand Club, Minneapolis & St. Paul, 1940.
13. Morley, "Friends, Romans..." The Ampersand Club, Minneapolis & St. Paul, 1940.
14. "Minneapolis Public Library—50 Years of Service," Minneapolis, 1939.
15. "Library Services for Youth in Minneapolis," included in Minneapolis Public Library Annual Report, 1941, Minneapolis Public Library.
16. "Junior High School Libraries—Whose Responsibility Are They?" included in Minneapolis Public Library Annual Report, 1941, Minneapolis Public Library.
17. Sheridan School PTA, Mrs. John F. Nagovsky, president, to Vitz, 8 March 1941, Minneapolis Public Library archives.
18. Minneapolis Public Library Annual Report, 1941, Minneapolis Public Library.
19. Minneapolis Public Library Annual Report, 1942, quoting Wilson Bulletin.
20. Minneapolis Public Library Annual Report, 1943, Minneapolis Public Library.
21. Minneapolis Public Library Annual Report, 1942, Minneapolis Public Library.

22. Minneapolis Public Library Annual Report, 1942, Minneapolis Public Library.
23. Minneapolis Public Library Annual Report, 1943, Minneapolis Public Library.
24. Minneapolis Public Library Annual Report, 1945, Minneapolis Public Library.
25. Minneapolis Public Library Annual Report, 1946, Minneapolis Public Library.
26. *Minneapolis Tribune*, 7 Dec. 1961.
27. Minneapolis Public Library Annual Report, 1956, Minneapolis Public Library.
28. Minneapolis Public Library Annual Report, 1951, Minneapolis Public Library.
29. Minneapolis Public Library Annual Report, 1950, Minneapolis Public Library.
30. Public Library Friends membership letter, 22 Oct. 1948, Minneapolis Public Library archives.
31. Minneapolis Public Library Annual Report, 1959, Minneapolis Public Library.
32. *The Minneapolis Star*, 15 Jan. 1959.
33. Helen Grouse to *Minneapolis Tribune*, 12 Jan. 1959.
34. Interview with author, 7 Sept. 1982.

CHAPTER 5   *Renewing Downtown*

1. Minneapolis Public Library Annual Report, 1944, Minneapolis Public Library.
2. Minneapolis Public Library Annual Report, 1944, Minneapolis Public Library.
3. *Minneapolis Tribune*, 10 Oct. 1944.
4. Civic Center Development Association, "Recommendation for Redevelopment of Lower Loop," 1945, Minneapolis History Collection, Minneapolis Public Library.
5. Civic Center Development Association, "Recommendation for Redevelopment of Lower Loop," 1945. Minneapolis History Collection, Minneapolis Public Library.
6. Library Board minutes, 10 April 1947, Minneapolis Public Library.
7. Library Board minutes, 10 April 1947, Minneapolis Public Library.
8. *Minneapolis Tribune*, 9 Feb. 1950.
9. *Minneapolis Tribune*, 13 June 1954.
10. Minneapolis Public Library Annual Report, 1956, Minneapolis Public Library.
11. *Minneapolis Tribune*, 20 Aug. 1955.
12. *The Minneapolis Star*, 17 Sept. 1955.
13. *Minneapolis Tribune*, 6 Oct. 1955.
14. *Minneapolis Tribune*, 5 Oct. 1957.
15. *Minneapolis Tribune*, 5 Feb. 1961.
16. *Minneapolis Tribune*, 31 Jan. 1961.
17. *Minneapolis Tribune*, 5 Feb. 1961.
18. Library Board minutes, 15 Dec. 1960, Minneapolis Public Library.
19. "Survey of organizational, personnel and fiscal areas," George Fry and Assoc., Minneapolis, 1962, Minneapolis Public Library.

20. "Survey of organizational, personnel and fiscal areas," George Fry and Assoc., Minneapolis, 1962, Minneapolis Public Library.
21. Library Board minutes, 8 Feb. 1963, Minneapolis Public Library.
22. *The Minneapolis Star*, 11 Feb. 1963.
23. Library Board minutes, 8 Feb. 1963, Minneapolis Public Library.
24. Minneapolis Public Library Annual Report, 1963, Minneapolis Public Library.
25. *The Minneapolis Star*, 26 Aug. 1975.

CHAPTER 6   *Challenge and Change*

1. *Minneapolis Tribune*, 10 May 1964.
2. *Minneapolis Tribune*, 1 June 1966.
3. *The Minneapolis Star*, 2 June 1966.
4. *Minneapolis Tribune*, 26 June 1967.
5. *The Minneapolis Star*, 7 July 1967.
6. Quoted by Don Morrison, *The Minneapolis Star*, 8 July 1967.
7. *Minneapolis Tribune*, 3 Oct. 1970.
8. *Minneapolis Tribune*, 1 Oct. 1970.
9. *Minneapolis Tribune*, 9 Oct. 1970.
10. *Minneapolis Tribune*, 12 Oct. 1970.
11. *Minneapolis Tribune*, 12 Oct. 1970.
12. *Minneapolis Tribune*, 9 Sept. 1974.
13. Minneapolis Public Library Annual Report, 1970, Minneapolis Public Library.
14. Minneapolis Public Library Annual Report, 1970, Minneapolis Public Library.
15. Minneapolis Public Library Annual Report, 1971, Minneapolis Public Library.
16. *Minneapolis Tribune*, 9 Sept. 1974.
17. *Minneapolis Tribune*, 18 Feb. 1968.
18. *Minneapolis Tribune*, 27 March 1968.
19. Minneapolis Public Library Annual Report, 1967, Minneapolis Public Library.
20. Minneapolis Public Library Annual Report, 1973, Minneapolis Public Library.
21. Minneapolis Public Library Annual Report, 1957, Minneapolis Public Library.
22. *Minneapolis Tribune*, 7 Oct. 1970.
23. *Minneapolis Tribune*, 11 June 1974.
24. Interview with author, 1 Sept. 1981.
25. *Skyway News*, 4 June 1975.
26. Interview with author, 1 Sept. 1981.
27. Interview with author, 1 Sept. 1981.
28. Interview with author, 1 Sept. 1981.
29. Thompson, "Public Library Administration," 22 May 1929, Minneapolis History Collection, Minneapolis Public Library.
30. Interview with author, 1 Sept. 1981.

CONCLUSION   *Learning for the Future*

The verbal material in the conclusion is from interviews with the author in 1981, 1982, and 1983.

Anderson, Chester G., ed. *Growing Up in Minnesota: Ten Writers Remember Their Childhood.* Minneapolis: University of Minnesota Press, 1976.

Atwater, Isaac. *History of the City of Minneapolis, Minnesota.* 2 vols. New York: Munsell & Co., 1893.

Burnquist, Joseph A. A., ed. *Minnesota and its People.* 4 vols. Chicago: S. J. Clarke, 1924.

Chapman, Louise. "History of the Minneapolis Athenaeum." WPA Minnesota Writers' Project, 1940. Minneapolis History Collection, Minneapolis Public Library.

Community Bookshelf. House organ of Minneapolis Public Library. 1922-1931. Minneapolis Public Library.

Conant, Ralph W., and Kathleen Molz, eds. *The Metropolitan Library.* Cambridge: MIT Press, 1972.

Countryman, Gratia A. Papers. Minneapolis Public Library archives. Minneapolis Public Library.

——. Papers. Minnesota Historical Society Research Center, St. Paul.

——. "Safeguards of the Suffrage." Paper, 1889, Minneapolis. Gratia Countryman papers, Minnesota Historical Society Research Center, St. Paul.

——. "We Select Books With Care." Parent-Teacher Broadcaster, February 1931. Clipping, Minneapolis History Collection, Minneapolis Public Library.

Ditzion, Sidney H. *Arsenals of a Democratic Culture: A Social History of The American Public Library Movement in New England and the Middle States from 1859 to 1900.* Chicago: American Library Association, 1947.

DuMont, Rosemary Ruhig. *Reform and Reaction: The Big City Public Library in American Life.* Westport, Connecticut: Greenwood Press, 1977.

Dyste, Mena C. "Gratia Alta Countryman, Librarian." Master's thesis, University of Minnesota, 1965.

Engebretson, Betty L. "Books for Pioneers — The Minneapolis Athenaeum." *Minnesota History* 35 (1957): 222-232.

Flanagan, John T. "Bayard Taylor's Minnesota Visits." *Minnesota History* 19 (1938): 399-418.

Freestone, Robert G. "Minneapolis Public Library and T. B. Walker: The Politics of Library Location 1918-1923." *Hennepin County History* 37 (Summer 1978): 4-13.

——. "Minneapolis Public Library from 1885: The First Library." *Hennepin County History* 39 (Spring 1980): 3-9.

——. "Minneapolis Public Library from 1885: The Long, Hard Road Toward a New Central Library." *Hennepin County History* 39 (Winter 1980-81): 12-19.

——. "Spatial Evolution of the Minneapolis Public Library System 1885-1977." Master's thesis, University of Minnesota, 1977.

Fry, George, and Associates. "Survey of organizational, personnel and fiscal areas." Minneapolis, 1962. Minneapolis History Collection, Minneapolis Public Library.

Garrison, Dee. *Apostles of Culture: The Public Librarian and American Society 1876-1920.* New York: Free Press, 1979.

Goldstein, Harold, ed. *Milestones to the Present: Papers from Library History Seminar V.* Syracuse: Gaylord Professional Publications, 1978.

Harris, Michael H., ed. *Advances in Librarianship.* Vol. 8. New York: Academic Press, 1978.

Harris, Michael H. "The Role of the Public Library in American Life: A Speculative Essay." University of Illinois Graduate School of Library Science Occasional Paper 117, 1975.

Holmquist, June Drenning, ed. *They Chose Minnesota: A Survey of the State's Ethnic Groups.* St. Paul: Minnesota Historical Society Press, 1981.

Hosmer, James K. *The Color Guard: Being a Corporal's Notes of Military Service in the Nineteenth Army Corps.* Boston: Walker, Wise & Co., 1864.

——. *History of the Louisiana Purchase.* New York: D. Appleton & Co., 1902.

——. *The Last Leaf: Observations, During Seventy-Five Years, of Men and Events in America and Europe.* New York: G. P. Putnam's Sons, 1912.

——. Papers. Minneapolis History Collection, Minneapolis Public Library.

——. Papers. Minneapolis Public Library archives. Minneapolis Public Library.

——. *A Short History of Anglo-Saxon Freedom.* New York: Charles Scribner's Sons, 1890.

Hudson, Horace B., ed. *A Half Century of Minneapolis.* Minneapolis: Hudson Publishing Co., 1908.

Jackson, Donald D. *Gold Dust.* New York: Alfred A. Knopf, 1980.

Kane, Lucile M. *The Waterfall That Built a City: The Falls of St. Anthony in Minneapolis.* St. Paul: Minnesota Historical Society, 1966.

Lowry, Goodrich. *Streetcar Man: Tom Lowry and the Twin City Rapid Transit Company.* Minneapolis: Lerner Publications Co., 1979.

Mearns, David C. "Herbert Putnam; Librarian of the United States." *D. C. Libraries* 26 (January 1955): 1-22.

Minneapolis Athenaeum Annual Reports, 1859-1983. Minneapolis Public Library.

Minneapolis Athletic Club Gopher. July 1937. Clipping, Minneapolis History Collection, Minneapolis Public Library.

Minneapolis Public Library Annual Reports, 1890-1983. Minneapolis Public Library.

Minneapolis Public Library: Fifty Years of Service, 1889-1939. Minneapolis: Minneapolis Public Library, 1939.

Minnesota Academy of Natural Science. Bulletins, correspondence, archives. Minneapolis History Collection, Minneapolis Public Library.

Morley, Christopher D. *Friends, Romans...* Minneapolis and St. Paul: The Ampersand Club, 1940. Minneapolis History Collection, Minneapolis Public Library.

Nelson, Clara W. An unpublished biography of T. B. Walker. Possession of Louise Walker McCannel, Minneapolis.

Northwest Architect, January-February 1954. Clipping, Minneapolis History Collection, Minneapolis Public Library.

O'Brien, Frank. *Minnesota Pioneer Sketches.* Minneapolis: H.H.S. Rowell, 1904.

Old Rail Fence Corners. 2d. ed. Austin, Minnesota: Daughters of the American Revolution, F. H. McCulloch Printing Co., 1914.

Olle, James G., ed. *Library History.* 2d ed. Hamden, Connecticut: Archon Books, 1971.

Phelps, Gary. "The St. Paul Public Library and Its First 100

Bibliography

Years." *Ramsey County History* 18 (1982): 3-23.

"Recommendation for Redevelopment of Lower Loop." Civic Center Development Association, 1945. Minneapolis History Collection, Minneapolis Public Library.

Richardson, Anna S. "A Living Library." *Woman's Home Companion*, April 1935, 11-41.

Rohde, Nancy F. "Gratia Alta Countryman: Evangel of Education." Draft of article. n.d. Minneapolis History Collection, Minneapolis Public Library. Article appeared in *Women of Minnesota: Selected Biographical Essays.* St. Paul: Minnesota Historical Society Press, 1977.

Stevens, John H. *Personal Recollections of Minnesota and Its People and Early History of Minneapolis.* Minneapolis: Tribune Job Printing Co., 1890.

Thompson, Ruth. "Public Library Administration." Manuscript, 22 May 1929. Minneapolis History Collection, Minneapolis Public Library.

Toffler, Alvin. *The Third Wave.* New York: Morrow, 1980.

Totterdell, Barry, ed. *Public Library Purpose.* London: Clive Bingley, 1978.

Walker, T. B. "Character as Related to Citizenship and Public Welfare." Speech before Men's Forum of Hennepin Avenue Methodist Church, 5 April 1914. Minneapolis History Collection, Minneapolis Public Library.

———. "The Contribution of Capital to the Public Welfare." *Fair Play.* 19 June 1915. Reprint in Minneapolis History Collection, Minneapolis Public Library.

———. "Memories of the Early Life and Development of Minnesota." Collection of the Minnesota Historical Society, vol. 15, 1915. Minnesota Historical Society Research Center, St. Paul.

Williams, Thomas Hale. Papers. Minnesota Historical Society Research Center, St. Paul.

———. *Sketch of St. Anthony and Minneapolis, Minnesota Territory.* St. Anthony: W. W. Wales, 1857.

Wilson, Bess M. "The Library and the Good Life." *Journal of the American Association of University Women*, June 1934. Reprint for American Library Association. Minneapolis History Collection, Minneapolis Public Library.

Wilson, Pauline. *A Community Elite and the Public Library: The Uses of Information in Leadership.* Westport, Connecticut: Greenwood Press, 1977.

Index

This book was composed in eleven point Paladium on thirteen point leading, printed by Colwell/North Central Inc. on eighty pound Consolith Gloss and sixty pound Mountie Matte, an acid free paper for permanence and durability, and bound at West Publishing Co. with endsheets of eighty pound Strathmore Rhododendron and cover of Holliston Roxite B cloth, #53663 linen finish, foil stamped in gold.